Disciplines and Movements

'This book goes significantly beyond traditional studies of cultural influences, encounters, understandings, or misunderstandings which have till recently dominated the agenda of comparative cultural studies. It widens the fields of studies between the German-speaking world and India, and moves methodologically decisively beyond the study of representations that still influence culture studies. The essays in the book focus on intellectual entanglements, transdisciplinary fields of investigation, and are a net addition in terms of scope, quantity, and quality of investigation to the work done in the past decade by scholars and scientists from the German-speaking world and India. In addition to shedding new light on Indological, sociological, philosophical, and psychoanalytical involvements, we have absorbing essays on the fields of aeronautical sciences, physics, nationalism, and fascism here.

Taken together, the essays in this book will initiate a welcome shift of perspective that can help us to historically analyse knowledge production and critically redefine the comparative and transnational study of culture and science studies for an increasingly interconnected world.'

Anil Bhatti, Professor Emeritus,
Centre of German Studies, JNU, New Delhi

'This volume of essays represents a milestone in the understanding of scholarly encounters and the circulation of ideas between India and the German-speaking world. It moves far beyond traditional accounts of East-West dialogue and offers significant insights into the formation of disciplines in a transnational context, and thus into the globalisation of knowledge in the age of disciplinary science. While its thematic range is breath-taking, the book remains focused on the key aspects of this process. A remarkable scholarly achievement!'

Juergen Renn, Director,
Max Planck Institute for the History of Science, Berlin

Disciplines and Movements

Conversations between India and the German-speaking World

EDITORS

HANS HARDER
DHRUV RAINA

Orient BlackSwan

DISCIPLINES AND MOVEMENTS: CONVERSATIONS BETWEEN INDIA AND THE GERMAN-SPEAKING WORLD

ORIENT BLACKSWAN PRIVATE LIMITED

Registered Office
3-6-752 Himayatnagar, Hyderabad 500 029, Telangana, India
e-mail: centraloffice@orientblackswan.com

Other Offices
Bengaluru, Chennai, Guwahati, Hyderabad, Kolkata, Mumbai, New Delhi, Noida, Patna, Visakhapatnam

First published Orient Blackswan Private Limited 2022

ISBN 978-93-5442-180-8

Typeset in
Minion Pro 10.5/12.5
by Shine Graphics, Delhi 110 094

036459

Printed in India at
Thomson Press, New Delhi 110 020

Published by
Orient Blackswan Private Limited
3-6-752 Himayatnagar, Hyderabad 500 029, Telangana, India
e-mail: info@orientblackswan.com

Dedicated to the memory of Roddam Narasimha (1933–2020)
and Dietmar Rothermund (1933–2020)

Contents

Preface

This book originated in a conference on 'Philosophy and Science: Indo-German Dialogues and Dimensions', sponsored by the Indian Council of Cultural Relations (ICCR), which was held at the South Asia Institute (SAI), Heidelberg University, in July 2013. The occasion was the celebration of Swami Vivekananda's 150th birth anniversary. In a meeting between ICCR and SAI staff a year ahead of the event, there had been a general feeling that we should attempt to go beyond the diplomatic and celebratory exchange of oratory that such occasions tend to trigger. Thus, the present editors, aided by others and particularly by Axel Michaels, started giving shape to the idea of looking at what was to become the title of this book, namely 'disciplines and movements' between India and the German-speaking countries in Europe.

In addition to frequently discussed themes such as German Indology and its reception by such prominent nationalist thinkers in India as Vivekananda, we thought it would be important to venture into the fields of psychology, aeronautics, philosophy, or sociology, etc., and thereby present a more diverse tableau of the interactions between the regions. The scope would be to look at different sites of encounter rather than furnishing a comprehensive survey. Above all, they were to be critical in their assessment of those exchanges, true to the spirit of free enquiry that motivated many of our protagonists in the pages that follow.

As we present the result of this venture to the public, we believe that these aims have borne fruit. Far from being comprehensive, many of the accounts included in the book do explore themes that are not usually in the limelight. Most are indeed critical in moving beyond commonly held perceptions, and, we hope, will add new angles and perspectives to the history of interactions between India and the German-speaking world.

We thank the ICCR for initiating and funding the conference that got us started; the erstwhile director of the Tagore Centre in Berlin, Dr Shivaprakash, for his support and his active and creative participation in the conference; and Ms Anna Baumann and Mr Saravanan Ganesan for organising the event and taking good care of the participants. We are also grateful to our contributors who have borne with the long delay until the book has finally come out, and untiringly updated, revised, and proofread more than one version of their chapters. The Orient BlackSwan team, particularly Proteeti Banerjee and Nilanjana Majumdar, have coached us well through the editing process. Thanks also to their designer Mishta Roy for the Einstein-Tagore collage of the cover, based on an idea that Anna Baumann had originally designed for the conference poster.

Last but not least, our deepest gratitude and respect for two senior colleagues and teachers who are no longer with us, Dietmar Rothermund and Roddam Narasimha, who encouraged us in this venture from the very start.

HANS HARDER and DHRUV RAINA
New Delhi/Heidelberg, January 2022

Abbreviations

ALH	Advanced Light Helicopter
Caltech	California Institute of Technology
CSIR-NAL	CSIR National Aerospace Laboratories, Bangalore
GALCIT	Guggenheim Aeronautical Laboratory at Caltech
GDR	German Democratic Republic
GoI	Government of India
HAL	Hindustan Aircraft Limited
IISc	Indian Institute of Science
LCH	Light Combat Helicopter
LUH	Light Utility Helicopter
STOL	Short Take-off and Landing

One | Introduction

Hans Harder and Dhruv Raina

Several years ago, a workshop on 'Philosophy and Science: Indo-German Dialogues and Dimensions' was convened at Heidelberg University. The event was sponsored by the Indian Council for Cultural Relations to commemorate Indo-German relations in the academic sphere. Our idea as organisers had been to expand the scope beyond the circle of Indian Germanists and German Indologists often put in charge on such occasions, and to include specialists from many different academic fields. From the very start, a tacit consensus developed quite naturally among the participants to understand 'German' as denoting the German-speaking academic and public sphere rather than any particular State, thus also encompassing the various past and present political formations apart from Germany, particularly Austria. India's denomination was less problematic, since pre-Partition British India and independent India proved a valid bracket for all the cases at hand. Hence, it was decided to recast the 'Indo-German' dialogues of the workshop in a more careful phrasing and to call the book *Disciplines and Movements: Conversations between India and the German-Speaking World*. As editors, we apologise to our contributors and thank them for their patience in putting up with the inordinately long delay in finalising the chapters. However, most were able to revise and rework their chapters to bring them up to date, and all, we assert, have their own currency of concern.

Critical indeed were the papers read at the workshop and the chapters later presented to the editors. True to the idea of this project, the themes of the majority diverge substantially from the customary concerns of events commemorating East–West dialogue. Thus, displacing the focus makes sense because disciplinary histories offer an alternate lens. The disciplinary approach enables a perspective leading beyond evaluations of the place of Indology and German Indomania and their impact on nineteenth- and early twentieth-century Indian nationalist imagery, focussing on the dimension of intellectual exchange and engagement rendered possible in an environment of scientific internationalism. Traditions of 'national science' were on the rise in the period concerned, but simultaneously its limitations were clearly recognised (Dubos 1950). The hiccups marking this phase of internationalism are discussed in some of the chapters, as they attempt to carve out a slice of internationalist engagement within these exchanges.

Most of the chapters in this volume, partly including those on the development and state of Indology, address moments in the history of disciplinary evolution. Broadly speaking, the nineteenth century was the century of disciplinary institutionalisation, characterised by diverse mechanisms and strategies. Intra- and interdisciplinary collaboration were among these mechanisms. But the actual unfolding of this process was marked by distinct trajectories, generating different logics of collaboration within and across disciplines, regions, and nations. Most contributors to this book recognise that the mechanisms of the circulation of knowledge were embedded within institutionally laid-out tracks, shaped by distinct ways of framing encounter and interpretation.

By the end of the nineteenth century, several of the concerned disciplinary formations were institutionally stable. In India, the modern university as a 'teaching and examining body'—an instrument of colonial governmentality—was, through local efforts and struggles, progressing towards an institution of postgraduate teaching and research. Multiple conduits for the circulation of knowledge and ideas passed through the portals of universities (Wallerstein, et al. 1995; Weingart 2010). Despite such institutionalisation, the period between the end of the nineteenth and the middle of the twentieth centuries was marked by a major institutional transition. Various disciplines were still quite fluid, but a process of crystallisation had set in and was transforming that fluidity, eventually leading towards the institutionalisation of disciplinary identities in South Asia. The chapters in this volume are situated in their respective concerns at this historical moment, and close with the end of colonial rule in India, and the end of World War II in Europe. This moment again signals a new beginning, both in India and Germany.

Against this backdrop of the globalisation of scientific institutions, it is interesting to examine a set of transnational encounters between

German and Indian thinkers, Indologists, sociologists, physicists, engineers, and psychoanalysts during a rather fateful period of world history. With specific reference to the chapters appearing here, it could be argued that while this circulation of knowledge was framed within the national and colonial regimes of the first half of the twentieth century, there were emergent modes of non-governmental, spontaneous internationalisation and disciplinary collaboration based on institutional and collegial ties forged across national boundaries (Elzinga 1996; Schott 1993). The standard master narratives of such encounters have been structured along three axes: the tension between Eastern and Western knowledge forms; centre-periphery relations; and the politics of knowledge (Goonatilake 1998; Nandy 1988; Raina 1996). The chapters in this volume attempt to transgress framings in terms of these customary binaries.

Lurking in the shadows is a concern with the internationalisation of the sciences and social sciences, across national borders and cultural boundaries (Wagner 2004). The chapters bring together diverse aspects of this encounter, reflecting the multiple rhythms of disciplinary evolution, shared intellectual and scientific concerns, and the place of colonial and other knowledge forms in constituting the identity of the modern sciences and social sciences. The chapters do not merely focus on the circulation and domestication of knowledge, ideas, and concepts, but also on the movement and meeting of scholars, the mode and content of communication, and the apprehension of the deeply mediated nature of all knowledge production. Does the relocation of knowledge result in the reframing of scientific practices and the forms of validation? What role, if any, does convention play in the staging of these encounters? The chapters form a collage of several transnational disciplinary encounters, and should be seen as such.

One dimension of the dialogues under consideration is the role of translation, understood as a wide range of practices, right from the nitty-gritty search for semantic equivalents in a philological context to the rather broad fashion in which ideas and ideologies are transmitted to a different cultural context. To begin with, very few of the interactions discussed in this book took place in either German or any South Asian vernacular language. Most commonly, it was English that came in as the medium of communication. In some of these cases, English had already become the undisputed medium of international scientific discourse—mathematics, for instance, was a field whose Anglophone character was beyond questioning—but in other cases, alternatives existed.

In the field of Indology, translation, right from its institutionalisation in 1818, was at the core of disciplinary engagements, and furnished the basis upon which coming dialogues would rest, even though they were mostly one-way exercises enabling an Indian past to speak to a European present. We may think of Schlegel's translation of the *Bhagavadgītā*, Friedrich Max Müller's various editions and translations, Deussen's renderings of the *Brahmasūtra* and *Upaniṣads*, and Garbe's *Sāṃkhya* translations (discussed in Malinar). On the other hand, there were protagonists like Bankimchandra Chattopadhyay who, in the 1880s and 1890s, attempted to (re-)introduce India-related scholarship into modern vernaculars, in his case Bengali, in an equally one-way attempt to take knowledge about India home to India. He, too, was later selectively translated into German or English by scholars like Paul Hacker and others (Hacker 1978; see also Harder 2001). This resulted, of course, not in a dialogue, separated as these interventions were by more than half-a-century, but in a long-lasting exchange on the status of modern Hinduism that, in many ways, has left traces leading up to the present.[1]

A more immediate sense of translation, however, with language weighing far less heavy in terms of an identity-bestowing entity, speaks out of the to-and-fro between German and English in the sciences. In physics, in the interwar period, German was the dominant disciplinary *lingua franca*, and while Satyendranath Bose and Meghnad Saha translated Albert Einstein's exposition of the Theory of Relativity into English, Einstein, in turn, translated Bose into German in order to publish him in the *Zeitschrift für Physik* (see Chapter 4, this volume). More was at stake in psychology, where cultural specificities could drop out of the common denominator of English (Chapters 9, 10, this volume). And in sociology, translation, rather than facilitating communication, sometimes distorted and prevented it, as Martin Fuchs demonstrates vis-à-vis the difficulties that the English renderings of Max Weber's writings pose.

[1] For the part Paul Hacker took in these debates, *cf.* Halbfass (1995).

The volume begins with two chapters on encounters between the South Asian and German-speaking scientific communities in physics and engineering. Dhruv Raina looks at the exchanges between Indian and German/Austrian scientists between the two World Wars, or 1920–1937, to be precise. This period coincided with a decisive phase of discipline formation in the sciences, as well as the boom of modern physics with its epicentre in Germany. Following the common distinction in the history of science between non-governmental or *autotelic* as opposed to intergovernmental or *heterotelic* internationalism, Raina sees the period in question as an autotelic one, driven by the individual initiative mostly of Indian scientists to connect to their German-speaking peers. Raina discusses the famous encounters of those years—Jagadish Chandra Bose and Johann Friedrich Haberlandt, Rabindranath Tagore and Albert Einstein (slightly off-track, but greatly significant), the connection between Einstein, Meghnad Saha, and S. N. Bose (among the first to translate Einstein's 'Principle of Relativity' into English), and also Max Born and C. V. Raman and the latter's attempts to bring Born, Schrödinger, and others to India in times of Nazi oppression. The Nazi regime and World War II interrupted these exchanges, and contacts transmuted into the rather government-driven, or heterotelic cooperations that have characterised collaboration since the later twentieth century.

The chapter that stretches beyond the chronological ambit of the majority of the contributions is the one by Roddam Narasimha (Chapter 3) discussing German engineering and the role of German engineering scientists in relation to the aeronautical sciences and technology in India. The chapter focuses on the postcolonial period, characterised by a new wave of institutionalisation and disciplinary renewal. While German engineering and German engineers had been a presence in modern India from the end of the nineteenth century, in the early twentieth century collegial ties were forged between German and Indian physicists (see Chapter 4, this volume). Within the sphere of engineering sciences so designated, these ties took some time to develop for two reasons. First, collaborative ties in the engineering sciences require an elaborate institutional architecture before they can be fruitfully enabled—part of the reason has to do with the cultural specificity of engineering science and its practice. Second, in the twentieth century under British colonial rule, collaborative ties with Germany were not encouraged for a variety of strategic and industrial reasons.

As India shrugged off the yoke of imperial rule, things began to change. Roddam Narasimha chronicles the role of the Indian engineer V. M. Ghatge, who went on to establish the first Indian academic programme in aeronautical engineering at the Indian Institute of Science, Bangalore. Ghatge had been a student of the German engineer-scientist, the renowned Ludwig Prandtl (1875–1953). The mobilisation of this network of scientists introduced some 'Göttingen flavour' into Indian aeronautical science. These networks need to be situated within a history of the internationalisation of engineering science education (Krige 2006; see also Bassett 2015). Some of the pioneers of aeronautical science, such as Theodore von Kármán and Hans Wolfgang Liepmann, were either students of Prandtl or came out of the Göttingen school and emigrated to Caltech. Amongst their students were Indians, including Narasimha, who played a major role in developing the aeronautical engineering programme in India. On the other hand, in the post-World War II context, India's burgeoning postcolonial strategic interests provided opportunities for leading engineering scientists from Germany, such as Kurt Tank. He himself had ties with another engineering school with a vocational focus on aeronautical engineering, namely the Madras Institute of Technology—the alma mater of Abdul Kalam, renowned space scientist and later President of India. It becomes evident that for the sciences and engineering, very specific institutional forms serve as grooves that facilitate the movement of ideas and practices.

The standard narrative of Indo-German academic exchange almost always commences with the beginnings of German Indology and its role in shaping a national consciousness in India.[2] Of late, some questions have been posed at an acute angle to this narrative. The two chapters by Axel Michaels and Angelika Malinar (Chapters 5 and 7, respectively) do not reject Sheldon Pollock's overdetermined reading of the political and ideological functions of German Ideology

2 For example, Schreiner (1978) discusses how what constitutes the academic discipline of Indian philosophy was influenced by German philosophy and Indology.

(Pollock 1993), but by using a big magnifying lens nuance our understanding of the evolution of German Indology. Malinar's contribution recognises German Indology's role in influencing what subsequently came to be institutionalised as Indian philosophy in university departments. The chapter begins with a discussion on Vivekananda's response to German philology and Indology. Vivekananda proposed a tripartite classification of the stages of development of German Indology, offering a left-handed compliment to the philological approach of Müller and Deussen, which he saw as playing an important role in preserving the integrity of the ancient scriptures, but unable to uncover the 'gems of thought and spirituality' in these very texts. Malinar perceives an echo of contemporaneity in his views regarding the limitations of philology, thus raising the need to redraw the boundary between philology and philosophy. What is noteworthy in Vivekananda's intervention is that, contrary to the idea of the diffusion of Western institutions and disciplines in South Asia, we have here what Kaviraj (1988) called a 'reverse commentary' on Western representations of Indian thought. In general, such reverse commentaries were *de rigueur* among a modernising and deeply politicised *Bhadralok* community. But we return to Malinar's discussion on situating Paul Deussen's and Richard Garbe's ideas about the essence of Indian philosophy. While both were agreed about its ontological status—Indian philosophy exists—they disagreed on its course. Deussen, like several other Bengali thinkers from the nineteenth century, saw the monistic idealism of the Vedānta as the core of Indian philosophy, while Garbe, in a more modernist reading, emphasised the rationalist dimension, particularly Sāṃkhya, as shaping the trajectory of the development of Indian philosophy.

The discussion on German Indology further strays into its relationship with the Nazi regime. The issue has been a thorn in the side of German Indologists in recent decades, especially in light of the radicalisation of social theory and cultural theory with regard to the politics of knowledge. Without being an apologist, Axel Michaels rightly points out that the designation 'German Indology' is indeed a simplification, bracketing something that at times turns out to be a rather transcultural and transnational field. In engaging with Pollock's paper, he shows that there were indeed Indological works of Germans that contributed towards an 'inward' Nazi project of Saidian Orientalism. This suggests that some Indologists of the period were predisposed to Nazism, but does not implicate all German Indologists within the Nazi ideology and agenda. The chapter also discusses the status of contemporary Indology and the need to think about its relationship to philology, which has been so fundamental to the definition and self-understanding of the discipline. This has a bearing on the more recent attempts to reinvent *Zukunftphilologie* (Pollock 2016). Axel Michaels concurs with Pollock's as well as Indologist Walter Slaje's argument that the intimate bonding between Indology and philology makes of the latter a European science. Unlike Slaje, however, he argues that Indology also needs to respond to the Zeitgeist, and calls for a situated philology that is sensitive to its academic context and, more generally, to issues of the embodiment of knowledge.

What, if any, is the family resemblance between Indian and German versions of *völkisch* nationalism? What conclusions can we draw from the history of the early twentieth-century movements without projecting the label 'fascism' onto them? Benjamin Zachariah (Chapter 6) reckons that fascism is not a uniquely German or European phenomenon, and Nazism is fascism in an extreme form. Further fascisms in the plural do not derive from an ur-fascism, for its different varieties emerged more or less contemporaneously and were not an inevitable outcome of a particular combination of factors. Zachariah sees global fascism as part of a worldwide Zeitgeist and not as a singular event or aberration. The exploration of fascism is extended over a larger time scale that explores the notions of the Volk. The author points out that cognate ideas of the Volk were not foreign to India, and were recognisable by both Indians and Germans. Thus, while there was a 'Nazi fascination with things Indian', this had little impact on the practice of Nazism.

A related issue that one must raise in the context of this transnational academic conversation is that the historiography of Indo-German ideological or cultural exchange, according to Zachariah, has been celebratory as States commemorate their association in the realm of high culture or ideas. One such volume commemorating Indian and French ties was *Passeurs d'Orient*, which appeared in the 1990s to coincide with French President François Mitterrand's visit to India (Pouchepadass 1991). In the Indo-German case, this has accorded

Germany an important place in India's intellectual development in the nineteenth and twentieth centuries. What is on offer is 'an undifferentiated, almost non-ideological description of Germany and India through selected incidents and individuals'. Zachariah's contention is that Indians too contributed to a 'fascist repertoire'. German academies in the 1920s and 1930s offered fellowships that may have facilitated the establishment of linkages with the Nazi movement. But the universities did not provide the glue for Indo-Nazi collaboration.

Moving from movements to larger concerns of social theory, Martin Fuchs takes up a more German disciplinary engagement with India. He asserts that despite the attraction towards different aspects of Indian life, the history of the sociology of India is a history of misunderstandings. The sociology of India, as perhaps anywhere else, has posed conceptual problems for scholars from within India and without—and this relates to the translatability of concepts and frames between and across cultures and societies. Fuchs feels that the central problematic arises from the fact that anthropology manifests a greater sensitivity in listening to the other, while sociology is still trapped in 'modernisation and modernity'. For Max Weber, India served as a contrast to the Judeo-Christian world, and the chapter explores in detail Weber's study of India devoted to explaining why, in regions other than Western Europe, there did not appear the 'ability and disposition of men to adopt certain types of potential rational conduct'. The chapter journeys through the omissions and commissions of this Weberian exploration.

If Fuchs' disciplinary engagement concerns sociology, Rajendra Dengle examines this encounter through the lens of media theory. Although courses on the so-called 'Germanistik' taught in Indian universities mention cultural encounters, Dengle contends that this is done in a manner of disseminating factoids. A comparison of different cultures of understanding suggests that the understanding of the other in these different frames is often neglected, and hence does not progress into a self-reflective research interest. When it does do so, is it manifest as postcolonial theory, anthropology, or ethnology? Hermeneutics makes it possible to probe the epistemological and metaphysical legacy of other cultures, indexing the canvas of knowledge and deepening our understanding of experience. Dengle discusses

Mauthner's *Buddha* and Hofmannsthal's *A Letter* as reflections on the crisis of the European subject, language, and communication. The hermeneutics of cultural understanding—understanding the other, another culture, a text—requires a framework of communication. Dengle turns to Flusser, whose 'Eastward' turn is very unlike that of Carl Jung and Mircea Eliade, but whose goal is to liberate himself from thinking, in order to overcome the self.

The linkages between disciplinary collaboration and cultural translation are addressed in two chapters on the development of psychological thought. While disciplinary psychological knowledge took a particular turn in Austria and Germany in the nineteenth and early twentieth centuries, in India—as occurred with other scientific disciplines as well—psychology underwent a process of institutionalisation in the 1920s following the establishment of an association and a society, and the launch of a journal. Christiane Hartnack (Chapter 9) points out that the transcontinental encounters of German-speakers and Indians working in the psychological sciences were embedded within well-defined institutional and political contexts, with quite distinct motivations for each of the interlocutors she discusses. Beyond the circumstances of the encounter, the biographies of the interlocutors were also very diverse. For German scholars, this encounter with South Asian knowledge(s) was stamped by '... celebration of an intellectual conquest ... resistance to seduction by Indian knowledge ... appropriation of intellectual findings ... and an aborted Orientalist fascination'. But for some German scientists, this encounter signified a quest for 'unusual human wisdom'. Hartnack's chapter pairs four German and four Indian psychologists, some of whom travelled through India and Germany, respectively. The form of these interactions between the two worlds was unstructured and quite in contrast to the world of physics, regulated by stronger and well-rehearsed institutional practices.

Hans Harder's chapter (Chapter 10) embarks on a detailed reading of the work of Girindrasekhar Bose (1887–1953), founder of the Indian Psychoanalytical Society. He probes Bose's writings on dreams and the *Yogasūtras*, and summarises and comments upon his exchange of letters with Freud. Here, too, the process of cultural translation, as well as the institutional dimension within which the dialogue with Freud is framed, are foregrounded. Harder examines the communicational mechanics shaping Bose's interactions with a Bengali-reading public, an English-reading audience, and of course Freud himself. Linked to Hartnack's and Ashis Nandy's discussions on Bose and his corpus of writings in terms of a colonial intellectual (Hartnack 2001; Nandy 1995), Harder focuses on Bose's colonial bilinguality and positionality. The first has to do with the relationship between Bose's writings in English and Bengali, and the second asks the question: On which level does the English vs Indian, coloniser vs colonised dichotomy prove insightful in looking at the Freud–Bose relationship?

Dialogue serves Harder as a robust rubric to probe Bose's writings. He draws a line from the Bengali book *Svapna* or *Dreams* (1928), written at an early stage of Bose's career, and *The Yoga Sutras*, an English examination of the role of psychology, authored at the end of Bose's life and published posthumously in 1957, to refute the fairly common notion that Bose used English for sober academic publications and Bengali for nationalist, identity-bestowing purposes; in fact, Harder shows that the revivalist aspects are far more pronounced in the later text. The Sigmund Freud–Girindrasekhar Bose exchange that Harder engages with shows, it may be remarked in passing, some parallels with the Albert Einstein–Satyendranath Bose collaboration. Both run into a roadblock when the student or apostle differs with the master. But whereas Freud bluntly writes to Bose about the latter's contrary views: 'I am not convinced by your arguments'—a remark that plays itself out in their estrangement—conversation continued in the case of the Bose–Einstein collaboration, despite Einstein's reservations regarding Bose's second paper.

If we summarise the exchanges under discussion in this book in the light of the original key notion of the project, the dialogue, we have to state that the sublime heights of the ideal dialogue in Gadamer's hermeneutics, as evoked in Dengle's contribution, were hardly ever actually attained. The Tagore–Einstein encounter of 1930[3] was certainly the most iconic and perhaps the only direct exchange undisturbed by institutional hierarchies, despite its inconclusive nature, and no matter how much it fell short of a 'communion in which we do not

[3] Republished in Pais (1994), cited in Raina and Habib (1996).

remain what we were' (Gadamer 2004, 171) as it turned out to be. Rather than institutional hierarchies, the dialogue had to meet a bias of expectations predetermined by tropes of the scientific West and the spiritual East (Raina and Habib 1996), but it turned out that neither of the two thinkers was ready to employ such simple dichotomies in their conversation. Even before he met Einstein, Tagore had recognised the inadequacy of characterising Einstein's thought along these lines and referred to him as a transcendental materialist.[4] Despite their different vocations and professional preoccupations as thinkers embroiled in the central political issues of their age, both were deeply sceptical of the idea of the nation-State. So, on the positive side, while there were fundamental premises that separated the manner in which Tagore and Einstein conceived the philosophical enterprise, there is in the dialogue a deep recognition that their starting points are different, and despite which their humanist visions converge.

In most other exchanges dealt with in this volume, subtle or not-so-subtle hierarchies played out. Sometimes these collapsed, in fact, in one-sided communication not so far from the genre of the instructive dialogue popular in colonial India;[5] at other times, they construed the interlocutor as the quite elusive voice of a whole tradition or religion (for example, Mauthner's Buddhism). To what extent this led to any 'fusion of horizons'—Gadamer's term for the process of understanding historical texts—remains open to debate (Gadamer 2004, 305).

As for the role of nationality—(British-) Indian, German, Austrian—in all these dialogues, whether successful or failed, we can state that it does not seem to be an all-determining factor, in the sense that the interlocutor's national belonging did not immediately delimit the nature of the exchange. Even when national self-assertion was at stake, the relative lack of political entanglements between South Asia and the German-speaking countries prevented the interlocutors from turning into opponents. In a sense, the absence of any direct relationship of colonial dependency did warrant an indeterminacy that potentially undercut cultural hierarchies. The South Asian and

4 Tagore quoted from his second dialogue with Einstein in Pais (1994, 107).

5 The most famous example of this kind of 'dialogue' is Gandhi's *Hind Swaraj* (1963 [1909]).

German-speaking spheres thus profited from an air of ambivalence between them that did of course at times lapse into stereotyping and prejudice, but could at others be transmuted into productive, open-ended, and forward-looking exchanges.

In any case, we hope that this collection of essays manages to point to the problematic aspects of these exchanges, as essays must in order to deserve to be called critical, but also to convey the spirit of disciplinary dialogue in a transnational context that some of these exchanges bear witness to. While the institutional, cognitive, and communicological aspects have been the focus of discussion, the role of convention, which is just as important, has been underplayed. But that is for another occasion.

REFERENCES

Bassett, Ross. 2015. *The Technological Indian*. Cambridge, Massachusetts: Harvard University Press.

Dubos, René. 1950. *Louis Pasteur: Free Lance of Science*. New York: De Capo Paperback.

Elzinga, Aant. 1996. 'Introduction: Modes of Internationalism'. In Aant Elzinga and Catharina Landström (eds), *Internationalism and Science*, 3–20. London: Taylor Graham.

Gadamer, Hans-Georg. 2004. *Truth and Method*, Joel Weinsheimer and Donald G. Marshall (trans.). London/New York: Continuum.

Gandhi, Mohandas Karamchand. 1963 [1909]. 'Hind Swaraj'. In *The Collected Works of Mahatma Gandhi*, Vol. X (November 1909–March 1911), 6–64. New Delhi: Director Publication Division, Navajivan Trust.

Goonatilake, Susantha. 1998. *Toward a Global Science: Mining Civilizational Knowledge*. New Delhi: Vistaar Publications.

Hacker, Paul. 1978. 'Der Dharma-Begriff des Neuhinduismus'. In Lambert Schmitthausen (ed.), *Kleine Schriften*, 580–608. Wiesbaden: Steiner.

Halbfass, Wilhelm. 1995. *Philology and Confrontation. Paul Hacker on Traditional and Modern Vedanta*. Albany: State University of New York Press.

Harder, Hans. 2001. *Bankimchandra Chattopadhyay's* Śrīmadbhagabadgītā*: Translation and Analysis*. New Delhi: Manohar.

Hartnack, Christiane. 2001. *Psychoanalysis in Colonial India*. New Delhi: Oxford University Press.

Kaviraj, Sudipta. 1988. 'Imaginary history'. NMML Occasional Paper on History and Society Issues, Second Series, No. VII.

Krige, John. 2006. *American Hegemony and the Postwar Reconstruction of Science in Europe.* Cambridge, Massachusetts: MIT Press.

Nandy, Ashis (ed.). 1988. *Science, Hegemony and Violence: A Requiem for Modernity.* New Delhi: Oxford University Press.

———. 1995. 'The Savage Freud: The First Non-Western Psychoanalyst and the Politics of Secret Selves in Colonial India'. In *The Savage Freud and Other Essays on Possible and Retrievable Selves.* New Delhi: Oxford University Press.

Pais, Abraham. 1994. *Einstein Lived Here.* Oxford: Clarendon Press.

Pollock, Sheldon. 1993. 'Deep Orientalism? Notes on Sanskrit and Power beyond the Raj'. In C. A. Breckenridge and P. van der Veer (eds). *Orientalism and the Postcolonial Predicament: Perspectives on South Asia*, 76–133. Philadelphia: University of Pennsylvania Press.

———. 2016. 'Philology and Freedom'. *Philological Encounters* 1, 4–30.

Pouchepadass, Jacques. 1991. 'L'Inde au miroir de l'histoire et des sciences du temps présent'. In F.Gros (ed.), *Passeurs d'Orient—Encounters between India and France*, 52–57. Paris: Ministry of Foreign Affairs.

Raina, Dhruv. 1996. 'Reconfiguring the Centre: The Structure of Scientific Exchanges Between Colonial India and Europe'. *Minerva* 34, 161–176.

Raina, Dhruv, and S. Irfan Habib. 1996. 'The moral legitimation of modern science: Bhadralok reflections on theories of evolution'. *Social Studies of Science* 26 (1), 9–42.

Schott, Thomas. 1993. 'World Science: Globalization of Institutions and Participation'. *Science, Technology, & Human Values* XVIII (2).

Schreiner, Peter. 1978. 'The Indianness of Modern Indian Philosophy as a Historical and Philosophical Problem'. *Philosophy East and West* 28 (1), 21–37.

Wagner, Peter. 2004. 'Introduction to Part I'. In Christophe Charle, Jürgen Schriewer, and Peter Wagner (eds), *Transnational Intellectual Networks: Forms of Academic Knowledge and the Search for Cultural Identities.* Frankfurt/New York: Campus Verlag.

Wallerstein, Immanuel, et al. (eds). 1995. *Open the Social Sciences: Report of the Gulbenkian Commission on the Restructuring of the Social Sciences.* Stanford: Stanford University Press.

Weingart, Peter. 2010. 'A Short History of Knowledge Formations'. In Robert Frodeman, Julie Thompson Klein, and Carl Mitcham (eds), *The Oxford Handbook of Interdisciplinarity*, 3–14. Oxford: Oxford University Press.

Two

Sociological Entanglements

Max Weber's Comparative Engagement with India

MARTIN FUCHS

The history of the sociology of India is a history of misunderstandings, even when authors were led by an attraction towards its philosophical, religious, or cultural traditions. Today, Western as well as Indian scholarship is still debating the right approach to the study of India, and the approach to the comparative study of civilisations, societies, and cultures in general.[1] The relationship between Western and Indian social sciences is still not balanced. Western scholarship has tended to include India and other cultures as subsidiary or contrasting cases, assuming the universality of its own concepts and tools. At the same time, Indian social scientists had to struggle with the concepts and theories deliberately or involuntarily imposed on them. Social and cultural *comparison* does not start in a vacuum, but has to be aware of the pre-constituted nature of every research relationship. The relationship with the field of study rests on pre-existing social, cultural, and political relationships between the contexts that are being compared, which have evolved historically. Research, in particular, is inescapably implicated in relations of authority and power, and confronted by value disparities. What we have to consider is not just the (post-)colonial context per se, but also the different and changing forms of episteme involved in the modes of data generation and processing.[2] This includes various forms of objectivation of people,

1 As attested by Arnason and Hann (2018).

2 First systematically addressed in Cohn (1968). Later, in an effort to characterise the mode of governance based on such data, Nicholas Dirks (2001) coined the term 'the ethnographic state' for this kind of colonial rule.

practices, and ideas, as it encompasses the traditions of Orientalist and philological scholarship.

In more general terms, at issue is the mode of translation between and across contexts, and this operates on two levels: on the one hand, the translation between different social and cultural contexts and the languages and semiotics involved, and on the other, the translation of ideas, concepts (explicit as well as implicit concepts), and practices encountered in social life, cultural activities, or texts (or sedimented in other cultural artefacts) into scholarly language and theories. Among the widely used concepts that display an inbuilt bias towards Western constellations and self-understanding, and which are under fire today, are concepts such as 'religion', 'belief', 'civilisation', 'secularisation', or 'individual and society'. The aim of the comparison also matters: Is it meant to define and demarcate the other, or is it meant to listen to the other? Is the intention to appropriate the other intellectually, perhaps to use the other as one's mirror, or is comparison receptive to possible modifications of one's own viewpoints?

The pictures that individual social science disciplines provide show differences, however. While anthropology, for example, has become more self-critical following postcolonial critique and shows a greater inclination to listen to others and foreground the perspectives of people on the ground (Berg and Fuchs 1993; Clifford and Marcus 1986), comparative sociology has much greater difficulty in letting go of frames of thought that generalise selective experiences and (often normative) notions of modernisation and modernity. Even basic sociological propositions like the theoretical concepts of social praxis, agency, and intersubjectivity still take their cues largely from Western sources.

In contrast to other Western countries, Germany has not played a leading role in the conceptual development of anthropology or in postcolonial studies, while it has done so in the field of sociology. The towering figure here is that of Max Weber. Weber stands for a comparative approach that operates on the macro level. India is his favourite case of contrast with the Judaic-Christian world. To do so, he takes India as a civilisational entity, to be approached in an imperial manner in order to grasp its essentials, its core. In some ways, Weber is torn between a fascination for the many facets of India, its political history and social structures, its religious diversity, its intellectual systems, even its scientific achievements, *and* the attempt to cut research short, to put the manifold reality in a nutshell, in order to then return to the only global success story, as he sees it—that of the West. This may sound harsh to some, and one could even make the argument that Weber, when he died, had been on the verge of developing greater doubts regarding the teleological Western-centric models of world history. But this is speculation and we have to deal with his writings as he left them behind, which is also how they have been received in India. Weber, one should mention here, never visited India or any other Asian country.

CIVILISATIONAL AGENDAS

When looking at the ways in which Weber dealt with religion and society in the Indian subcontinent, we primarily have to take into consideration the agenda—or rather, agendas—underlying his comparative essays on world religions (*Gesammelte Aufsätze zur Religionssoziologie [GARS]*). This includes three volumes, the second of which is the one on India, titled *Hinduismus und Buddhismus*. It was first published in 1916/17 in the form of a journal contribution, as the second encompassing case study (after 'Konfuzianismus und Taoismus') of 'Die Wirtschaftsethik der Weltreligionen' ('The Economic Ethics of World Religions'). Weber himself prepared the book edition which was published in 1921, after his death; this contained only minor changes.[3]

---

[3] The study on Hinduism and Buddhism appeared first in three parts in the *Archiv für Sozialwissenschaft und Sozialpolitik* 41 (3), April 1916, 613–744; 42 (2), December 1916, 345–461; and 42 (3), May 1917, 687–814. The book edition appeared in January 1921 as Vol. 2 of *GARS* (RS II). The only English translation of the book so far (by Hans H. Gerth and Don Martindale) was published in 1958 under the title, *The Religion of India: The Sociology of Hinduism and Buddhism*. This translation was not licensed and contains numerous and, in some cases, serious mistakes (*cf.* Kantowsky 1985 and 1986).

The three volumes of *GARS* were never translated completely into English. Unaware of the composition of *GARS*, English-language readers tend to miss

How did Weber proceed with comparison in his study of India? At the outset, Weber was particularly interested in what can be called a case of negative causality.[4] He wanted to explore why, in regions other than Western Europe, modern forms of capitalism, and especially what he calls the 'capitalist spirit'—or, more generally, the 'ability and disposition of men to adopt certain types of *practical rational conduct* [*Lebensführung*; emphasis mine]'—did not develop on their own. This spirit or disposition was, in the case of Western Europe, formed by religious ethics, as Weber argued in his study *The Protestant Ethic and the Spirit of Capitalism* (RS II, 4; 359/1958, 4; 325; RS I, 1; 11–12, 17–206/2004c, 109; 2009). This is his first agenda.[5] However, while conducting studies on non-European regions and religions, Weber broadened the scope of his approach to not only include the other side of that 'causal' relationship, namely the role of economics and social stratification in the development of economic ethics (RS I, 12–13/2004c, 110),[6] but also to undertake a wholesale civilisational comparison as part of the second agenda.[7] To do so,

out on the context of Weber's case studies as laid down by Weber in the three conceptual chapters of Vol. 1 of *GARS*, the 'Vorbemerkung' or 'Prefatory Remarks to the Collected Essays in the Sociology of Religion' to GARS, the 'Einleitung' or 'Introduction' to the 'Wirtschaftsethik der Weltreligionen' ('Economic Ethics of the World Religions'), and the 'Zwischenbetrachtung' or 'Intermediate Reflection on the Economic Ethics of the World Religions' (*cf.* Weber 2004a, b, c).

4 S. Munshi (1998) makes this the main point of his critique of Weber's study on India.

5 *Die protestantische Ethik und der Geist des Kapitalismus* (*The Protestant Ethic and the Spirit of Capitalism)* was first published in 1904/05 in Vols 20 and 21 of the *Archiv für Sozialwissenschaft und Sozialpolitik.* Weber revised the text for the 1920 publication of the study as part of the first volume of GARS. The first English translation by Talcott Parsons appeared in 1930, and a new translation by Stephen Kalberg in 2001 (*cf.* Weber 2009).

6 He considers the economic interests impacting on religious actors. These economic interests, however, can assume particular shape once they have been translated into a specific religious idiom or perspective.

7 Weber's term for civilisation is 'area of culture (*Kulturkreis*)' (RS I, 12/2004c, 109), that is, 'cultural world' or 'cultural area' (Arnason 2003, 87).

he anchored this comparative approach in a universal, evolutionist theory of rationalisation, which includes a theory of differentiation of 'value-spheres' or 'life-orders' (*Wertsphären, Lebensordnungen*),[8] the development of each sphere bringing to the fore its respective 'autonomous logics' (*innere Eigengesetzlichkeiten*; RS I, 541).[9]

Both these agendas expect, and establish, a specific relationship between religion and economics, or social (that is, this-worldly) life in general. While emphasising on the one hand the differentiation or dissociation of value-spheres, each governed by sphere-specific rationales and supposedly leading to increased tensions between them, especially between religion and the other spheres, Weber on the other hand expects religions in pre-modern days to have had a particular hold over the non-religious spheres.[10] Regarding his first objective or agenda, he considers those religious values that have an impact on economic action to be of particular social significance. This assumption is based on both a model of social action and a specific idea of the person that he obtains from his study of (Puritan) Protestant ethics, and which he generalises.[11] It takes such religion as pragmatic, that is,

8 Weber distinguishes six 'value-spheres', or 'life-orders', with religion as the originally encompassing one: politics, economics, knowledge or science, the aesthetic, and the erotic.

9 'Autonomous logics' is Johann Arnason's translation of *Eigengesetzlichkeiten*; he also suggests rendering *Wertsphären* or *Lebensordnungen* as 'world orders' (2003, 153; 230). Sam Whimster translates '*innere Eigengesetzlichkeit*' as '*internal and autonomous working* ... of the individual spheres' (Weber 2004a, 219). Weber expounds his theory of the increasing tensions between the six value-spheres in the *Zwischenbetrachtung* at the end of Vol. 1 of *GARS* (for the English translation, see Weber 2004a). This was meant to be the first theoretical conclusion of his comparative civilisational studies.

10 This hold seems broken only in post-Protestant modern societies.

11 The requirement of a specific attitude towards life and work (self-control and self-monitoring; 'disinterested' interest in worldly pursuits) as the ground for rationalisation in the economic field is based on the assumption that such an attitude ('ethics') requires transcendental sanction as well as gratification. A further underlying assumption is that of consistency of a person across spheres of action. And it is being assumed that specific ideas tend to instigate particular (lines of) action.

geared towards controlling (or placing demands on) and formatting practices and values in other spheres.

Viewed from this angle, in the end only one culture, one religious tradition, looks fully authentic to Weber (Arnason n.d., 8; Fuchs 1988, 279).[12] To find a way out of this conundrum of turning a particularistic religious constellation into the general model, Weber somewhat relativises his claim. He maintains in the first sentence of the 'Vorbemerkung' to the GARS, the last piece he wrote,[13] that this type of religion, together with other related cultural phenomena, represents a development of '*universal* significance and *validity*', as 'we' (that is, people in the West) specifically '*like to think*' (RS I, 1/2004c, 101; emphasis mine). This qualifier of the claim for universality already points to the third agenda.

This concerns the fact that Weber, at the very same time, had discovered a cultural diversity of rationalisations in the various social spheres, even within the same culture region. He then started looking systematically for alternative routes of rationalisation, and this became what I would call his third agenda: 'One can in fact "rationalize" life,' Weber writes in the revised version of *Protestant Ethic*, 'from a vast variety of ultimate vantage points. Moreover, one can do so in very different directions' (RS I, 62/2009, 88). 'Hence rationalizations of the most varied character have existed in various departments of life and in all cultural areas' (RS I, 11f, that is, the *Vorbemerkung*/2004c, 109; see also RS I, 266, that is, the *Einleitung* to the *Die Wirtschaftsethik der Weltreligionen*. This has been omitted in the translation [Weber 2004b]). The third agenda or approach is the one that involves the fewest presuppositions. It starts with realising that tendencies towards rationalisation can vary within each sphere

12 Schluchter (1979, 34, 37), who claims a '*Sonderstellung*', a special status, for modern Western culture, and sees it as representing '*eine ausgezeichnete Auslegung des Kulturmenschentums*', a particularly distinguished variant of the existence of cultural human beings, forcing all others (non-Western cultural women and men) to 'relate to' this variant.

13 Probably written in the winter of 1919–1920 (RS I, 1–16). Translated into English first by Talcott Parsons and recently by Sam Whimster (Weber 2004c).

of life. The third approach not only allows for rationalisations in the plural, but even more importantly, it allows for specific developments (rationalisations) in specific areas or contexts (for example, single religious traditions) and does not have to apply to an entire culture, religion, society, or civilisation.

Weber's three comparative agendas delineated above show a scholar whose thought was still evolving. For a long time, most comparative sociologists favoured one of the first two agendas, or a combination of both. I do agree that these dominated Weber's position as it stood in 1920, but I do not subscribe to them. I insist that we also take adequate account of the third and more open or pluralist orientation wherever it appears in Weber's work.

Weber amasses a wide range of religious, social, economic, and political facets from the different Indian regions. However, he did not do so in order to undertake region- and time-specific case studies, but to illustrate and argue certain general points, thereby constantly moving back and forth across wide geographical and temporal distances. Hence, he took the various time- and region-specific facets of Indian social history as parts of *one* playing ground, one shared general structure, and thus as expressions of structural continuity. The approach that Weber had chosen allows for only one source of Indian civilisation (the north-Indian Vedic tradition), and can on principle not accommodate other sources from either within the subcontinent (for example, the Tamilian traditions) or from without.

ANALYSING INDIA: SOCIAL AND CULTURAL DIMENSIONS

Let me now look somewhat closer into the main aspects of Weber's study. I will concentrate on the structure of the sociological argument pursued by him in his book on Indian religions and Indian civilisation. I will touch upon (*i*) the analysis of India's political systems; (*ii*) the analysis of India's social structure, especially caste; (*iii*) the analysis of Indian religions; and wind up with (*iv*) a discussion on the ways he engages with Indian systems of knowledge.

THE POLITICAL INSTITUTION OF INDIAN SOCIETY[14]

Weber was one of the first comparative social scientists to emphasise the significance of the separation of political authority and the priesthood in India; he also acknowledged that this had occurred at an early stage in India's history (Weber RS II, 139–142, 144–146/1958, 141–143, 145–146).[15] Weber emphasised both the structural and the ethical significance of the separation of the two functions and their related spheres. Acknowledging the thorough and independent rationalisation of the political in India, he regrets that adequate ethical controls (natural law and human rights concepts) did not develop alongside it (RS II, 142–144/1958, 144–145). Weber's position, however, is not fully consistent. On the one hand, he states that politics was 'theorised in perfectly "Machiavellian" manner' in India (RS II, 3; 1958, 3) and, with reference to, *inter alia*, Kauṭilya's *Arthaśāstra*, that the 'power pragmatics ... were altogether left here to follow their autonomous logics [*Machtpragma ... war hier, gerade von der Theorie, ganz und gar seinen eigenen Gesetzen überlassen*]' (RS II, 146, translation mine; 1958, 146). On the other hand, he contradicts himself, stating in the 'Vorbemerkung' that 'all Asiatic political thought was lacking in a systematic method comparable to that of Aristotle, and, indeed, in the possession of rational concepts' (RS I, 2; 2004c, 101).[16] We will see later, with reference to Indian

---

14 I have commented on Max Weber's study of India and Indic religions at several instances (see, among others, Fuchs 1987, 1988, 2017, 2020, forthcoming).

I will limit my comments on Weber's discussion of Indian politics here to points that play a systematic role in my argument.

15 Louis Dumont later made this aspect a central instance of his own comparative conceptualisation of Indian society, without giving Weber, whose study of India he knew well, the credit due to him for already having brought this up (Dumont 1980, 66ff, 287ff; see Fuchs 1988, 363ff, 454ff).

16 This seems a strange remark. According to Weber's own (evolutionary) theory of rationalisation, Machiavellianism and the full-fledged pursuit of the autonomous logical possibilities (*Eigengesetzlichkeit*) of the political would represent a more advanced stage than Aristotelian systematisation. Thus, logically speaking, the *Arthaśāstra* would have to be seen to anticipate a developmental stage that was only reached much later in Europe.

scientific developments, how Weber again shies away from the full consequences of his own theoretical insight.

The case for the separation of the religious and political functions and spheres is, however, not that straightforward. While each value-sphere can develop and be rationalised independent of the other, this does not exclude the possibility that a ruler may keep cosmological functions, be vested in a special relationship with some god(s), protect his subjects as well as the *dhārmic* order, and/or act as a ritual agent in relation to nature (Conrad 1986; Derrett 1976).[17] Nor does it imply that Brahmins cannot pragmatically engage in worldly matters. Differentiation and rationalisation on the categorial level and within certain schools of thought do not mean that these processes are automatically mirrored on the level of social institutions and social interaction.

Analytically, Weber himself addresses the institutional aspect of authority or rule (German: *Herrschaft*) from a more politico-economic angle. Yet, it is rather difficult to pin down Weber's view of Indian structures of dominance and governance. While he considers India to have been dominated by patrimonialism over major periods of its development (for roughly two millennia, from the time of the Mauryas until the beginning of British colonisation),[18] he also states that India kept oscillating (*schwanken*) between 'feudal organisation and patrimonialism' (RS II, 73; 1958, 72). On the one hand, he asserts that it was the coalition between patrimonial rulers and Brahmins that led to the framing and fixing of the caste system and forever closed the possibility of other developmental options without external (that is, colonial) intervention (RS II, 128, 131, 318f; 1958, 128, 130f, 292). On the other hand, he found in the Middle Ages 'elements of truly feudal

---

17 Besides, a general equation of Brahmins and priesthood seems problematic in the Indian case: 'Not only have there been, after Vedic times, many classes of priests other than brahmins, but vast numbers of brahmins were not priests in any recognizable sense' (Derrett 1976, 602). Rather, Brahmins working as priests are considered socially degraded compared to the scholarly or renunciatory Brahmins (Fuller 1979; Heesterman 1985).

18 In RS II, 108; 1958, 109, Weber talks of the 'patrimonial church-state structure of the old kingdoms'; see further RS II, 72, 75, 253; 1958, 71, 74f, 235.

social structure ... in most parts of India, particularly in the west, often in quite occidental form' (RS II, 67; 1958, 66; translation adapted).[19] Finally, even when asserting the patrimonial character of India's political structure, it does not look as if Brahmins and Brahminism were natural (or 'electively affine') coalition partners: according to Weber himself, the first full-fledged patrimonial state in India, that of Ashoka, used Buddhism as the 'means of mass domestication' (RS II, 260; 1958, 240), and Jainism, too, it seems, was a suitable 'official state religion' (RS II, 210, 216; 1958, 199, 203). What, according to Weber, brought patrimonial rulers and Brahmins together was their joint interest in smashing the merchant cities, with whom the earlier patrimonial state had cooperated, but which then, he argues, had become too politically and financially strong, and moreover had become sites in which the non-Brahmanic religious movements had been thriving.

The treatment of feudalism and patrimonialism is one of the most jumbled parts of Weber's work. The patrimonialist diagnosis of the Indian political system dominates in Weber's writing, even though the ground the diagnosis stands on appears somewhat shaky. The predominance of both patrimonialism and the patrimonialism-Brahmanism cooperation play a core part in Weber's systematic argument about India. On this highly general level of analysis, Weber does not differentiate, but treats the various historical empires and kingdoms, whose religious engagements reflect the whole array, from Buddhism, Jainism, and Hinduism to Islam (he basically takes note of the Mughal Empire), as being of one type (RS II, 69–71; 1958, 67–69).[20]

19 Weber's usage of the 'middle ages' periodisation in his study on India is extremely vague. It may or may not include the Maurya period at one end, and it may or may not include Islamic rule at the other (*cf.* Fuchs 1988, 96). The reference to India's west relates especially to Rajput rule.

20 In *Economy and Society*, his other major work, Weber emphasises the systematic difference, and the consequences of the distinction, between feudalism and patrimonialism, not without once again blurring that distinction: Patriarchal patrimonialism and feudalism 'shaped strongly divergent political and social ideologies and through them a very different style of life [*Lebensführung*]' (W&G, 650; 1978b, 1104). However, at other

THE CULTURAL INSTITUTION OF INDIAN SOCIETY

Not unlike his investigation of political structures, Weber's analysis of India's social structure(s) is characterised by a major tension: Weber's historical sense seems constantly at odds with his idea of the continuity, if not immutability, of Indian society, a characteristic he claims to have gained from his colonial-ethnological as well as Indological sources.

Weber sees cities, and along with them capitalism, as having flourished for over roughly one millennium, starting from the seventh century BCE (RS II, 86; 1958, 86), but alleges that these left little lasting social or economic traces (other than affecting the features of individual castes). Reducing the long phase of urban development in India to a historical interlude, Weber took India as basically 'a country of villages', fully in accordance with the colonial scholarship of the day (for example, authors like Henry Baden-Powell). 'India, in contrast to China, has been, and remains, a land of villages . . .' (RS II, 1; also 109; 1958, 3; also 111).[21] He joins Karl Marx in his judgement that 'the peculiar position of the artisan in the Indian village—his dependence upon fixed payment in kind instead of upon production for the market . . .' has to be regarded 'as the reason for the specific "stability" of the Asian peoples' (RS II, 109; 1958, 111).

Of all the institutions in India, it is obviously caste that takes up the most space in Weber's book. Weber tackles caste from different angles: he tries to pin down the social unit to which the term applies, and he tries to place caste within his theoretical and categorial framework; he further looks for a mechanism that drives castes and would historically explain their forms and functioning; and he looks for a shared ideology, or a shared structure of meaning, that keeps people attached to the 'system' and thus sustains it. To cut

places in the same work, the feudatory relationship appears to him not so much as opposite to patrimonialism as just a 'marginal case' of patrimonialism (W&G, 624, 636; 1978b, 1069, 1086).

[21] Only to add, 'But at the same time it was a land of trade, foreign, particularly with the Occident, as well as domestic . . .' (RS II, 2–3; 1958, 3). This ignores the flourishing urban economy of later days, destroyed by colonialism.

the analysis short:[22] for Weber, castes represent an extreme form of status groups (*Stände*); considering both their hereditary and closed or self-contained character and the 'magical distance[23] between castes in their mutual relationships', there existed even 'deadly jealousy and hostility' amongst them (RS II, 4, 36f, 40, 42; 1958, 4, 34, 38, 39). He first tries to catch this by employing the notion of *Gentilcharisma*, 'clan charisma', that is, charisma affixed to, and handed down via a line of descent.[24] However, there is a second and better-known principle that Weber believes could help us understand the ways castes, considered an order or even a system, operate: the *karman-saṃsāra* (retribution-rebirth) doctrine. For him, this doctrine provides the only reason why people would accept their specific *dharma*, that is, the social role and status accorded to them, as well as all obligations connected with it.

Weber takes on thoughts and ideas that had been repeatedly brought forward in the orientalist, colonial, and missionary discourses on India. However, it is interesting how he handles them. As a prefabricated figure of thought ('*Gedankengebilde*'; not included in Weber 1958) and as 'theodicy'—the 'product of rational ethical thought'—*karman-saṃsāra*, he supposes, is an invention of the dominant caste of Brahmins (RS II, 131; 1958, 131; translation adapted). Although this theory represents a somewhat voluntaristic foundation of the origin and perpetuation of the caste system, it did not keep him from jumping to a very culturalist conclusion: this system of thought had 'irresistible power over the thought and hope of the people embedded in it' (RS II, 131; 1958, 131; translation corrected). The '*Geist*', that is, the spirit of the system, permeates

22 For more detail, see Fuchs 1988, 33–81.

23 For Weber, this includes ritual barriers.

24 It is this principle that, for him, lies behind, and even already includes, the institutional base of the caste phenomenon: 'As clan charisma supported the caste so caste, in turn, supported the charisma of the sib' (RS II, 57; 1958, 54). It was the *Gentilcharisma* that differentiated social groups from each other and alienated them as a result. The problem with this analysis is that Weber fails to accurately distinguish between exogamy (of clans, lineages) and endogamy (the circle of intermarriage) (Fuchs 1988, 43f; Rösel 1975, 70; 1982, 95).

society like ether, overruling all the empirical intricacies.[25] Individual rules and difficulties cannot explain why economic rationalisation was obstructed in India; rather, 'the core of the obstruction was the "*spirit*" [*Geist*] of the whole system' (RS II, 110; 1958, 112; emphasis mine).[26] Nor did it matter if the 'individual devout Hindu' understood the *karman* doctrine and its presuppositions; the system existed independently of what a given person actually thought and believed: the individual Hindu 'was incarcerated in a cage [*Gehäuse*, in the German original], which made sense only in this ideational context, and the consequences of this burdened his actions' (RS II, 120f; 1958, 121; translation mine).[27] It was the combination of 'ritual law' (both the *dharmaśāstras* and group-specific rules) and the 'promise of rebirth' that turned this into a 'closed system' (RS II, 110, 130, 131; 1958, 111, 130, 131). The doctrine of *karman* is for Weber 'the most consistent theodicy ever produced by history', turning the world 'into a strictly rational, ethically-determined cosmos' (RS II, 120; 1958, 121).

In Weber's hands, the *karman-saṃsāra* concept is given enormous social weight. It determines the thought and action of those exposed to it, and in this way safeguards and reproduces the social order. It combines, so he claims, the poles of individualistic and social

25 He acknowledges that 'this consequence [that human beings, going through an endless chain of rebirth and re-death, determine their own fate only by their own actions] was not always maintained', and was himself fully aware that the *śraddha* ceremony, which is intended to influence the fortunes of the dead, 'contradicted' (his words) the *karman-saṃsāra* doctrine (RS II, 119; 1958, 120; translation adapted).

26 Weber had earlier applied the notion of 'Geist' to the ethics of Protestantism (in the formula, '*Der Geist des Kapitalismus*'; RS I, 17; Weber 2009), with which he compares all the other major religions.

27 Just a few pages earlier, he had made the empirically stronger claim that *saṃsāra* and *karman* define the dogmatic core of all Hinduism and that no Hindu would deny these (RS II, 117). Note the similarities between this characterisation of the spirit claimed to permeate the Indian world and Weber's depiction of the capitalist spirit in the case of the West, resulting in a '*stahlhartes Gehäuse*', 'steel-hard casing', also translated as 'shell as hard as steel' or 'iron cage', operating on its own, independent of what people think and feel (RS I, 203; 2009, 158).

principles—the postulate of the individual's own responsibility for his/her destiny and the demand to submit to social norms.

What Weber practises here is a kind of objectivist, culturalist hermeneutics by defining a consistent and closed system of thought and ascribing it to all those who are deemed to belong to a specific 'religion'. It offers a rational, consistent theodicy as it provides the main support for the 'organic', that is, the graded social ethics of Indian society, and so becomes the mental nucleus of society, its ideational basis. And it ostensibly unites the perspectives of participants and observers. The *saṃsāra-karman* doctrine thus becomes the pivotal category in Weber's analysis of Indian society, in the manner of Marcel Mauss' '*fait social total*'.

Weber is grossly overstating both the internal consistency and the role and significance of the *karman* and *saṃsāra* 'doctrine'.[28] First, *saṃsāra-karman* is neither employed nor accepted throughout the Hindu segment of the Indian population.[29] It therefore does not seem

[28] We know today that castes have been very fluid and versatile groupings, and actually have never been of one kind (see, for example, Bayly 1999). Between the lines, Weber seems to acknowledge how difficult, if not impossible, it actually is to find the one and only master key for an explanation of caste, and more than that, of the 'system' of caste (RS II, 45–49, 98, 100f, 108; 1958, 44–48, 100, 102f, 109; *cf.* Fuchs 1988, 34, 39, 61). Insofar as Weber himself feels dissatisfied with a notion of India 'as sum of its parts' (Cohn 1968, 16), he tends to look for general formulas, like the one discussed above (the '*Geist*' of the whole system).

[29] Sometimes the *karman-saṃsāra* concept is not known, and in other cases, it is met with scepticism or even rejected. This is especially the case with people at the bottom of the social ladder (Berreman 1967; Cohn 1959; Juergensmeyer 1980; Kolenda 1964). Additionally, *karman* is not unanimously interpreted in classical, textual traditions, among social actors, or in everyday life. In everyday life, the concept of *karman* is often employed retrospectively, only to rationalise failure; if related back to the actions of an 'identical' past Ego, this is often not interpreted in the sense of a personal moral responsibility. The interpretation of *karman* oscillates between a 'deterministic' and a 'voluntaristic' perspective (S. Daniel 1983; Halbfass 1980; Keyes 1983a; Sharma 1973). Finally, one finds alternative, and to some extent rival, models of explaining the 'residual' (Babb 1983) of what practical reasoning cannot give reasons for, such as events in one's life, especially the blows of fate and suffering (feeling under someone's spell; actions of deities;

to be the basic driving force of Indian society, and does not have the clear-cut consequences on action that Weber claims. Second, Weber errs with regard to the ways in which *karman* functions, and the role it plays in the actions of Indian people.[30] If *karman* is understood strictly causal-ethically, it is connected with the quest for salvation and less with orienting 'inner-worldly' action.[31] When included in social interactions, it loses its ethical acuity. *Karman* can be transferred and corrected. Social and individualistic principles cannot be united without contradictions. If all this is the case, then Weber's contentions regarding the kind, extent, and strictness of the influence of the *saṃsāra-karman* doctrine on Indian society and its (economic) development cannot be maintained.[32]

The image that Weber evokes regarding India's social structure is of certain seeds sown at the outset which developed partially organically and partially by intelligent and somewhat malicious Brahmanical design into a full-blown closed system, which then froze (*Gentilcharisma*, particularist *dharmas*, that is, group-specific moral rules). This system then combined with an idea of theodicy that allowed nobody, not even those most disadvantaged, to cultivate any idea of dissent. In addition, Weber lacked sensitivity towards the conditions of the so-called 'Untouchables' and the modalities of

predeterminations through destiny—*bhāgya* [Hindi], *viti* [Tamil]) (Babb 1983; E. V. Daniel 1983; Hiebert 1983; Sharma 1973).

30 *Karman* does not have to be understood as certain results ('retribution') mechanically and inflexibly following from the individual's action. Rather, *karman* can be transferred and corrected in the eyes of many Indians; it gets a social character. In the Hindu context, such transferences happen especially between close relatives, and in the Buddhist context in the form of merit transfer between *bhikkhus* and lay people. A specific instance is the exercise of influence on the destiny of dead ancestors in connection with the *śrāddha* ceremony (S. Daniel 1983; Dumont 1980; Kane 1953; Keyes 1983a, b; O'Flaherty 1980; Sharma 1973; Wadley 1983).

31 The *karman* doctrine 'pushes for wresting oneself free from the world of the collective and points to individual salvation. [...] the consequence of the *karman* doctrine means nothing less than the call for dismantling the world' (Heesterman 1984, 78).

32 For a detailed critique of Weber's handling of *karman* and *saṃsāra*, see Fuchs (1988, 64–81).

humiliation and stigmatisation. He was unable to distinguish between the general social mechanisms of group formation and differentiation (caste), *and* specific modes of exclusivism (and inclusivism).

The sociology of pollution or impurity does not play a central role in Weber's depiction of India. Weber takes the fact of 'ritual impurity' as given, referring in particular to the work with leather, sweeping or scavenging, and the consumption of beef. Considering ritual impurity as 'magical', he makes no attempt to understand the logic of this phenomenon, be it in a relational or substantial sense, but develops a theory of original non-belonging: he tries to derive the existence of groups included through exclusion or 'negative privileging' from the fact that these had supposedly been tribal groups originally, which then became 'guest tribes' and were thus only partially integrated into Hinduistic society. Not only does he not take the purity-impurity, Brahmin-Untouchable hierarchical opposition as the basis of the caste 'system', as Louis Dumont later did (Dumont 1980), but he also followed an argumentative strategy contrary to that which later became common. For him, it was the sociological mechanism of exclusion (which led people to not fully belong) that established the basis for stigmatisation, rather than stigmatisation being the basis for exclusion. But this also means that Weber, unlike Dumont after him, did not completely amalgamate the issue of the ascription of impurity and stigmatisation with the mechanisms of caste in general, which also include endogamy and intra-group solidarity.[33] Weber reduces the entire issue of stigmatisation and degradation to a question of admittance to ranks in a given normatively designed order.

INDIAN SOTERIOLOGIES

The conception of a germination-growth-and-freezing model is even clearer in Weber's work when it comes to Indian religions of salvation. Not involved in the executive function of political dominance, the

33 Regarding the term 'Pariah', Weber states that the term is not really valid in the Hinduistic context—'[a]s far as the Hindus are concerned', it would be 'quite incorrect' to use this term (RS II, 12, fn.; 1958, 12).

priests or Brahmins—regarded by Weber as a rather homogenous group—established India's core religion.[34]

Weber sketches a two-stage developmental process of Indic religion: from ritualism—which Weber also calls *magic* (*Magie* and *Zauberei*)—to soteriology, as formulated in the Upaniṣads (the earliest approximately between the seventh and fifth centuries BCE). Weber regards Brahmins, whom he takes in their entirety as both the 'genteel literati' *and* 'magicians' or priests[35] (RS II, 60f, 136f, 147, 149f; 1958, 58, 139, 147, 149f), as the carriers (*Träger*)[36] of this development.[37] Monkhood and 'professional' asceticism appear as a largely Brahmanical achievement, which developed out of the classical magical Brahmanic asceticism (RS II, 157–162; 1958, 155–158).[38] Intellectually and spiritually, the Upaniṣads represent the culmination and, in a way, the conclusion of the evolution of religious speculation in India (RS II, 162, 175ff; 1958, 158, 169ff). What followed over the next more than 2,000 years did not seem to challenge this basic frame.[39]

---

34 Weber's remark about Brahmins pursuing 'other professions' does not make clear if he thinks that those who fall in rank do so within the Brahmin category, or if they lose their Brahmin status (RS II, 64; 1958, 62f) altogether.

35 Weber treats priests and magicians as equivalents.

36 The 1958 translation provides the word 'vehicle' (1958, 147), or 'to champion' (ibid., 183) for 'Träger'.

37 Weber's equation of priests with magicians, and the reductionist understanding of ritual as just magic, is highly problematic. Hans Joas, discussing Weber's attitude to Catholicism, regards this as a Protestant legacy (Joas 2010, 446). Weber knows, in principle, of the existence of non-Brahmanic priests, and acknowledges that this may be an expression of opposition to Brahmins, but shares the Brahmanical view that the non-Brahmanical priests have to be regarded as 'degraded' (RS II, 64; 1958, 62).

38 Weber translates *sādhu* and *sannyāsī* (or *saṃnyāsī*) as 'monk', but also uses *bhikshu* (*bhikkhu*). He connects '*Altersasketen*' ('senior ascetics', referring to the fourth stage of life) with '*Berufsasketen*' ('professional ascetics'). The first Brahmanical monasteries, *maṭhs*, may have been emulations of heterodox (especially Buddhist) institutions.

39 For Weber, this includes the fact that Brahmins, in their priestly role, retained dimensions of the magic of their origin (RS II, 136f; 1958, 139).

The soteriology of what Weber calls classical-orthodox Hinduism is the 'contemplative mysticism of a Gnostic type' (RS II, 148; 1958, 148; translation adapted), its goal the 'absolute salvation from the world as such' (RS II, 172; 1958, 167; translation adapted). Essential for this idea of salvation are, in Weber's view, the non-personal character of the Divine or Absolute and the rejection of the world, not because of its sinfulness or its imperfection, but because of its transience (RS II, 149–151, 154, 162, 167–178; 1958, 148–150, 152f, 158, 163–172).

Still, Weber had to accommodate deviant developments:

(i) The *Bhagavadgītā* (between 200 BCE and 100 CE), developing alongside the writing of the Upaniṣads, introduced non-classical elements into Indian society, namely *bhakti*, that is, the concept of God's grace and thus the belief in 'the super-worldly personal God' or in a Saviour.[40] The (inner-worldly) ethical message of the Gita is that of 'world-indifference' (RS II, 194)—to act 'without regard to results and without personal interest' in one's acts (RS II, 199; 1958, 189). Weber considers this the 'crown of classical ethics of Indian intellectuals' (RS II, 194; 1958, 185) and the acceptance of concurrent ways towards salvation (*Heilswege*), that is, *jñānayoga*, *karmayoga*, besides *bhaktiyoga*, as an acknowledgement of classical Gnosis (RS II, 195; 1958, 185).

(ii) Buddhism and Jainism merely represent intellectual variations of the Indian soteriological paradigm. Weber includes these as heterodox forms opposed to Brahmanical orthodoxy, a status these soteriologies never lost for him. 'Professional monks' (*Berufsmönche*) became the carriers (*Träger*) of these religions. Buddhism, for Weber, was an 'ethic of nonaction', which marks the 'culmination' of the 'soteriologies of the distinguished/genteel Hindu intellectuals' and represents the 'ultimate [lit., 'most extreme'; translation mine] ethic of world-rejection' and 'the most radical form of striving for redemption which is conceivable' (W&G, 483; 1978b, 627; RS II, 220f, 235,

40 Throughout, Weber regards Krishna as *avatāra*, which he takes to mean the 'human incarnation' of the 'supreme divine being' or 'redeemer', saviour; he nowhere regards Krishna as being himself the Supreme Being (RS II, 191; 1958, 182).

251; 1958, 206, 217f, 233; translation adapted). Weber found certain similarities between Jainism and Christian Puritanism, but in the absence of a transcendental god, Jainism did not provide a comparable ethics (RS II, 212–217; 1958, 200–204). Buddhism too provided no ethical guidance for 'lay people'; rather, Mahayana Buddhism as well as Jainism retained aspects of 'magic' in his eyes (RS II, 217, 278; 1958, 204, 255).

(iii) Post-*Gītā* notions of *bhakti* are viewed by Weber as symptoms of decline, leading to a 'plebeisation' of Indian soteriology. He begins his overview of *bhakti* by defining it as 'passionate devotion to the redeemer and his grace', which he at the same time regards as being characterised by a 'deep intimacy to God' (RS II, 337; 1958, 307; translation corrected). From the point of view of soteriology, the 'adjustment' to 'plebeian religious needs' (and, significantly, not interests) of the lay people, plebians, or masses (RS II, 255, 326; 1958, 237, 297), signifies a de-rationalisation and 'plebeisation' of the Brahmins (RS II, 352ff; 1958, 320ff), while seen from the other end, it stands for a certain degree of rationalisation and 'sublimation' of earlier folk practices (RS II, 324, 326, 369; 1958, 296, 297, 335). Weber mentions the new relationship between believers and God (continuing what he saw in the *Gītā*) as well as the *universalisation* of chances of salvation (*Universalisierung der Erlösungschancen*)—the 'religious equality of all human beings, also of women' (Lingayats) (RS II, 334, 342, 343f; 1958, 304, 311, 312; translation adapted). He also acknowledges the 'permission of the lower castes to achieve *guru* status' (Kabir and Raidas) or the 'indifference toward caste distinctions' (the Tenkalai branch of Shrivaishnavism) (ibid.).

However, these observations fade beside the two other aspects that upset him: the orgiastic character of Shaivism, Shaktism, and Vaishnavism, as he sees it—above all, in the form of sexual, but also alcoholic, meat, and blood orgies (RS II, 135, 257, 324, 326, 333; 1958, 138, 239, 296, 298, 303)[41]—and 'anthropolatry', the veneration of 'corporal living

[41] Weber also emphasises what he regards as the continuity of human sacrifice within Shaivism and Shaktism (RS II, 333; 1958, 303).

saviours', *gurus*, or other 'magical dispensers of grace', and the 'deification' of 'all sect founders' (RS II, 351, 359, 369; *cf.* 159, 187; 1958, 319, 325, 335; *cf.* 156, 179). 'Adoration of the living saviour was the last word of Hindu religious development', 'the characteristic type of Asiatic piety' (RS II, 357, 369; 1958, 324, 335).[42] All said and done, Weber continued to regard Brahmins as the carriers of Hinduism, Hinduism still taken in the singular: 'The *guruhood* now constituted the typical role of the Brahman. As a *guru* the Brahman is a living god (*thakur*)' (RS II, 351; 1958, 319).

(iv) Islam, which had been present in India for over a millennium and, as specified by Weber, claimed about 20 per cent of India's population as its adherents around the turn of the twentieth century (RS II, 5; 1958, 5), is kept out of his account of Indian religions. Weber insists, just like the Hindu nationalists of today, that Islam in India means '*Fremdherrschaft*', 'foreign domination' (RS II, 4, 358; 1958, 4, 324), thus excluding a large section of the Indian population and Indian culture from his assessment of India. Weber elides all grounds that made Islam a compelling religious option in the Indian context, as well as the various ways that Islam and Hinduistic religious ideas and practices have (or had) blended in many regional contexts.[43]

India's religions play a central role in Weber's civilisational comparison. For him they are the main contrasting case of Western Christianity, and thus of a religion that in his view supports the rationalisation of inner-worldly action. It should be noted that Weber sees religions as *systems*, as dogmatic units; he does not take the perspectives and agency of ordinary, everyday social actors into account.

42 Weber makes a connection between Krishna and gurus or heads of sects as 'human saviours', up to the point of identifying both phenomena (RS II, 191, 197, 351/1958, 182, 187, 319). *Cf.* n40 above.

43 He states that the fact that 'numerous Hindu castes worship Islamic saints alongside Hindu deities, [...] and that Indian Islam absorbed numerous ritual practices of Hindu provenance' does not occupy him in this work (RS II, 21; 1958, 20; translation corrected).

On the level of ideal types, Weber contrasts the idea of a universal, transcendent (*überweltlichen*), and almighty personal God, who places ethical demands on humans and emphasises individual sin, with the idea of a non-personal Supreme Being or Order which, nevertheless, can also be experienced as world-immanent, but for Weber is linked to the idea of the transience (*Vergänglichkeit*) and futility (*Sinnlosigkeit*) of the world. Important here are the (psychological) consequences. The first position favours an attitude according to which human beings are ultimately god's instruments. This may lead to disciplined action within the (social) world 'against' the world. The second approach leads to a search for mystical experiences, to attempts to reduce or even flee action, or to act as non-involved (*innerlich unbeteiligt*) (RS I, 'Einleitung' and 'Zwischenbetrachtung'; 2004b; 2004a; 1978b, chapter on the Sociology of Religion [Religious Groups]; see Fuchs 1988, 153–156). In Weber's eyes, Indian religions (or better yet, Indic religions, to use a contemporary terminology) provide the best examples of this second ideal type. The Indian forms of world rejection that attempt to curtail involvement in worldly matters range from world indifference (*Weltindifferenz*), even while acting 'in the world' (for example, *Bhagavadgītā*; RS II, 367; 1958, 332f), to 'absolute flight from the world' (*absolute Weltflucht*) (RS II, 359; 1958, 326). India became the 'cradle of theoretically and practically the most world-denying (*weltverneinend*) forms of religious ethic that the world has ever known' (RS I, 536; 2004a, 215; translation corrected). Weber emphasises the 'Gnostic', 'aristocratic notion of salvation [*heilsaristokratisch*]' and the asocial and apolitical character of Indian religiosity (RS II, 148, 167, 199, 364–366, 369; 1958, 148, 162, 188, 330–332, 334).

Weber himself had stated that the 'belief in a supreme, personal, benevolent/merciful [*gütig*] Lord of Creation' arose again and again in India (RS II, 173, translation mine; *cf.* 1958, 168). But taking Indian religions as they are actually practised as representing a circumscribed ideal type of the kind just described foreclosed the possibility of giving full recognition to the Indian concepts as well as practices of unmediated access to a personal, universal God. It prevented Weber from detecting the numerous forms of individual interaction between devotees (*bhaktas*) and God that had become possible, and from seeing that other stances or attitudes towards the world (*Welteinstellungen*) had been generated in India, ones that represent a positive and affirmative relation to the world. Friedhelm Hardy, in his work on (Tamil) Krishna *bhakti* and Shrivaishnavism, speaks of the 'positive attitude to the world' (1983, 234), a 'this-worldly attitude' (ibid., 314), and the 'world-positive' (ibid., 447). Karen Pechilis Prentiss, in her work on Tamil Shaiva Siddhanta, talks of '(b)hakti's positive valuation of action in the world' as 'a constitutive premise of bhakti's thesis on embodiment' (1999, 18f).

Instead, Weber's final judgement was: '... from such mysticism [Weber relates to gnostic mysticism; translation mine] no ethic for life within the world could be deduced' (RS II, 178; 1958, 172). There was no connection possible for him between this 'otherworldly' soteriology and life in the world (RS II, 367; 1958, 333). According to Weber, this meant that the process of rationalisation in India got stuck (before attaining modernity).[44]

Knowledge Systems of India

As mentioned above, for Weber, the spheres of religion and politics were (conceptually) differentiated in India fairly early on. Weber further extends this idea of differentiation to other spheres in the Indian context. Since he does not look into the Indian aesthetic and erotic spheres, of which he knew little, the main sphere he covers, besides religion, economics, and the political order, is that in knowledge and science. Here, we encounter the most extreme contradiction in Weber's India study. Weber makes statements that appreciate Indian achievements in a wide range of fields, from algebra and arithmetic to grammar, from medicine to metallurgy, and from politics to philosophy, especially logic. Hinduism, he says, was able 'to do individual justice to each sphere of life and of knowledge and

---

44 Weber takes the macro- and the micro-levels of social life as isomorphic, so that basic attitudes or stances, *Stellungnahmen*, towards the world informing the outlook of individuals—world rejection (*Weltablehnung*), world flight (*Weltflucht*), world affirmation (*Weltbejahung*), world dominance (*Weltbeherrschung*)—also reflect the general or predominant attitude characteristic of a civilisation, that is, its collective worldview.

thus establish true/actual [*wirkliche*] specialised scientific disciplines [*Fachwissenschaften*]' (RS II, 146; translation mine; *cf.* 1958, 146). As we have seen, politics in his view had been elaborated on the conceptual level, according to its autonomous logics.

However, there are other statements where Weber tries to turn these very findings on their head: 'The factual inner orders of the real world of nature as of art, ethics, and of economics remained concealed to the distinguished/genteel strata', 'the strata of the wise and educated', in Asia in general and in India in particular, 'because for them those orders seemed bereft of any interest' (RS II, 378; 1958, 343; translation corrected). To Weber, this was the case because 'individual striving for redemption' 'functioned as barrier to the development of specialised scientific disciplines as well as to the development of intellectual questions in general' (RS II, 146f; 1958, 147; translation corrected).

On the one hand, processes of rationalisation in India appear to be the perfect illustration of an open relationship between the different value-spheres, as discussed in the *Zwischenbetrachtung*. India, and especially Indian religions, seemingly allowed (that is, did not hinder) each sphere to discover and then follow its *Eigengesetzlichkeiten*, autonomous logical possibilities. On the other hand, Weber sees Indian religions as actually obstructing rationalisation in other spheres. To prove this last position, Weber puts up two very different arguments. The first argument states that Indians under the spell of religion were indifferent towards, if not ignorant of, things and processes in the 'real' world, including nature. The other argument suggests a lack of strong ethical demands on social action in the Hindu tradition, and thus of an intensification of tensions between religion and the world. Hinduism, according to this argument, did not create any 'principles for an ethical universalism which would raise demands for life in the world in general' (RS II, 147; 1958, 147; translation adapted).

All this means that the dominant paradigm of Weber's theory of rationalisation (agenda 2), which seemed unequivocal, is unable to provide clarity when applied to specific cases—or to the case of a non-Western society—with regard to the relationship between religion and other life spheres.

CONCLUSION: THE IDEA OF CULTURE IN CIVILISATIONAL COMPARISON

Civilisation in Weber's hands is culture writ large:

> ... the 'worldviews' that have been created by ideas have very often, like switch points, decided the lines on which the dynamic of interests has propelled behaviour. It is the worldview that has directed 'from what' and 'for what' one would be 'saved' and, let us not forget, could be saved .... (RS I, 252; 2004b, 69)

In the final analysis, we thus see that Weber's prior theoretical commitment (*Vorentscheidungen*) and disposition foreclose the possibility of doing full justice to the wide cultural and soteriological range as well as the plurality of rationalisations in India or other non-Western contexts. Hermeneutics, in the sense that we understand it today, means engagement with something or someone other, on the textual level, but also on the practical and experiential levels; it means to be taken in by the other (the ideal of reflexive cultural anthropology in particular, and of interpretive social sciences in general). Weber allows for hermeneutical engagement to a certain extent on the level of 'intellectual' traditions, although even here he comes to the final conclusion that behind the 'mysterious' and 'secretive' character of the impression made by Indian intellectuals, and Asian ones in general, no deeper meanings are hidden (RS II, 374f; 1958, 339f). Weber completely refuses to hermeneutically engage with the traditions of the majority of the population. It is the non-elite Indians who thus become the radical 'Others'.

Weber did not own up to the hermeneutic character of comparison, nor did he take the chance, implied in his third, pluralist agenda, of seeing comparison as a two-way and long-term process. To us today, it looks more and more likely that the cognitive, economic, and political dominance of 'the West' was one particular episode in world history. This alone should be sufficient reason why we can no longer avoid taking the relational and reciprocal character of comparison much more seriously than Weber did.

Weber sets out to understand and analyse India on par with the select few other grand civilisations, and what he considered the respective 'world religions'. He acknowledged India's sophistication and the alternatives inscribed within its philosophical and metaphysical systems. He was one of the first to acknowledge the conceptual differences between kingship and priesthood at an early stage in Indian history. Weber, however, was unable to distinguish systematically between Brahmanical priesthood and the carriers of the paths of liberation and renunciation, while his understanding of India's social and political dynamics exhibits a mix of conceptual clarity and confused thinking. His attempt to find and define a unitary political structure for India was unsuccessful, and he was especially misled by the very idea of a social system, turning caste into a watertight order from which there was no escape and which was based on one core element, the belief in *karman*. On the other hand, he developed no comprehensive understanding of the relational modalities and the constitutive role of discrimination, stigmatisation, and humiliation in social life in the Indian context. The biggest flaw in Weber's depiction of India concerns *bhakti* and the religious perspectives of wide sections of society. It is here that prejudices on his side, both moral and cognitive as well as epistemic ones, intersect with a lack of information and scholarship. Regarding *bhakti*, Weber missed the chance to rethink and revise a crude civilisational comparison and do justice to non-elite perspectives and their rationales. Belying his insights, he stuck to a unified picture of India, confirming the notion of India as the cradle of spirituality and characterised by a lack of concern for wordly things. If we accept this diagnosis for just a moment, it seems odd that Weber was seemingly unaware of the attempts made in his own time by Vivekananda and other Indian contemporaries to bridge the gap between the 'spiritual' and this-worldly orientations in the shape these had been given by the West under the auspices of colonialism.

It would have to be a toned-down version of Weber's concept of *Welteinstellungen*—attitudes towards the world—and processes of rationalisation that might today serve as a new agenda for a less-biased comparative approach of a Weberian kind. Such reconceptualisations could no longer relate to entire civilisations or transhistoric social units that survived the ages, but would have to allow for conceptual distinctions within themselves. Better still, in the Indian context, a new approach would have to make clearer distinctions between different religious and/or civilisational strands and components, and focus more on the modes of interplay between these, some of which could extend beyond the boundaries that presumably enclose a civilisation or cultural area like the Indian.[45]

Bibliography

Arnason, Johann P. n.d. 'Rationalisation and Modernity: Towards a Culturalist Reading of Max Weber', La Trobe University Sociology Papers 9. Melbourne: La Trobe University.

———. 2003. *Civilizations in Dispute: Historical Questions and Theoretical Traditions*. Leiden: Brill.

Arnason, Johann P., and Chris Hann (eds). 2018. *Anthropology and Civilizational Analysis: Eurasian Explorations*. Albany: SUNY Press.

Babb, Lawrence A. 1983. 'Destiny and Responsibility: Karma in Popular Hinduism'. In Charles F. Keyes and E. Valentine Daniel (eds), *Karma: An Anthropological Inquiry*, 163–181. Berkeley: University of California Press.

Bayly, Susan. 1999. *The New Cambridge History of India, IV, 3: Caste, Society and Politics in India from the Eighteenth Century to the Modern Age*. Cambridge: Cambridge University Press.

Berg, Eberhard, and Martin Fuchs (eds). 1993. *Kultur, soziale Praxis, Text: Die Krise der ethnographischen Repräsentation*. Frankfurt/Main: Suhrkamp.

Berreman, Gerald D. 1967. 'Concomitants of Caste Organization'. In George de Vos and Hiroshi Wagatsuma (eds), *Japan's Invisible Race: Caste in Culture and Personality*, 308–324. Berkeley: University of California Press, 2e.

Clifford, James, and George E. Marcus (eds). 1986. *Writing Culture: The Poetics and Politics of Ethnography*. Berkeley: University of California Press.

Cohn, Bernard S. 1959. 'Changing Traditions of a Low Caste'. In Milton Singer (ed.), *Traditional India: Structure and Change*, 207–215. Philadelphia: American Folklore Society.

———. 1968. 'Notes on the history of the study of Indian society and culture'. In Milton Singer and Bernard S. Cohn (eds), *Structure and*

45 For respective suggestions, see Fuchs 2018.

Change in Indian Society, 3–28. Chicago: Viking Fund Publications in Anthropology.

Conrad, Dieter. 1986. 'Max Weber's Conception of Hindu Dharma as a Paradigm'. In Detlef Kantowsky (ed.), *Recent Research on Max Weber's Studies of Hinduism: Papers Submitted to a Conference Held in New Delhi, 1–3 March 1984*, 169–192. München: Weltforum.

Daniel, E. Valentine. 1983. 'Conclusion: Karma, the Uses of an Idea'. In Charles F. Keyes and E. Valentine Daniel (eds), *Karma: An Anthropological Inquiry*, 287–300. Berkeley: University of California Press.

Daniel, Sheryl B. 1983. 'The tool box approach of the Tamil to the issues of moral responsibility and human destiny'. In Charles F. Keyes and E. Valentine Daniel (eds), *Karma: An Anthropological Inquiry*, 27–62. Berkeley: University of California Press.

Derrett, J. Duncan M. 1976. 'Rajadharma'. *Journal of Asian Studies* 35 (4), 597–609.

Dirks, Nicholas B. 2001. *Castes of Mind: Colonialism and the Making of Modern India*. Princeton: Princeton University Press.

Dumont, Louis. 1980. *Homo Hierarchicus. The Caste System and its Implications*. Chicago: University of Chicago Press, complete rev. English edn.

Fuchs, Martin. 1987. 'Fremde Kultur und soziales Handeln. Max Webers Analyse der indischen Zivilisation'. *Kölner Zeitschrift für Soziologie und Sozialpsychologie* 39 (4), 669–692.

———. 1988. *Theorie und Verfremdung. Max Weber, Louis Dumont und die Analyse der indischen Gesellschaft*. Frankfurt/Main: Peter Lang.

———. 2017. 'India in Comparison: Max Weber's Analytical Agenda'. In Thomas C. Ertman (ed.), *Max Weber's Economic Ethic of the World Religions: An Analysis*, 223–266. Cambridge: Cambridge University Press.

———. 2018. 'Indian Imbroglios: *Bhakti* Neglected; Or, The Missed Opportunities for a New Approach to a Comparative Analysis of Civilizational Diversity'. In Johann Arnason and Chris Hann (eds), *Anthropology and Civilizational Analysis: Eurasian Explorations*. Albany: SUNY Press.

———. 2020. 'Weltreligionen, Welteinstellungen, Zivilisationen: Max Webers vergleichende Religionssoziologie und die Analytik indischer Religiosität'. In Volkhard Krech and Hartmann Tyrell (eds), *Religionssoziologie um 1900: Eine Fortsetzung*, 595–629. Baden-Baden: Ergon.

———. Forthcoming. 'World Religions, World Attitudes, and Civilizations: Max Weber's Comparative Sociology of Religion and the Analysis of Indian Religiosity'. In Alan Sica (ed.), *Max Weber Handbook*. Abingdon and New York: Routledge.

Fuller, Chris J. 1979. 'Gods, Priests and Purity: On the Relation between Hinduism and the Caste System'. *Man* (n.s.) 14 (3), 459–476.

Halbfass, Wilhelm. 1980. 'Karma, apūrva, and "natural" causes. Observations on the growth and limits of the theory of saṃsāra'. In Wendy Doniger O'Flaherty (ed.), *Karma and Rebirth in Classical Indian Traditions*, 268–302. Berkeley: University of California Press.

Hardy, Friedhelm. 1983. *Viraha-bhakti: The Early History of Kṛṣṇa Devotion in South India*, Delhi: Oxford University Press.

Heesterman, J. C. 1984. 'Kaste und Karma. Max Webers Analyse der indischen Sozialstruktur'. In Wolfgang Schluchter (ed.), *Max Webers Studie über Hinduismus und Buddhismus: Interpretation und Kritik*, 72–86. Frankfurt (Main): Suhrkamp.

——. 1985. 'Brahmin, ritual, and renouncer'. In J. C. Heesterman, *The Inner Conflict of Tradition: Essays in Indian Ritual, Kingship, and Society*, 26–44. Chicago: University of Chicago Press.

Hiebert, Paul G. 1983. 'Karma and Other Explanation Traditions in a South Indian Village'. In Charles F. Keyes and E. Valentine Daniel (eds), *Karma: An Anthropological Inquiry*, 119–130. Berkeley: University of California Press.

Joas, Hans. 2010. 'Review of Anthony J. Carroll, *Protestant Modernity: Weber, Secularization, and Protestantism*'. *The Journal of Religion* 90 (3), 445–447.

Juergensmeyer, Mark. 1980. 'What if the Untouchables don't believe in untouchability?' *Bulletin of Concerned Asian Scholars* 12 (1), 23–28.

Kane, Pandurang Vaman. 1953. *History of Dharmaśāstra (Ancient and Medieval Religious and Civil Law in India)*, Vol. 4. Poona: Bhandarkar Oriental Research Institute.

Kantowsky, Detlef. 1985. 'Die Fehlrezeption von Max Webers Studie über "Hinduismus und Buddhismus" in Indien: Ursachen und Folgen'. *Zeitschrift für Soziologie* 14 (6), 466–474.

—— (ed.). 1986. *Recent Research on Max Weber's Studies of Hinduism: Papers Submitted to a Conference Held in New Delhi, 1–3 March 1984*, 169–192. München: Weltforum.

Keyes, Charles F. 1983a. 'Introduction: The Study of Popular Ideas of Karma'. In Charles F. Keyes and E. Valentine Daniel (eds), *Karma: An Anthropological Inquiry*, 1–24. Berkeley: University of California Press.

——. 1983b. 'Merit-Transference in the Kammic Theory of Popular Theravada Buddhism'. In Charles F. Keyes and E. Valentine Daniel (eds), *Karma: An Anthropological Inquiry*, 261–286. Berkeley: University of California Press.

Kolenda, Pauline Mahar. 1964. 'Religious Anxiety and Hindu Fate'. *The Journal of Asian Studies* 23 (Supplement), 71–81.

Munshi, Surendra. 1988. 'Max Weber on India: An introductory critique'. *Contributions to Indian Sociology* (n.s.) 22 (1), 1–33.

O'Flaherty, Wendy Doniger. 1980. 'Karma and Rebirth in the Vedas and Purāṇas'. In Wendy Doniger O'Flaherty (ed.), *Karma and Rebirth in Classical Indian Traditions*, 3–37. Berkeley: University of California Press.

Prentiss, Karen Pechilis. 1999. *The Embodiment of Bhakti*. New York: Oxford University Press.

Rösel, Jakob. 1975. 'Über die soziale Gewalt von Wirklichkeitsbildern. Das sanskritistische Indienbild und seine koloniale Verwirklichung. Am Beispiel der Indien-Studie Max Webers'. *Internationales Jahrbuch für Wissens- und Religionssoziologie* 9, 45–76.

——. 1982. *Die Hinduismusthese Max Webers. Folgen eines kolonialen Indienbildes in einem religionssoziologischen Gedankengang*. München: Weltforum.

Schluchter, Wolfgang. 1979. *Die Entwicklung des okzidentalen Rationalismus. Eine Analyse von Max Webers Gesellschaftsgeschichte*. Tübingen: Mohr.

Sharma, Ursula. 1973. 'Theodicy and the Doctrine of Karma'. *Man* (n.s.) 8 (3), 347–364.

Thapan, Meenakshi (ed.). 1998. *Anthropological Journeys: Reflections on Fieldwork*. New Delhi: Orient Longman.

Wadley, Susan S. 1983. 'Vrats: Transformers of Destiny'. In Charles F. Keyes and E. Valentine Daniel (eds), *Karma: An Anthropological Inquiry*, 147–162. Berkeley: University of California Press.

Weber, Max. 1958. *The Religion of India: The Sociology of Hinduism and Buddhism*, Hans H. Gerth and Don Martindale (eds and trans.). Glencoe: Free Press.

[W&G] Weber, Max. 1964 [1921/22]. *Wirtschaft und Gesellschaft. Grundriß der verstehenden Soziologie, Studienausgabe*, 2 vols, Johannes Winckelmann (ed.). Köln: Kiepenheuer & Witsch.

[RS I] ——. 1972 [1920]. *Gesammelte Aufsätze zur Religionssoziologie, Bd. I*, Tübingen: Mohr. New critical edition in Max Weber-Gesamtausgabe, vol. I/18 and I/19, Tübingen: Mohr, 2016 and 1989.

[RS II] ——. 1978a [1921]. *Gesammelte Aufsätze zur Religionssoziologie, Bd. 2: Hinduismus und Buddhismus*. Tübingen: Mohr. New critical edition in Max Weber-Gesamtausgabe, vol. I/20, Tübingen: Mohr, 1996.

——. 1978b. *Economy and Society: An Outline of Interpretive Sociology*, 2 vols, Guenther Roth and Claus Wittich (eds). Berkeley: University of California Press.

———. 2004a. 'Intermediate Reflection on the Economic Ethics of the World Religions'. In Sam Whimster (ed.), *The Essential Weber: A Reader*, 215–244. London: Routledge.

———. 2004b. 'Introduction to the Economic Ethics of World Religions'. In Sam Whimster (ed.), *The Essential Weber: A Reader*, 55–80. London: Routledge.

———. 2004c. 'Prefatory Remarks to the Collected Essays in the Sociology of Religion'. In Sam Whimster (ed.), *The Essential Weber: A Reader*, 101–112. London: Routledge.

———. 2009. *The Protestant Ethic and the Spirit of Capitalism with Other Writings on the Rise of the West*, Stephen Kalberg (ed.). New York: Oxford University Press, 4e.

Three | The German Connection in Indian Aeronautical Science and Technology

Roddam Narasimha

Introduction

The history of modern science and technology in India was generally dominated by British connections and objectives, right up to the end of British rule in 1947 and a couple of decades thereafter. In the second half of the nineteenth century, several British scientists who were brought to India by the government of the time distinguished themselves by the important contributions they made to science. Among these were Sir Ronald Ross, who won the Nobel Prize for his discovery of the source of malaria, then a much-dreaded disease; Sir Gilbert Walker, who did pioneering work on the monsoons, which included the discovery of the connections between the monsoons and phenomena in the Pacific Ocean, a precursor to what is now known as the El Niño-Southern Oscillation; Sir George Everest, whose leadership of the Survey of India led eventually to the discovery of the highest peak in the world, which came to be known (in his honour) as Mount Everest. What is interesting about this and other similar lists is that by and large, all of them had to do with the natural resources or earth science problems of the country. In the first half of the twentieth century, many Indian scientists went beyond the list and did outstandingly well in the fundamental sciences, often with the support of Indian princes, merchants, and professionals.

Indian aeronautics represents a particularly striking example of a branch of science and technology that developed through connections with a country other than the UK, in this case, Germany. It is unlikely that this occurred through careful planning on either side—it might well have been an unusual combination of circumstances that led to these connections. It, however, represents one facet of Indo-German relations that may be of interest. It is my purpose to describe here how it happened and why.

Early History of Aviation

Although aircrafts from Europe, in particular Britain, had been seen in Indian skies for some years, the first civilian transport service was the venture of the well-known House of Tatas, in particular the late J. R. D. Tata. The idea was to set up a Tata Air Mail service, along the route Karachi–Ahmedabad–Bombay–Bellary–Madras, connecting a weekly mail service from London to Karachi run by the British airline, Imperial Airways. The earliest aircraft used was a de Havilland Puss Moth. In 1929, JRD went on to obtain the first civil pilot's license (bearing No. 1) in India. In later years, several private airlines were set up for domestic air transport.

One can say that aeronautics, as distinguished from aviation, came to India during World War II. The large fleet of military aircraft from the British and American air forces operating in the Pacific theatre needed a support and maintenance system whose facilities were sufficiently far from the frontline. To meet this need, a private company called Hindustan Aircraft Limited (HAL) was set up at Bangalore by a far-seeing businessman from Gujarat, Mr Walchand Hirachand, in December 1940. The company was a partnership with the Government of the Maharaja of Mysore at that time. It undertook the production of a variety of American aircraft, including the Harlow trainer, a CurtissHawk fighter, and a Vultee bomber. A ten-seater troop-carrying glider, reportedly for dropping Indian troops behind Japanese lines in the Burma theatre, was also designed and developed, and flew in August 1941. However, the aircraft manufacturing programme was quickly given up and HAL became a repair and overhaul centre for the aircraft of the South East Asia Command.

Dr V. M. Ghatage

In 1942, the Indian Institute of Science (IISc), the brain-child of the pioneering and far-seeing industrialist and philanthropist of

Bombay, Jamsetji Tata, established in 1909 through a three-party agreement among the British Indian government, the Maharaja of Mysore, and the House of Tatas, started a Department of Aeronautical Engineering—the first in the country. The first Head of the Department was a pioneering Indian aeronautical engineer-scientist, Dr Vishnu Madhav Ghatage (Image 3.1), who moved from HAL, which he had joined at the time of its establishment in 1940. This is where India's German connection truly begins. Ghatage's excellent academic record at Bombay University enabled him to get a foreign scholarship from the University, and he went to the Kaiser Wilhelm Institute at Göttingen in 1933. Three years later, he obtained his Ph.D. as a student of the renowned German scientist Ludwig Prandtl, who may legitimately be called the founder of modern fluid dynamics, especially of the kind that was needed in aircraft technologies. In 1903 or 1904, shortly after the Wright Brothers had inaugurated powered-flight in the US in 1903, Prandtl read a profoundly original paper in the Third Congress of Mathematicians at Heidelberg. This paper combined careful observation of real fluid flows, a fundamentally new mathematical argument that developed later into what came to be called the method of matched asymptotic expansions, a willingness to use numerical methods to solve nonlinear differential equations that had no known closed-form solutions, and finally, an extraordinary

Image 3.1: V. M. Ghatage (1908–1991), seated in an aircraft
Source: Ajay Amrit Ghatage/IISc Archives.

power to see the significance of the conclusions to a wide variety of real flow problems that had remained unsolved till then. The paper transformed the subjects of hydraulics and aerodynamics into the rational scientific discipline of fluid dynamics, and eventually resolved many of the paradoxes that had been plaguing the study of fluid flows for a long time.

Interestingly, Ghatage's Göttingen thesis (accepted in 1936) was not on an aeronautical subject, but rather on one inspired by meteorology. This was because Prandtl had by then become deeply interested in atmospheric flows, and in particular the cold fronts that are such a characteristic feature of weather in Northern Europe. Ghatage's thesis reported model experiments on the motion of a cold mass of air over a warm one, simulating the cold fronts just mentioned. On his return to India, he taught physics at Pune. However, he was aware of the connections that had been built up by Prandtl's school with the aeronautical research, development, and design efforts in Germany, and so joined HAL to set up a design office when it was established in 1940. He must have realised that in war-time India, an aeronautical expert was in much greater demand than one on meteorology. With the advent of aeronautics at IISc, he was loaned by HAL to IISc in 1942 when the aeronautics programme started there.

At IISc, as Head of Department of Aeronautical Engineering till 1945, Ghatage started an educational programme in aeronautics for the first time in India. The course was at the Master's level. In the beginning, Ghatage was the only faculty member in the Department, so he taught a variety of subjects, including both solid and fluid mechanics. I believe he was able to do this because his adviser Ludwig Prandtl (Image 3.2), who headed the Department of Applied Mechanics at Göttingen, had himself done research in both solid and fluid mechanics. Ghatage also built a 5 ft × 7 ft closed-circuit wind tunnel at IISc, and made some preliminary measurements about the turbulence levels in the tunnel.

By 1948, soon after the end of British rule, HAL began to expand its design office, and Ghatage returned to HAL from IISc to take on greater responsibilities. He collected a group of engineers for the design office, most of them among the first graduating batches from IISc. In succeeding years, he led the design office step-by-step on a series of projects of gradually increasing complexity: the basic trainer HT-2, the

Image 3.2: Ludwig Prandtl (1875–1953)
Source: https://commons.wikimedia.org/wiki/File:Ludwig_Prandtl_1904.jpg.

flying club trainer Pushpak, an agricultural aircraft named Krishak (used as a military Air Observation Patrol and light passenger aircraft as well), and the very successful intermediate jet trainer HJT-16 (to which Raj Mahindra at HAL made major contributions). Ghatage was therefore a pioneer in both design and education, and (from everything I can recollect from my generally brief encounters with him in the mid-1950s and the 1960s), his approach revealed the strength of the scientific foundations that had been laid in his years in Göttingen, combined with a keen appreciation of the nature of engineering problems.

A personality that could combine these abilities with Sanskrit scholarship and love for golf made 'Doc' (as he was called by all his colleagues) an affectionately respected figure at HAL. He was honoured by the Indian government with a Padma Shri for his services to Indian aeronautics.

DR OSKAR TIETJENS

In 1948, IISc appointed Oskar Tietjens (Image 3.3) as the third Head of the Aeronautical Engineering Department. Tietjens was also a student of Prandtl, and was widely known across the world for having co-authored with Prandtl two books on hydro- and aero-mechanics, which taught generations of students all over the world both the fundamentals and applications of fluid mechanics as they had been developed largely in Germany under Prandtl's leadership. When I joined IISc as a graduate student in 1953, Tietjens was still Head of the Department, and taught the first course on fluid mechanics to entering students. The courses had a strong Göttingen flavour—to the extent that Tietjens would often mention how 'Professor' had handled that particular ticklish problem that was the subject of the day's lecture: for him, 'Professor' of course always meant Prandtl. The lectures laid great emphasis on the fundamentals, and introduced students to the Navier–Stokes equations, of which they had never heard in their undergraduate courses in hydraulics.

Tietjens initiated the project of building a 9 ft × 14 ft open-circuit wind tunnel at IISc: it still remains the biggest low-speed tunnel in the country.

Image 3.3: Group photo of faculty at IISc, including Oskar Tietjens (1893–1971), seated outside the Main Building

Source: IISc Archives.

Two personal memories of Tietjens stand out in my mind. Although rather formal in many ways, he cared for the students. All of us were invited once a year to his bungalow (No. 11) on campus for tea, accompanied (among other dishes) by the delicious ice-cream (home-)made by Mrs. Tietjens, with Indian flavours. Tietjens talked to us about which part of India each of us had come from, where we had studied, and so on. Some days before his departure for Germany, he sent an unusual message to me, asking me to see him. It turned out that he was curious about my future plans, and encouraged me to pursue a research career and go to either Göttingen or the California Institute of Technology (Caltech) to do a Ph.D. And he offered to help me in any way possible at either place. I was of course both pleased and relieved. (However, I stayed on in India to do a Master's by research at IISc with Dr Satish Dhawan before going to Caltech in 1957.) I was glad to have the opportunity to personally thank Tietjens in 1962 at his home in Friedrichsburg on my way back from Caltech with a Ph.D., and thank Mrs Tietjens for her coconut-flavoured ice-creams at Bungalow No. 11.

The Tietjens years at IISc saw the emergence of a strong faculty in both aerodynamics and structures. In particular, Dr Satish Dhawan had joined the Department in 1951 and proceeded to set up a high-speed aerodynamics laboratory with the country's first supersonic tunnels, and started a vigorous research programme in fluid mechanics. Dhawan had received his Ph.D. from Caltech, working at the renowned Guggenheim Aeronautical Laboratory at Caltech (GALCIT). Founded in 1928, GALCIT played a pioneering role in establishing modern aeronautical science in the US, under the leadership of the redoubtable Theodore von Kármán who, although Hungarian by birth, was very much an intellectual descendant of the Prandtl/Göttingen school. Dhawan's own adviser, Hans Wolfgang Liepmann, was a German physicist who had moved to the new fluid dynamics that had emerged from Göttingen, and joined von Kármán at GALCIT just months before World War II broke out in Europe. There was therefore a second-generation connection between Dhawan and Prandtl. Dhawan succeeded Tietjens as Head of the Department after the latter's departure in 1956, and rose quickly to the position of Director of the Institute in 1962. He went on to head the Indian space programme in 1972, and was in many ways the architect of the Indian Space Research Organisation as it has developed in the past several decades into one of India's most successful technology development agencies in the private or public sector.

DR KURT WALDEMAR TANK AND INDIA'S SUPERSONIC FIGHTER PROJECT

In the 1950s, the Government of India (GoI) started thinking about the design and manufacture of a supersonic Indian military aircrafts for the Indian Air Force. It was decided that this should be done at HAL, and the famous German designer and pilot, Kurt Tank (Image 3.4), was invited to lead the project at Bangalore. Dr Tank had designed a series of famous German aircraft at Focke-Wulf,

Image 3.4: Professor Kurt Tank (1898–1983), Head of HF-24 Design Team, HAL (1956–1967)

Source: https://en.wikipedia.org/wiki/Kurt_Tank#/media/File:Bundesarchiv_Bild_183-L18396,_Kurt_Tank.jpg.

including the FW-190, which had acquired a formidable reputation as one of the best fighters during World War II. When the German aircraft industry was virtually closed down as a result of post-war treaties, Tank joined many other compatriots who migrated to set up industries in Latin America. When this project began to face difficulties, he left to accept the Indian invitation rather than go to the US, as some of his associates had done. He arrived in Bangalore in August 1956 to head the military aircraft project. This necessitated a split in Dr Ghatage's painstakingly assembled Design Office, with one part working under Dr Tank on the new fighter project, and the other continuing under Dr Ghatage on the rest. This upset Dr Ghatage, who had carefully set up the Design Office from scratch. Furthermore, his 'step-by-step' philosophy appeared to have been abandoned.

The aircraft, known as the HF-24 (entering service as *Marut*, Sanskrit for wind or tempest), was intended to be a supersonic fighter-bomber, capable of achieving Mach 2. This was the first attempt outside the major aeronautical powers in the world to build such an advanced aircraft. It was a bold and ambitious attempt, as at the time of Tank's arrival in Bangalore, the only experience that India had had been with the basic trainer HT-2, designed under Ghatage's leadership. Tank and his assistant Mittelhuber proceeded to recruit new engineers, make preliminary designs, conduct wind tunnel tests at IISc, and make an assessment of the chosen configuration with flight tests on an air-launched glider. If I may strike a personal note, I recall Kurt Tank's visits to the old 5 ft × 7 ft tunnel built at IISc by Dr Ghatage: I was at that time a research student of Satish Dhawan, who had become the Head of the Department in 1955, following Tietjens. Tank usually liked to collect test results as soon as the tests were completed, so he was a not infrequent visitor to IISc. I had the opportunity to listen in on some of the discussions that took place between Tank and Dhawan, as the laboratory where I was working adjoined the test section of the 5 ft × 7 ft tunnel. My own Master's research project at the time concerned the transition from laminar to turbulent flow, and was inspired by the worries of Dhawan and Tank regarding the Reynolds numbers in the 5 ft × 7 ft tunnel being generally in the fluid-dynamically awkward transitional range, making it difficult to extrapolate tunnel data to flight conditions. Incidentally, Tank wanted to keep his academic links alive (he was often *Professor* Tank), and used to give lectures at the Madras Institute of Technology, where the students included Abdul Kalam, who went on to lead national space and missile projects and was elected President of India in 2002.

The HF-24 had its first flight in 1961—five years after Tank's arrival. Supersonic-level flight demanded a jet engine with reheat, which unfortunately was not available from the British Orpheus engines that powered HF-24. The British manufacturer (Bristol) who had plans for a reheat variant found no support for it in Britain, and agreed to undertake the project only if India fully funded it. As GoI found that the required resources were not available, the HF-24 airframe was modified to house a reheat version developed within the country; however, a crash of the prototype with the reheat version (killing the respected test pilot Suranjan Das during take-off) put an end to efforts to give the aircraft full supersonic capability (it did cross Mach 1 in shallow dives). The aircraft saw action in the 1971 Indo-Pak war. Kurt Tank returned to Germany in 1967 at the end of his contract. The last Marut was withdrawn from service in 1985.

Image 3.5: The HF-24 Marut in a German Museum
Source: Used with the permission of Simon Watson. <www.aviation-bookshop.com>.

Curiously, the possibility of achieving supersonic capability in the HF-24 was revived around 1976. The proposal was to replace the Orpheus by a Russian engine, and I happened to head this 'HF-25' project at HAL, on partial leave from IISc (which I had joined in 1962). However, the project was closed in 1980. Interestingly, the Anglo-French SEPECAT Jaguar (initiated in 1966), which India decided to buy and build under licence in 1978, has a planform uncannily close to that of the HF-24, suggesting that the overall aerodynamic design of the HF-24 was ahead of its time in 1957.

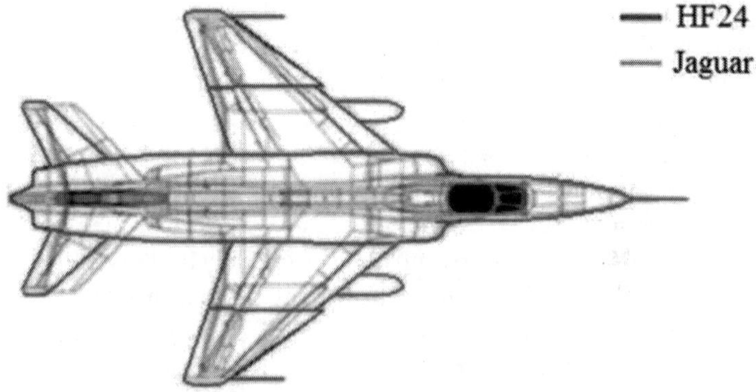

Image 3.6: Marut and Jaguar planforms compared
Source: Image drawn by Roddam Narasimha for a public lecture at the Indian National Science Academy, New Delhi.

In summary, the bold initiative that the country took in the mid-1950s under Tank's leadership could not, for one reason or another, come to full fruition, but a useful aircraft still emerged from the project and provided good support to the Indian Air Force in conflicts with Pakistan.

The Advanced Light Helicopter 'Dhruv'

Perhaps the most successful Indo-German aeronautical project is the HAL Advanced Light Helicopter (ALH). The ALH concept was mooted by the Indian Air Force in the 1970s, and was driven by the need to provide material and logistic support to India's mountainous regions, particularly around the Himalayan border areas. This requirement led to the consideration of a 5-tonne class multi-role utility helicopter, of the kind then being mooted in several other countries as well (including the US), but with a more severe requirement on operability at higher altitudes (6–7 km, 18,000–21,000 ft), under the hot-high conditions prevailing in Ladakh. (It has been said that Leh is one of those rare places in the world where one can die from an attack of both sunstroke and frostbite at the same time, with feet stretched under the shade of a tree and body in the sun.) A project was finally approved by the government in 1976, as continuation of a 1970 agreement for collaboration signed by the GoI with the French company SNIAS (more familiar as part of Aérospatiale) on a single-engine helicopter. However, US experience in Vietnam had shown that a single-engine configuration was too vulnerable to ground fire, so IAF changed the requirement to a twin-engine version. After much debate on the advantages of continuing with a long-familiar French company versus obtaining newer technologies, the GoI opened the doors to other potential collaborators, and opted eventually for the well-known German firm MBB. (Incidentally, Kurt Tank had become a consultant at MBB after his return in 1967 from the HF-24 assignment in India, and SNIAS and MBB, along with another of Tank's old haunts, Focke-Wulf, later merged to form Eurocopter, which in turn has become Airbus Helicopters since January 2014.)

The German team arrived promptly in Bangalore soon after an agreement was signed in 1984. The pattern of collaboration was similar to that earlier pursued in the HF-24 project: a small German team provided technical leadership and guidance to a much larger Indian team, some of whom were deputed to Germany for training as part of the programme. The first flight of the first prototype took place in 1992, and four prototypes were flying by 1995. This completed the task envisaged under the agreement, and the MBB team returned to Germany the same year. It had been led first by D. Bender as Programme Manager, and towards the latter half of the period by F. Och. On the Indian side, key roles were played in the beginning by Raj Mahindra at HAL and Mahesh Sarin in the Ministry of Defence, and by Dr C. G. Krishnadas Nair, K. Baweja, and K. S. Sudheendra in the later stages. (But there were some successful sociocultural projects as well, when three members of the German team found their future wives among the Indian nurses they met in a Bangalore hospital, where a colleague had been undergoing treatment for a kidney problem!)

However, the ALH project continued in HAL, although it was plagued by delays due to a variety of reasons, including design changes, the 1991 budget crisis, and US sanctions following the Pokhran II

Indian nuclear explosion in 1998. Eventually ALH received provisional military certification in 2001, and entered service the next year under the name 'Dhruv' (Sanskrit for pole-star, meaning steady, sure, ever there; see Image 3.7). Dhruv was specially suited to Indian needs: it could operate from unprepared fields in mountainous terrain, had a capacity of twelve passengers (in addition to two crew members), could lift and drop bulky payloads, and had a service ceiling of 6,000 m (achieving a world record for highest flying altitude of 7,520 m). Since 2007, the ALH flies on two Shakti engines, developed jointly by HAL and the French aircraft gas turbine company Turbomeca, as a more powerful variant of an earlier Turbomeca engine that had been used on the previous variants of ALH. The Air Force, Army, Navy, and Coast Guard variants of ALH were all certified, as were the civilian variants. A well-known US consulting firm had made the assessment in the 1980s that the ALH had no equal in its class anywhere else in the world at the time.

Image 3.7: Dhruv Mk 3 (with Shakti engines) over Siachen

Source: Reproduced with the permission of Colonel Ajai Shukla (Retired), Broadsword blog (ajaishukla.com).

All of this was achieved because the ALH technology level was advanced: 29 per cent of the airframe was made of carbon-fibre composites, and the aircraft had a glass cockpit, a hinge-less rotor with fibre-glass composite rotor blades, and an automatic flight control system. By August 2013, more than 200 Dhruvs had been made, and were selling at US$ 6 million per unit, about 15 per cent cheaper than its rivals. Dhruv has been exported to Ecuador (for its Air Force) and to Nepal. It definitely had a much greater export potential, but I think India was not commercially or diplomatically ready for the aggressive marketing that would have been needed to achieve that potential.

In recent years, the programme has led to several new derivatives, including the Light Combat Helicopter (LCH) and a Light Utility Helicopter (LUH) being developed by HAL, and the ALH Mark 4 called HAL Rudra. Three civil variants have also been certified and are operational.[1] There is also a 2+14 pax variant, and a 2+5 VIP version.

THE DORNIER 228

This is a twin turboprop STOL (short take-off and landing) utility aircraft manufactured by the German company Dornier during 1981–1998. HAL bought a licence for its production of the aircraft in 1983, and subsequently manufactured 125 aircraft. The aircraft was intended for use by both the Indian Air Force and Indian Airlines, and has served a variety of roles in the country, including air taxi, commuter services, and executive transport.

In 2009, RUAG started manufacturing Dornier 228 New Generation in Germany, with fuselage, wings, and tail unit manufactured by HAL Kanpur. In October 2014, HAL obtained orders for twelve Do228 worth Rs 1,600 crore from the Indian Navy, and in February 2015 for fourteen Do228 worth Rs 1,090 crore from IAF: the aircraft is still 'alive'.

1 See https://en.wikipedia.org/wiki/HAL_Dhruv (accessed October 2021).

Do228 was also used in civil airline operations by a new airline, Vayudoot, established in 1981 to serve short-haul routes connecting smaller towns across the country, and jointly owned by Indian Airlines and Air India. Vayudoot, in its early years, was advertised as 'the fastest growing airline in the world', but it soon ceased to be profitable, and was closed down in 1993.

HAL currently has worldwide marketing rights for the HAL-Dornier 228.

RESEARCH AND DEVELOPMENT

The CSIR National Aerospace Laboratories in Bangalore (CSIR-NAL) have had a long-standing collaborative arrangement in R&D with the German Aerospace Research Establishment, DLR. This agreement became particularly active during the mid-1980s and early 1990s, and led to several interesting projects, including composite structures (for example, a carbon-fibre fin for the Do228), flight mechanics, wind tunnel test techniques, and experimental and computational fluid dynamics.

CONCLUSIONS

I hope the above account has shown how varied and rich the connections between Germany and India have been in aeronautics. These connections have ranged from the inspiration that German aeronautical science provided in the earliest years of the aircraft industry and aeronautical education and research in India, in particular through students who imbibed the spirit and philosophy of the extraordinary scientific achievements in fluid dynamics attributable to the genius of Ludwig Prandtl, to programmes where German technical expertise provided leadership in early phases of aircraft projects to Indian technical teams, and to continued collaboration in R&D. Although direct commercial transactions involving purchase and/or licence for production of aircraft, for example, have been dominated by manufacturers in other countries, none of them matches the breadth and depth of Indo-German connections. Recent decades have seen massive consolidation in Europe of earlier well-known national industries into such ventures as Airbus, Eurocopter, and Airbus Helicopters. Nevertheless, one cannot help thinking that the two countries have not fully utilised the possibilities for building more ambitious collaborations on the foundations of their unusually successful experiment in working with each other in the field of aeronautics.

REFERENCES

Dhawan, S., and R. Narasimha. 1958. 'Some properties of boundary layer flow during transition from laminar to turbulent motion'. *J. Fluid Mech.* 3, 418–437.

Krishnadas Nair, C. G., A. K. Baweja, and K. S. Sudheendra. 2007. *Dhruv, India's Advanced Light Helicopter*. Bangalore: Harishree.

Mahindra, Raj. 1992. 'Aircraft Industry Pioneer: An Obituary of Vishnu Madhav Ghatge'. *Current Science* 62 (9), 637–638.

Narasimha, R. 1957. 'On the distribution of intermittency in the transition region of a boundary layer'. *J. Aero. Sci.* 24, 711–712.

———. 2004. 'Divide, Conquer and Unify'. *Nature* 432, 807.

Sen, Alka. 1998. *Glimpses into Indian Aviation History, 1910–1997*. Bombay: Indian Aviation News Service, and London: Aviation News Service.

Four

Late Colonial India and Weimar Germany

Physicists in Conversation

Dhruv Raina

The history of science, perhaps marginally more than other genres of historical narrative, has been preoccupied with the exchange and transmission of scientific ideas. This chapter addresses two decades in the history of an exchange, namely 1920–1937, a period marked by the finalisation of the disciplinary identities of research schools of physics in Germany (Kumar 2009). On the other hand, in late colonial India within the university system, the period is marked by the onset of processes of institutionalisation of the disciplinary identity of physics research (Raina 2011; Raina and Jain 1997; Sen 1991). Naturally, the direction of transmission of knowledge and institutional practices is determined by the idea of temporal precedence, and historians of science are prone to evoke percolation or trickle-down models to serve as a kind of Hempelian covering law that explains the flow of knowledge in one direction. More nuanced readings, dissatisfied with purely internal accounts and reckoning instead with the politics of scientific knowledge, evoke centre–periphery explanations to characterise this exchange and the influences that shape the emergence of modern science at the periphery (Dasgupta 2015; Raina 1996).

This chapter deals with the conversations between a small group of Indian physicists and a philosopher-poet on the one hand, and the iconic figures of the quantum revolution from Germany and Austria in the first three decades of the twentieth century on the other. But before discussing the actual engagements and the fields of the engagement, an institutional preface is required since certain kinds of institutional settings beyond the idea of the nation-State provide a stage for very specific kinds of interactions, and the field of science was one such highly specific one (Raina 2011).

More than the postcolonial history of science that is concerned with the imbrications of knowledge and power as a variant of an imperialist sociology of knowledge (Pinch 1999), this chapter attempts to illustrate some of the conventions of the discourse and the circulation of knowledge (Boltanski and Thevenot 1991). Drawing upon the discussion of its institutional setting, the intent is to localise the engagements of Indian physicists with German physicists, specifically between 1900 and 1935. One of the difficulties with the centre–periphery models, as much as with the colonial science model proposed by Basalla, is that they differentiate between the two-way flow of knowledge between centre and periphery or metropolis and province—in terms of raw or uncooked information or data flowing one way, and knowledge or theory flowing the other. Consequently, from the perspective of the conventional philosophy of science or even from the sociology of scientific knowledge, this order of things needs to be reconfigured (Prasad 2014; Raina 1996, 1999). A reconfigured understanding of this bi-directionality of flows of scientific knowledge has often escaped the attention of historians of science. The chapter then proceeds to engage with the conversations between German-speaking physicists—from Germany and Austria—and their Indian colleagues between 1920 and 1937.

During this period, more specifically between 1900 and 1935, physicists in Europe were creating a new identity for a sub-discipline of physics that in the textbooks is referred to as 'modern physics', an identity constructed around the three revolutions in physics of the first three decades of the twentieth century. What about the physics between Galileo and the end of the nineteenth century—that large swathe of physics, elaborated upon between the seventeenth and nineteenth centuries, came to be called classical physics, while the physics of the twentieth century alone was inscribed and reproduced in textbooks as modern physics (Jungnickel and McCormmach 1986, 2017)? The epicentres of this movement were Berlin and Göttingen, Zurich, Cambridge and Paris, and by the 1920s, it could be argued, came to include the city of Calcutta as well. Two spatial settings are very important for this exchange—the modern city and the university. The history of the university is inseparable from that of the city, as several histories of the rise of the modern university have suggested (Jungnickel and McCormmach 2017). The discussion that follows focuses upon a period in the history of modern physics when Calcutta was the capital of science in India; and on the other hand, since the establishment of the Humboldtian university, Berlin gradually acquired a central place in the history of the new physics, alongside Göttingen, at least in Germany.

The idea of the university for teaching and research was itself in a phase of globalisation and was being naturalised in a myriad national contexts (O'Boyle 1983; Turner 1980). The stage, then, for this engagement is the university embedded as an essential element in the life of the city and its civilities, where a specialised group of individuals was pursuing what Weber would call science as a vocation (Weber 1922). The tentacles or networks of a global science, and in this case modern physics, were indeed expanding rapidly (Renn 2012). In the case of India, different scientific disciplines entered the phase of institutionalisation at different moments; the process commenced with chemistry in the last decades of the nineteenth century (Guay 1986; Raina, et al. 1995). A prerequisite was the presence of a critical number of researchers in the particular field, which would trigger the process. In the case of mathematics research, the process had begun in the first decade of the twentieth century, and for physics, it has been suggested by many that the decade of institutionalisation of research was the 1920s. In each case, the presence of a strong iconic personality whose research contributions were recognised in the West triggered the process—although this iconic personality himself may not have been involved in the process (Raina and Gupta 1998).

In terms of the historiography of science, the distinction between the internal and external history of science (despite the fact that the demise of this distinction has long been announced), comes back to haunt us again and again (Shapin 1992). While the opening clarification of this distinction in Hessen's landmark paper on 'The Social and Economic Roots of Newton's "Principia"' inaugurated the social history of science, another equally important paper published exactly forty years later was Paul Forman's 'Weimar Culture, Causality and Quantum Theory 1918–1927: Adaptation by German Physicists and Mathematicians to a Hostile Intellectual Environment', which also in a way prompted work on the cultural studies of science (Hessen 1971 [1931]; Forman 1971). Forman had argued that 'cultural values prevalent in a given place and time could influence the results of discipline bound research, i.e. the very content of scientific knowledge' (Carson, et al. 2011); this thesis is contested even today. He described the cultural climate in an economically depressed World War I Germany— thus a widespread sense of social crisis manifested itself as a 'crisis in science' (ibid., 2). This reflection on the conceptual foundations of science elevated the place of intuition and indeterminacy. 'Mechanical determinism, or the causality principle, came under special criticism as being too rationalistic and indeed, mechanical.' Physicists and mathematicians accommodated their disciplines to the new 'Zeitgeist by abandoning or restricting the validity of causality in physics'. A causality was proclaimed 'the fundamental scientific principle of the new quantum mechanics of atoms and electrons' (ibid.). Differences on the nature of science proliferated in factious debates, the most dominant one being that between the proponents of the Copenhagen interpretation and the realist interpretation of quantum mechanics. In this debate on measurement and foundations, the Austrian physicist Erwin Schrödinger turned to the resources of Indian philosophy, not spirituality, in the hope of clarifying some of the causal anomalies that the Copenhagen interpretation was quite resigned to accepting.

However, the other frame that structures this discussion is that of internationalism in science. The literature on scientific internationalism is very vast, and there are at least five distinct dimensions to it, but the one of salience here is that it was recognised

> ... as a set of ecumenical traditions and ideals common to the scientific profession: that scientific knowledge was universally valuable, that the methods and practice of science must remain unaffected by culture and politics, that unresolved scientific exchange among professionals of all nations or peoples was critical to the progress of ... human civilization, and that science itself was a kind of lingua franca that promoted a cosmopolitan perspective, unified goals, and an order based on merit that crossed international boundaries. (Manzione 2000, 25)

The dominion of international science began expanding in the nineteenth century with the spread of international conferences and the movement of physicists across national boundaries (Elzinga and Landström 1996). Several thousand kilometres away in colonial India, an Act permitting postgraduate teaching and research in the University, passed in 1904, gave a fillip to research in the University, and gradually inserted scholars into international networks of communication and exchange (Raina 2011).

However, historians draw a distinction between two kinds of internationalism in science—*non-governmental* or *autotelic*, organised by communities of scientists themselves to serve a common transnational aim, and *intergovernmental* or *heterotelic* internationalism that entails promoting science for extra-scientific purposes, wherein science is a mere vehicle of politics by other means (Elzinga and Landström 1996, 3–4). It can be seen that the beginnings of Indo-German collaboration in the realm of physics commenced during the phase of autotelic internationalism, as different from the internationalism of the post-World War II years, which was largely heterotelic in nature and for which the institutions inspired by the League of Nations provided a scaffolding. While heterotelic forms of international collaboration began to crystallise shortly after World War I, the discussion that follows is concerned primarily with the autotelic phase.

A POET AND A PHYSICIST OPPOSE THE WAR

Against this backdrop, the form and content of Indo-German scientific exchanges in physics was shaped by this international ethos of science, battered though this ethos may have been by a resurgent nationalism, as well as the attempts to redefine physics as modern physics. More than anything else, the institutionalisation of physics in late colonial India opened up avenues for internationalisation—despite the fact that weak institutionalisation posed impediments for collaboration (Raina and Gupta 1998; Sen 1991). However, the exchanges involved the circulation not only of ideas, but also of scientists between a variety of institutions and organisations, a circulation which, when narrativised, travesties historiographies of percolation on the one hand, and those of the scientific West and the spiritual East on the other. World War I delivered a blow to the internationalism of science. At the end of the War, as Kragh suggests, there was an informal boycott of the German scientific community, a boycott that extended from 1919 to about 1928; the nature of the boycott was such that it limited German participation at international conferences. The boycott was probably near total for the first two years only (Kragh 2001, 145).

There is a need to qualify the kind of internationalism that prevailed in the world of physics. Till the 1920s, internationalism in physics was largely Euro-American internationalism. By the 1920s, new actors began to trickle into these networks of physics, coming in from India, China, and Japan, among other places. How these existing communities and networks responded to the research publications of the newcomers has been the subject of reception studies as well as the politics of knowledge (DeVorkin 1994; Raina 1996; Singh 2001). The centre-periphery model emphasised the undervaluation of the research contributions coming in from the periphery when compared to those from the centre; the greater the disparity in the state of institutionalisation of the concerned disciplines at the periphery, the greater the undervaluation of the research publications. Despite the fact that at the time India was a British colony with well-established collegial ties with disciplinary networks in universities in England—Oxbridge and, in the sciences, Cambridge in particular—the attempts to forge relationships with Germany arose from the fact that Germany had, since the last decades of the nineteenth century, ascended to a position of leadership in the new mathematical physics, particularly quantum theory, and theoretical mathematical physics, more generally (Jungnickel and McCormmach 1986, 2017).

However, a substantial number of Swedish scientists at the time had trained in Germany and, as Heilbron points out, were less committed to the boycott. During these decades the Swedish chemist Svante Arrhenius stands out, for, as Aant Elzinga writes, while World War I marks a rupture in the social relations of science, one of the features of this break reflects a complex intertwining of research with the realm of politics. In this environment, Arrhenius reignited the possibilities of internationalism (Elzinga 1997). After the war, Arrhenius worked towards repairing the damage done to the relations between German scientists and their colleagues in the victorious countries. A decade earlier, as a chemist he had reviewed Acharya P. C. Ray's *History of Hindu Chemistry*, and rejected Bertholet's charge that Ray's history was a nationalist one (Raina 1997). In the work, Ray had challenged some of the chronologies of alchemical procedures that Bertholet had proposed. What is of relevance is that when one of India's first modern physicists-turned-biologists, J. C. Bose, visited Sweden in

1920, Arrhenius goaded him to visit Berlin and meet Johann Friedrich Haberlandt—then Germany's leading plant physiologist. This Bose proceeded to do, and from Bose's letter to Arrhenius, we learn that he was particularly satisfied (Singh 2007).

On the German side, the arrival of a scientist from the British empire less than a year after the declaration of the boycott was indeed very reassuring, and an isolated Haberlandt was to reminisce: 'We Germans feel ourselves to be allied in spirit with the Indian people' (quoted in Singh 2007, 335). However, the matter did not stop there as far as J. C. Bose was concerned, because the Ministry of External Affairs in Berlin learned in 1926 that the League of Nations Committee on Intellectual Cooperation had invited Bose to Europe. Writing to the German Counsellor's office in Calcutta, they sought to gauge Bose's view of the Committee on Intellectual Cooperation and Germany. But they failed, and in any case decided to invite him to Munich to deliver a few lectures (ibid., 336). And while science was certainly politics by other means, this gradual shift from the autotelic impulse of collaboration signalled the identity of the community of physicists as part of an international fraternity.

Speaking of an international fraternity, we shall briefly move from the world of physics to the much-discussed Einstein–Tagore encounter, for this too commenced in Berlin. In his book *Einstein Lived Here*, the historian of physics Abraham Pais devoted an important chapter to Einstein's India connection, highlighting Einstein's interest in other cultures and the profound concerns that Gandhi, Tagore, and Einstein shared about humanity's future (Pais 1994, 100). Einstein and Tagore met for the first time in Berlin very shortly after the end of World War I, and their conversation on that occasion has since come down to us through Tagore's reminiscences. They met on 14 July 1930 at Einstein's summer house in Caputh near Berlin, and held a philosophical colloquy that was published both in India and the USA (ibid., 99). The next meeting was on 14 December 1930 in New York, and from the ship Einstein sent Tagore a telegram: 'May it be given to Tagore also on this occasion to work successfully in the service of his ideal of bringing nations together' (ibid.). Einstein jokingly referred to Tagore as Rabbi Tagore.

The contents of the meeting at Caputh were jotted down by a friend present on the occasion, and the subject of discussion was the nature of

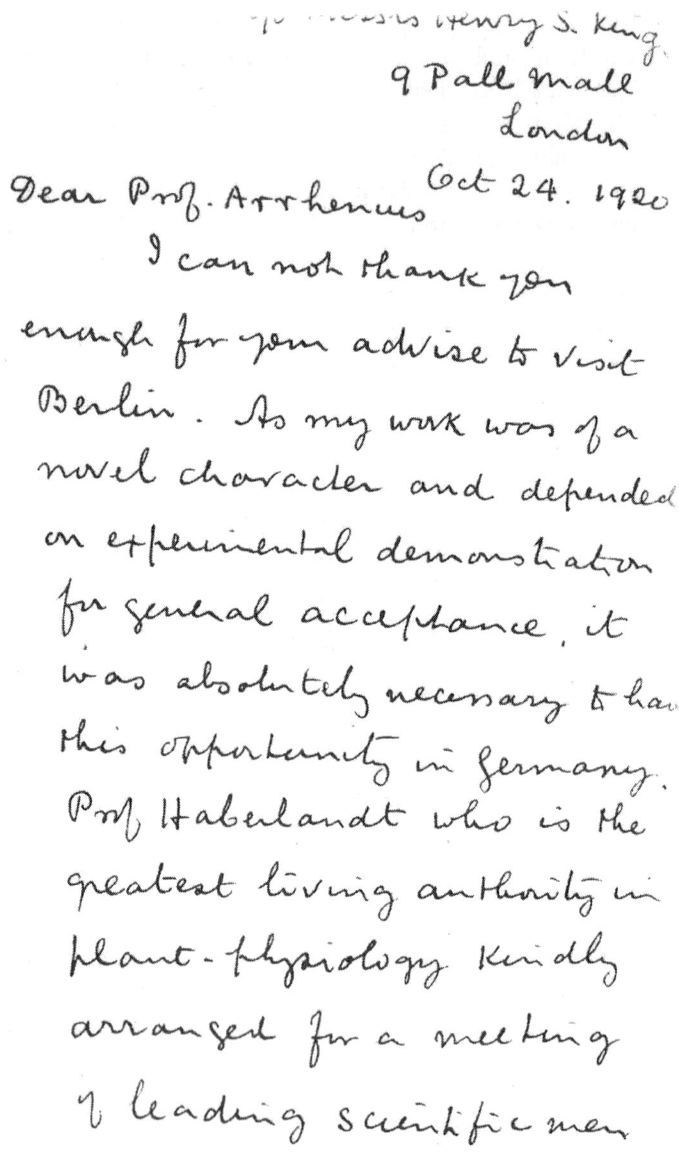

c/o Messrs Henry S. King.
9 Pall Mall
London
Oct 24. 1920

Dear Prof. Arrhenius

I can not thank you enough for your advise to visit Berlin. As my work was of a novel character and depended on experimental demonstration for general acceptance, it was absolutely necessary to have this opportunity in Germany. Prof Haberlandt who is the greatest living authority in plant-physiology kindly arranged for a meeting of leading scientific men

Image 4.1: Letter from Bose to Arrhenius, informing the latter of his visit to Professor Haberlandt in Germany

Source: S. N. Bose National Centre for Basic Sciences.

causality. On reading through the exchange, we discover that the two men 'talked past each other, without any understanding as to what the other was driving at' (Pais 1994, 105). When read closely, the exchange disappoints, for there is a pre-history of expectations and a horizon that is framed by the trope of the meeting of the scientific West and the spiritual East. But neither of the two thinkers concerned were used to thinking in such simple dichotomies. Even before he met Einstein, Tagore recognised the inadequacy of characterising Einstein's thought along these lines and referred to him as a transcendental materialist. Despite their different vocations and professional preoccupations as thinkers embroiled in the central political issues of their age, both were deeply sceptical of the idea of the nation-State (Bhattacharya 2012). And while there were fundamental premises that separated the manner in which they conceived the philosophical enterprise, there is in the dialogue a deep recognition that their starting points are different, despite which their humanist visions converge.

Einstein too recognised that the philosophical dialogue was a failure. In a letter he wrote in response to the French writer Romain Rolland, who had earlier written to Einstein seeking a contribution for a book to be presented to the Poet on his seventieth birthday, Einstein pointed out:

> I shall be glad to sign your beautiful text and to add a brief contribution. *My conversation with Tagore was rather unsuccessful* because of difficulties in communication and should, of course, never have been published. In my contribution, I should like to give expression to my conviction that men who enjoy the reputation of great intellectual achievement have an obligation to lend moral support to the principle of unconditional refusal of war service .... (Einstein, in Nathan and Norden 1960, 112)

Nevertheless, Einstein went on to write the Preface to Romain Rolland's collected work, called *The Golden Book of Tagore*. In the Preface, Einstein would write:

> You are aware of the struggle of creatures that spring forth out of need and dark desires. You seek salvation in quiet contemplation and in the workings of beauty. Nursing these you have served mankind by a long, fruitful life, spreading a mild spirit, as has been proclaimed by the wise men of your people. (Einstein, in Pais 1994, 108)

Tagore was grateful for the Preface and wrote to Einstein: 'The same sun is newly born in new lands, in a ring of endless dawn' (quoted in ibid., 105–107). Tagore went on to write about Einstein:

> He is a good and friendly man who has withdrawn himself from the world and its superficialities. He is devoted to peace and the wellbeing of mankind. He has pledged almost his entire life to those ideas. In his speeches in America he has stressed the harm of war and the benefits of peace. He is one of the greatest thinkers of our time. In my opinion he is in no way fanatic about race. He looks upon all people as equal and is fully prepared to serve humanity. (Tagore, in ibid., 108)

Rolland, Einstein, and Tagore were signatories to a manifesto that was realised on 12 October 1930, strongly arguing against conscription and the military training of youth (Pais 1994, 108). If the philosophical discussion turned out to be a damp squib, the discussion on music was more engaging, even though here, the differences were quite marked.

AUTOTELIC COLLABORATION DURING THE INTER-WAR YEARS

Normally, when discussing the life of C. V. Raman, the name of Einstein rarely comes up, although the names of many other leading German physicists of the time do; this is only partially explained by the circumstance that Raman was essentially an experimentalist and Einstein was a theoretical physicist. But this does not mean that there was no relation between their works. In fact, Raman did perform some experiments in 1922 that were among the many experiments carried out throughout the world confirming the wave or quantum nature of light.

The beginnings of the Indo-German encounter in the domain of physics research are traceable to the ties forged by D. M. Bose between Indian and German physicists. Bose had studied with Max von Laue in Berlin in the 1910s (Singh 2016). Debendra Mohan Bose had arrived in Berlin just before World War I and completed his doctorate in physics during the War years under the supervision of Erich Regener at the Humboldt University. Evidently, during the

Berlin years, which extended over the entire duration of the War, he was in touch with the leading Berlin physicists of the time—which, in addition to Einstein, included Max Planck, Walther Nernst, Heinrich Hertz, and Max Born. Max Born would have a special relation with India in the 1930s. The conversations that ensued between physicists in Germany and India during these two decades set the pace and tone for a collaboration during the autotelic phase of internationalism. Collaborative ties were forged across long distances between India's first Nobel Prize-winning physicist, C. V. Raman, and the German physicist Arnold Sommerfeld, and later, Max Born. This encounter is further embellished by the collaboration between Satyen Bose and Albert Einstein—that in fact merits a separate paper in light of the reconsideration of the nature of the collaboration. As one researcher was to write, the effort itself was possible because

> ... all the necessary ingredients were there at the right moment! The right passion for the understanding of nature, a common language (English and mathematics), the freedom to pursue this research leading to progress in the future not influenced by narrow minded funding agencies aiming at ephemeral technology transfer. (Putlitz 2000, 24)

And while the term 'internationalism' is used to designate the rubric under which these autotelic collaborative relations were worked out, we must not forget that the encounter was still deeply problematic for the new entrants into the world of international science.

By the 1920s, as it has been pointed out, the German physics community first began to take notice of the work of the fledgling community of Indian physics researchers (Singh 2001, 1490). As already stated, D. M. Bose had enrolled at Humboldt University in 1914 and submitted his dissertation in Berlin in 1918. He returned to India and assumed his position of Rashbehari Ghosh Professor in 1919. While in Berlin, he had already established contact with Germany's leading physicists, which included Max Planck, Albert Einstein, Peter Debye, Walther Nernst, Heinrich Hertz, and Max Born (Roy 2010, 491). In the next decade, S. N. Bose published his papers on quantum statistics and Meghnad Saha published his papers on theoretical astrophysics—some of this work was published in what we would today call the high-impact factor journal, *Zeitschrift für Physik*.

By 1924, Saha had already published twenty-seven papers on thermal ionisation and stellar formation and was nominated as Fellow of the Royal Society (Singh 2001, 1490). In short, then, speaking transnationally, the 1920s was a great decade for physics. Not without reason did Jagdish Mehra refer to it as the 'golden age of theoretical physics' (Mehra 2001). Physicists in Berlin, Göttingen, Paris, Cambridge, and Copenhagen were forging the quantum revolution; more than 5,000 miles away, a group of the Calcutta School of Physics had joined the club and had received eponymous recognition in the conceptual vocabulary of physics—the Raman effect, Saha ionisation formula, and Bose–Einstein statistics. This, in short, was the institutional context of international collaboration.

Amongst the German physicists acquainted with the researches of this generation of Indian physicists was Arnold Sommerfeld, a well-known, leading mathematical physicist of the old school in Germany, a professor of theoretical physics at Munich, and an early supporter of Einstein's work; as a member of the old school, he ended up supporting so much work on the new physics that one wonders why he is still counted amongst the old school. While not a member of the core group that invented quantum mechanics, he applied it to the study of atomic phenomena. He was to travel to India in the late 1920s, but this is not the place to discuss Sommerfeld's itinerary in India; I will, however, cite a passage from his 'Indische Reiseeindrücke' published in the *Zeitwende*, which in a way reviews his limited perception of the state of physics research in the early decades of the twentieth century: 'The sturdy shoots of modern physics have sprung up in recent years on this ancient and cultural soil and scientific research in India has suddenly begun to compete on equal terms with research in America and Europe' (quoted in Singh 2001, 1491). This impression is derived from the eponymous recognition of the work of the physicists he met on the trip to India. Clearly this group of physicists in India was not representative of the entire community at the time. The networks of collaboration were thus enclaved.

Saha's and Bose's exposure to German physics commenced in the late 1910s when P. J. Brühl, Professor at Sibpur Engineering College, who had a rich collection of advanced books and physics journals, introduced them to Max Planck's *Theorie der Wärmestrahlung* and von Laue's *Relativitätsprinzip*, which they read in the German. Following

Eddington's confirmation of Einstein's prediction of the bending of light rays in the presence of strong gravitational fields, Bose and Saha translated Einstein's papers on the General Theory of Relativity into English—these were possibly among the first such translations into English[1] (Wali 2009, xx). In a short biography of Einstein written in Bengali, Bose was to mention their discovery of Einstein's physics:

> The Calcutta University had started postgraduate classes in science. Three of us, Dr. Meghnad Saha, Professor Prasanta Mahalanobis and I selected the main papers on the new theories and translated them from the original German into English, and the Calcutta University published them as a book. Initially this book was the only one in which English translations of the main papers of relativity were available. Other translations followed and this book is now no longer available. (Bose 2000 [1965], 32)

In 1923, Bose had sent what later was to become his landmark paper to the journal *Philosophical Magazine* in England and the referee rejected the paper—so much for referees. In 1924, Bose then sent his paper with the famous postcard to Albert Einstein (*cf.* Image 4.3, left), making a strange request to somebody to whom he was writing for the first time—namely to translate the paper and arrange for its publication in nothing less than the *Zeitschrift für Physik*. Bose wrote: 'Though a complete stranger to you, I do not feel any hesitation in making such a request because we are all your pupils though profiting only by your teachings through your writings.' Einstein responded on 2 July 1924, heaving read, translated, and communicated the paper to *Zeitschrift für Physik* (Letters reprinted from the Einstein archive, in Wali 2009, xx–xxxvi). The rest is now history—the birth of Bose–Einstein statistics. But there remains much to be explained. Convinced about his derivation, despite the rejection from *Philosophical Magazine*, Bose sought the imprimatur of the master himself, and rather than opt for another physics journal published in English, opted for nothing less than the *Zeitschrift für Physik*. Within a week of having received Bose's paper, Einstein went on to write a paper, 'On the Quantum Theory of Monatomic Gas', extending the work of Bose, and then another

[1] This was *The Principle of Relativity: Original Papers by A. Einstein and H. Minkowski*, translated into English by M. N. Saha and S. N. Bose, with a historical introduction by P. C. Mahalanobis, Calcutta University, 1920.

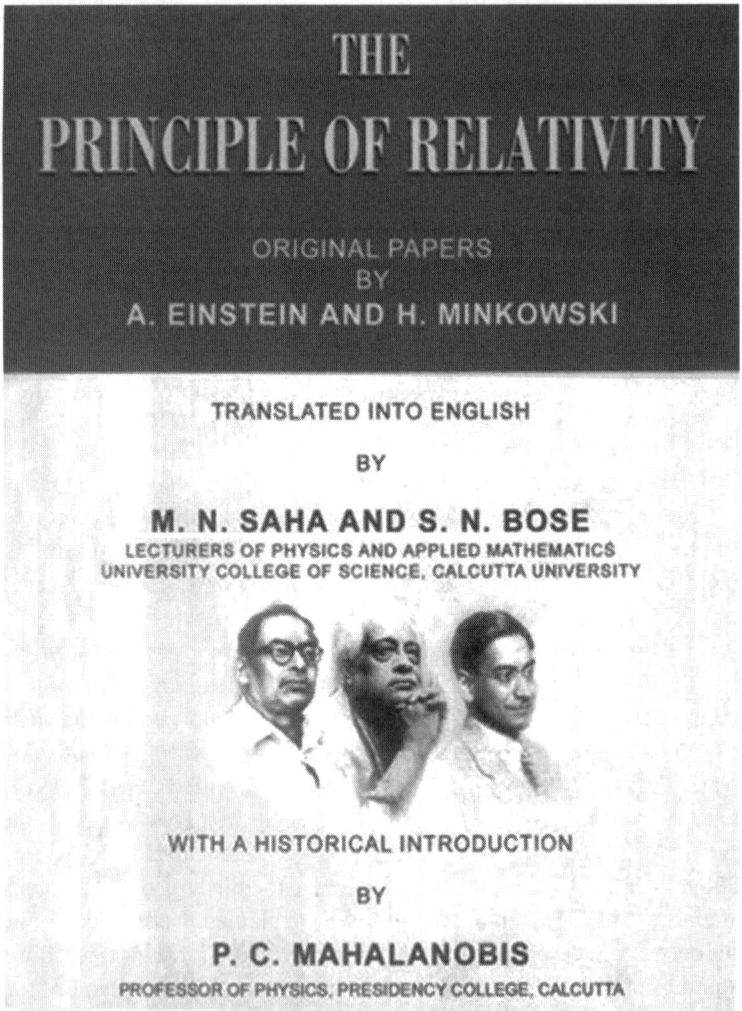

Image 4.2: Cover of the reprint of Saha and Bose's translations of Einstein's papers on relativity (2000 [1920])

one in 1925, predicting a new state of matter—the Bose–Einstein condensate, whose existence was established in the 1990s (ibid., xxii; *cf.* also Rempe 2000, 37–42).

Einstein's postcard earned Bose a grant from his university to travel to Paris and Berlin and a visa from the German consulate marked gratis

(Wali 2009). Before setting out, Bose sent another paper to Einstein and in his letter, now dropped the more formal 'Respected Sir', to the more familiar 'Respected Master', the English equivalent of the Bengali '*ādaraṇīya ācārya*'. Bose wrote: 'I have ventured to send you the typewritten paper in English ... I shall be glad for its publication in Zeit fur Physik or any other German journal ...' (quoted in ibid., xxiii). Here again, Bose in Calcutta professes a lack of familiarity with the civilities in the metropolis (Image 4.3).

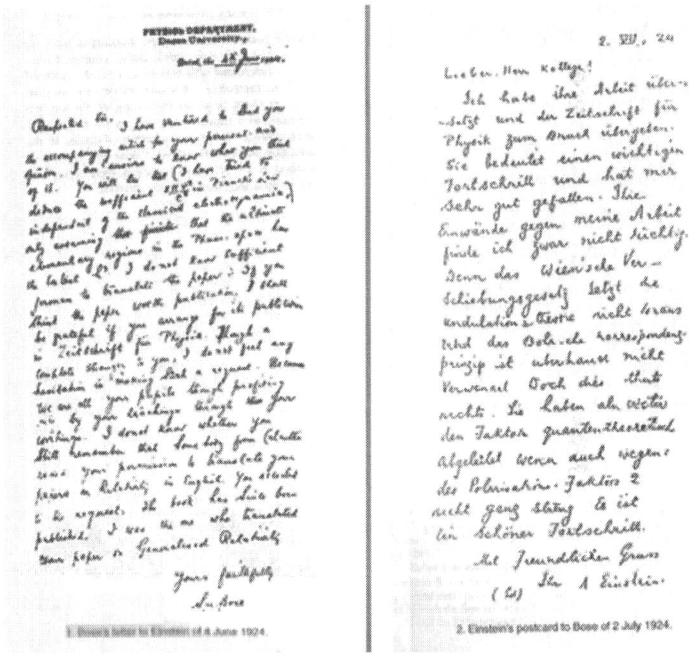

Image 4.3: Letters exchanged between S. N. Bose and Albert Einstein

Source: S. N. Bose National Centre for Basic Sciences.

While Einstein translated and communicated the second paper, which was published, in a letter dated 3 November he also voiced his disagreements with Bose's argument. In response, Bose wrote a third paper that he sent to Einstein. This paper was never published and no trace of it exists at the Albert Einstein Archive at Hebrew University (ibid., xxvi). In any case, Bose spent time with Einstein in Berlin and delivered several talks in 1925. He fondly writes: 'I arrived in Berlin in

1925. The Einsteins then lived in a flat on 5 Haberland-Straße. I was fortunate to be able to visit him often and have long discussions with him on many matters' (Bose 2000 [1965], 33). Amongst the many things they discussed was the ongoing freedom struggle in India. I extract a dialogue from one such discussion, as reported by Satyen Bose himself:

> E: I think Englishmen are better than other Western colonial nations, and I feel that they are far better than the French and the Dutch. You should not be surprised at a German like me praising the English [after the War]. Now, tell me, do you really want the British should quit your country?
>
> B: Of course, we all want to determine our destinies ourselves.
>
> E: Suppose, there was a button near you and all the Englishmen would quit India if you were to press it. So would you press the button?
>
> B: If God, were to grant me such an opportunity, I will not hesitate even for a moment to press it.
>
> E: Really? [... silence for sometime]
>
> B: Well, why do you Jews then want to establish a new Israeli state? Even you seem to be fairly inclined in its favour.
>
> E: I have, of course, now understood what you are saying—it is an emotional matter and cannot be explained by logic. (Bose 2000 [1965], 34)

Again, this is not the place to delve into the silences and ironies that marked the discussion, but Bose's remarks in this discussion close with a shared tragedy of both thinkers, namely the Holocaust in Europe and the bloody Partition of India. Returning to the lectures on physics that Bose delivered in Berlin, Bose was certainly not immune to the excitement surrounding the new developments in physics and was to write to Jacqueline Zadoc-Kahn:

> ... everybody seems to be quite excited in Berlin the way things have been on with Physics ... Einstein seems quite excited about it, the other day coming from the colloquium, we found him jumping in the same compartment, in the same compartment, where we were ... he talked almost all the time, unconscious of the interest and wonder that he is exciting in the mind of the passengers. (Bose, letter quoted in Wali 2009, xxvii)

Bose went on to spend time at the Kaiser Wilhelm Institute in Dahlem in Berlin, where Hermann Mark attended his seminars and later remarked in an interview on Bose's lectures:

> ... I think he gave it [the Seminar] in German because he was fluent in German.... Then Einstein said: 'Well, I think this is one of the most important works of the last few years'. He talked about it and then asked a few questions.... The discussion on this specific seminar took a few hours! Then of course Karman, Leo Szilard, Eugene Wigner also asked questions. We were young and he was young—so we quickly became friends and we invited him to the Kaiser Wilhelm Institut in Dahlem and give us the same seminar to continue the discussion. (quoted in Wali 2009, xxviii)

There was a process of forging a new confraternity of modern physics in the specific sense of 'modern' employed by physicists. Max Planck was once asked how he and his colleagues convinced the older generation of quantum theory. Planck responded: We could not convince them, they just died out. In any case, amongst the core group of those who participated in creating the new physics, the Indians were present in numbers disproportionate to the number of practising physicists in India.

Rajinder Singh, in his doctoral thesis on Raman, is right in pointing out that Sommerfeld and other German physicists had a very romantic idea of the state of physics in India in the 1920s. They encountered the *crème de la crème* and generalised from this the supposed landscape of physics research (Singh 2004). They did not know that under colonial rule infrastructure for research was lacking and poorly supported, research positions, if they existed at all, were very few, the university of teaching and research was barely twenty years old, the institutionalisation of scientific research in the university had just about commenced, and the two necessary conditions for institutionalisation—that is, a large enough number of scientists to sustain a community around common interests and the possibility of replenishment—were not adequately met at the time. In India, as I have argued elsewhere, the system was sub-optimal till the 1960s (Raina 2007). A 'true' picture of the depth and scale of Indian physics and the conditions under which it was pursued did not reach Germany till the mid-1930s. This gradually became evident when German physicists—Jewish and non-Jewish—fleeing Nazi Germany began looking for positions elsewhere. The German physicists Max Born and Rudolf Peierls actually considered making the Indian Institute of Science, Bangalore their home.

By 1934, Max Born had left Germany via Italy, and through the help of the Academic Assistance Council, obtained a lectureship in Cambridge. Raman, then director of the Indian Institute of Science, wished to develop theoretical physics in India and wrote to Born in January 1934 that he needed

> a first rate Mathematical Physicist who would guide and inspire the work of the institute on the theoretical side … I am writing to ask whether you could possibly think of coming to Bangalore if a full professorship of Theoretical Physics were created for you'. (Raman's letter to Born, dated 27 January 1934, quoted in Singh 2001, 1493)

Before taking a decision, Born wished to spend some time exploring the IISc. But the institute administration was already beginning to take steps to torpedo Raman's proposal.

Max Born arrived in India in 1936 and lectured on molecular optics and the quantum theory of radiation, but he writes that during the period he spent in India, there was nothing scientifically spectacular to report as far as his own research was concerned. He wrote to the leading Cambridge physicist Paul Dirac that his asthmatic condition had improved and that his wife Heidi was '… very happy in India'. He further expressed his unhappiness with his refugee status in England and wished to settle down (Singh 2004, 130–132).

However, his own work suffered since he had to build theoretical physics from scratch; despite his recollections in his Memoirs, retrospective evaluations of the work done during this time indicate that the work was not pathbreaking but substantial, as would be expected of a physicist of great competence. It must have been difficult working with Raman, and although their relation was amiable, differences in their approaches to lattice dynamics erupted in a scientific controversy that later became known as the Born–Raman controversy. This lasted for quite some time and strained their relationship, if not their friendship. But much before the controversy reached the level that it did, the administration of the Institute turned down Raman's proposal to offer the chair to Max Born. The Irwin Committee had pointed out that: 'Modern mathematical physics, with its collective fields of speculation and experiment, has little direct contact with industry, and in this respect cannot compete with chemistry as a subject likely to be of service to India' (Singh 2004, 135).

The Professor of Electrical Engineering, Aston, rejected Raman's proposal at the meeting of the Council where Born was also present. Born writes in his memoirs: 'Aston went up and spoke in a most unpleasant way against Raman's motion, declaring that a second-rank foreigner driven out from his country was not good enough for them ... I was so shaken that when I returned to Heidi I simply cried' (Born, quoted in Venkataraman 1988, 264). Born returned to Cambridge, Raman's problems with the administration multiplied, and slighted by the administration, he resigned from the Institute in a huff. Several years later, he lamented his inability to bring Erwin Schrödinger, Rudolf Peierls, and Paul Peter Ewald. When asked why he wished to recruit them, he spoke of his opposition to the recommendations of the Hill Committee Report to send Indians abroad to be initiated in scientific research

> ... because it would have been done in an environment so completely different from what exists in India. This type of training could have made them useless in our country. If great minds like Born and Schrodinger could have been provided a home here, a real scientific movement could perhaps have started in the country. (Raman, quoted in ibid., 265)

However, beyond a restrictive colonial policy and an underdeveloped infrastructure for scientific research, the counterfactual that needs to be posed is: Could these émigrés have stayed on? Again, in his memoirs Max Born was quite sceptical:

> The Jews will never consent to assimilate with the Indians and help build the Indian nation.... They regard themselves as representatives of righteousness upon the earth—the chosen race. The myth of race superiority is almost as strong in Jews as it is in the Nazis. (Born, quoted in Singh 2004, 134)

There is a despondency in this remark, a breakdown of any faith in an international community; to use a term coined by Salman Rushdie—sperectomy, the draining of hope.

There is a second aspect of the exchange between India and the German-speaking world that I would like to have discussed but leave for another occasion; this has to do with the two important Viennese physicists Ernst Mach and Erwin Schrödinger, both of whom turned to Indian philosophy to reflect on the epistemological dimensions of their science. Mach's preoccupation with Buddhism is well-known, but it is to Schrödinger I would have liked to turn: he is more relevant since he belongs to the core group of quantum theorists that we have been discussing. While training as a physicist, he had always shown an interest in philosophy—the Pre-Socratics, Hume, and more importantly, Ernst Mach, Kant, Spinoza, and Schopenhauer, with whom he shared his concerns on Indian philosophy. These reflections on philosophy and ontology are best articulated in his book, *My View of the World* (1951), particularly in the section titled 'What is Real'. I leave that discussion for a future paper, while pointing out that the finest work on the subject is authored by the French philosopher of physics, Michel Bitbol, titled *Schrödinger's Philosophy of Quantum Mechanics* (Bitbol 1996).

In any case, this exchange was interrupted during the war years. By the 1950s, the processes of decolonisation were well underway. The Cold War had begun to structure the formats of scientific exchange between the developing and developed worlds. The new political regime in India, rather than dismantle the institutional architecture of colonial science, began to reorient it to the developmental goals of the postcolonial State. This also entailed a massive project of State-led institutional building and investment in infrastructure—a humungous project perhaps never repeated by the State in India in the following six decades. In these developmental schemes, the post-war League of Nations organisations like the UNESCO and governments rushed in to usher in the era of heterotelic collaboration, wherein science did in fact become a form of politics by other means. In this scheme, Germany joined the nations who invested time and resources in founding one of the five elite Indian Institutes of Technology (IIT)—during what is referred to as the long 1950s. A new phase of scientific collaboration had commenced, and a new dynamics came to characterise the world of science—which was more team- and group-centred rather than individual-centred, even though individuals continued to matter.

A new institutional structure had emerged in German physics by the 1910s, the Kaiser Wilhelm Institute of Physics and gradually a hub of physics research began to crystallise around the area of Dahlem that was being planned as the Oxford of Germany. This geographical relocation was witnessed by some of the Indian physicists I mentioned between the 1920s and 1930s. By the 1930s, with the emigration of physicists from Germany to the UK and USA, and with the movement of Raman himself from Calcutta to Bangalore, the respective capitals of physics in the two countries also shifted. I have deliberately tried to tell this story by institutionally embedding these contacts and engagements within a university-based internationalism, but the cultural dimensions of this internationalism cannot be separated from the romance and history of the city itself.

BIBLIOGRAPHY

Bhattacharya, Sabyasachi. 2012. *Talking Back: The Idea of Civilization in Indian Nationalist Discourse*. New Delhi: Oxford University Press.

Bitbol, Michel. 1996. *Schrödinger's Philosophy of Quantum Mechanics*, Boston Studies in the Philosophy of Science. Netherlands: Springer.

Boltanski, Luc, and Lauren Thévenot. 1991. *On Justification: Economies of Worth*. New Jersey: Princeton University Press.

Bose, S. N. 2000 [1965]. 'Einstein'. In Stephan F. von Welck (ed.), *Crossing Borders, Stretching Boundaries: The Bose-Einstein Lectures on Indo-German Cooperation in Science, Technology and Environment*, 29–35. New Delhi: Manohar.

Carson, Cathryn, Alexei Kojevnikov, and Helmuth Trischler. 2011. 'The Forman Thesis: 40 Years After'. In Cathryn Carson, Alexei Kojevnikov, and Helmuth Trischler (eds), *Weimar Culture and Quantum Mechanics: Selected Papers by Paul Forman and Contemporary Perspectives on the Forman Thesis*, 1–6. London: Imperial College Press.

Dasgupta, Deepanwita. 2015. 'Stars, Peripheral Scientists and Equations: The Case of M. N. Saha'. *Physics in Perspective* 17 (2), 83–106.

DeVorkin, David H. 1994. 'Quantum Physics and the Stars (IV): Meghnad Saha's Fate'. *Journal for the History of Astronomy* XXV.

Elzinga, Aant. 1997. 'From Arrhenius to Megascience: Interplay between Science and Public Decision-Making'. *Ambio* 26 (1), 72–80.

Elzinga, Aant, and Catharina Landström. 1996. 'Introduction: Modes of Internationalism'. In Aant Elzinga and Catharina Landström (eds), *Internationalism and Science*, 3–20. London: Taylor and Graham.

Forman, Paul. 1971. 'Weimar Culture, Causality and Quantum Theory, 1918–1927: Adaptation by German Physicists and Mathematicians to a Hostile Intellectual Environment'. *Historical Studies in the Physical Sciences* 3 (1), 1–115.

Guay, Y. 1986. 'Emergence of Basic Research on the Periphery: Organic Chemistry in India (1907–1926)'. *Scientometrics* 10 (1–2), 77–94.

Hessen, Boris. 1971 [1931]. 'The Social and Economic Roots of Newton's "Principia"'. In *Science at the Cross Roads*, with a Preface by Joseph Needham and Introduction by P. G. Werskey. London: Cass.

Jungnickel, Christa, and Russell McCormmach. 1986. *Intellectual Mastery of Nature: Theoretical Physics from Ohm to Einstein*, 2 vols. Chicago: Chicago University Press.

———. 2017. *The Second Physicist: On the History of Theoretical Physics in Germany*. New York: Springer.

Kragh, Helge. 2001. *Quantum Generations: A History of Physics in the Twentieth Century*. New Jersey: Princeton University Press.

Kumar, Manjit. 2009. *Quantum: Einstein, Bohr and the Great Debate about the Nature of Reality*. New Delhi: Hachette India.

Manzione, Joseph. 2000. '"Amusing and Amazing and Practical and Military": The Legacy of Scientific Internationalism in American Foreign Policy, 1945–1963'. *Diplomatic History* 24 (1), 21–55.

Mehra, Jagdish. 2001. *The Golden Age of Theoretical Physics*, 2 vols. Singapore: World Scientific Publishing.

Nathan, Otto, and Heinz Norden. 1960. *Einstein on Peace*. New York: Schocken Books.

O'Boyle, Lenore. 1983. 'Learning for its Own Sake: The German University as Nineteenth-Century Model'. *Comparative Studies in Society and History* 25 (1), 3–25.

Pais, Abraham. 1994. *Einstein Lived Here*. Oxford, UK: Clarendon Press.

Phalkey, Jahnavi. 2013. *Atomic State: Big Science in Twentieth-Century India*. Ranikhet: Permanent Black.

Pinch, William R. 1999. 'Same Difference in India and Europe'. *History and Theory* 38 (3), 389–407.

Prasad, Amit. 2014. *Imperial Technoscience: Transnational Histories of MRI in the United States, Britain and India*. Boston: MIT Press.

Putlitz, Gisbert E. Zu. 2000. 'Satyendra Nath Bose and Albert Einstein: The Case of an Early Indo-German Scientific Cooperation'. In Stephan F. von Welck (ed.), *Crossing Borders, Stretching Boundaries: The Bose-Einstein*

Lectures on Indo-German Cooperation in Science, Technology and Environment, 17–27. New Delhi: Manohar.

Raina, Dhruv. 1996. 'Reconfiguring the Centre: The Structure of Scientific Exchanges Between Colonial India and Europe'. *Minerva* 96, 161–176.

———. 1997. 'The Early Years of P. C. Ray: The Inauguration of the School of Chemistry and the Social History of Science'. *Science Technology & Society* 2 (1), 1–40.

———. 1999. 'From West to Non-West?: Basalla's Three-Stage Model Revisited'. *Science as Culture* 8 (4), 497–516.

———. 2007. 'Science since Independence'. *India International Centre Quarterly: Special Issue—India* 60, 182–195.

———. 2011. 'Institutions and Knowledge: Framing the Translation of Science in Colonial South Asia'. *Asiatische Studien/Études Asiatiques* LXV (4), 945–967.

Raina, Dhruv, B. M. Gupta, and Rohit Kandhari. 1995. 'Evolutionary Trends and Collaboration in Indian Physics: A Study of Four Disciplines and Four Physicists'. *Scientometrics* 33 (3), 295–314.

Raina, Dhruv, and Ashok Jain. 1997. 'Big Science and the University in India'. In John Krige and Dominique Pestre (eds), *Science in the Twentieth Century*, 859–877. Amsterdam: Harwood Academic Publishers.

Raina, Dhruv, and B. M. Gupta. 1998. 'Four Aspects of the Institutionalization of Physics Research in India: Between Sociology and Bibliometrics'. *Scientometrics* 42 (1), 17–40.

Rempe, Gerhard. 2000, 'Bose-Einstein Condensation: From Theory to Experimental Observation to Application'. In Stephan F. von Welck (ed.), *Crossing Borders, Stretching Boundaries: The Bose-Einstein Lectures on Indo-German Cooperation in Science, Technology and Environment*, 37–42. New Delhi: Manohar.

Renn, Jürgen (ed.). 2012. *The Globalization of Knowledge in History*, Max Planck Research Library for the History and Development of Knowledge Studies 1. Open Access edition.

Roy, S. C. 2010. 'D. M. Bose: A Scientist Incognito'. *Science & Culture* 76 (11–12), 491–493.

Sen, S. N. 1991. *Scientific and Technical Education in India, 1781–1900*. New Delhi: INSA.

Shapin, Steven. 1992. 'Discipline and Bounding: The History and Sociology of Science as Seen through the Externalism-Internalism Debate'. *History of Science* 30, 333–369.

Singh, Rajinder. 2001. 'Arnold Sommerfeld—The Supporter of Indian Physics in Germany'. *Current Science* 81 (11), 1489–1494.

———. 2004. *Nobel Laureate C.V. Raman's Work on Light Scattering—Historical Contributions to a Scientific Biography*. Berlin: Logos Verlag.

Singh, Rajinder. 2007. 'India's Physics and Chemistry Nobel Prize Nominators and Nominees in Colonial and International Context'. *Notes Rec. R. Soc.* 61, 333–345.

——. 2016. *D. M. Bose, His Scientific Work in International Context.* Shaker Verlag GmbH.

Turner, R. Steven. 1980. 'The Prussian Universities and the Concept of Research'. *Internationales Archiv für Sozialgeschichte der deutschen Literatur* 5, 68–93.

Venkataraman, G. 1988. *Journey into Light: Life and Science of C.V. Raman.* Bangalore: IAS.

Wali, Kameshwar C. (ed.). 2009. *Satyendra Nath Bose: His Life and Times, Selected Works (with Commentary).* Singapore: World Scientific Publishing.

Weber, Max. 1962 [1917]. 'Science as a Vocation'. In B. Barber and W. Hirsch (eds), *The Sociology of Science*, 569–589. New York: Free Press.

Welck, Stephan F. von (ed.). 2000. *Crossing Borders, Stretching Boundaries: The Bose-Einstein Lectures on Indo-German Cooperation in Science, Technology and Environment.* New Delhi: Manohar.

Five

Sheldon Pollock and German Indology[1]

AXEL MICHAELS

INTRODUCTION

Let me begin with a caveat. I do not claim to be a specialist in the history of (German) Indology. What I have to offer in this chapter is no more than some thoughts on the production of Indological knowledge within Germany during the last approximately eighty years. I will often refer to Sheldon Pollock because he has stimulated my reflections through a number of thought-provoking articles, especially 'Deep Orientalism' (1993), 'The Death of Sanskrit' (2001), and 'Future Philology' (2009).[2] The first part of my chapter deals with the involvement of German Indology in the Nazi regime. The second part concerns the Indological scepticism in Germany about meta-theories in the humanities and social sciences.[3] In my view, both these aspects are connected.

---

[1] I am grateful to Christiane Brosius, Eli Franco, and Jan E. M. Houben for a critical reading of this chapter and for valuable additional hints.

[2] This is not the place to discuss the oeuvre of Pollock, which has been summarised and introduced by Bronner, et al. (2011, 1–22). Slaje (2014), in a sarcastic review, observed that the editors of this *Festschrift* did not list 'Deep Orientalism' among Pollock's major achievements and 'five broad areas' (p. 2) of his research, and he asks whether this debate on the involvement of German Indology in Nazi ideology and its murderous consequences must be seen as a confession of its failure.

[3] Jürgen Hanneder (2001, 239) speaks of 'the proclivity of American academia to meta-theorizing'; Walter Slaje (2003, 313) of '*Methodengeschrei und aller ohne Not geborener Theorienwut*' (screams of methods and unnecessary rage of theories).

Let me also say that I regard the term 'German Indology'[4] as a misnomer because it does not do justice to the many transcultural aspects of the discipline and the transnational life of Indologists. Take Max Müller, for example: Is he a German or an Englishman, given the fact that he spent most of his lifetime in Oxford? Or Otto Böhtlingk: born 1815 in St Petersburg into a family that originally came from Lübeck, he himself was a Dutch citizen, and later became a Russian citizen (Windisch 1919–1920, 239). Or Paul Thieme: he was born in Tübingen, became a teacher of French and German at Allahabad University in 1933, married Dorothy Learns, the daughter of a British officer, and returned to Germany in 1935. In 1941, he went to Russia as a soldier, joined the 'Indische Legion' of S. C. Bose in 1942, was imprisoned by the Americans in 1945, escaped from the German Democratic Republic (GDR) in 1953, went to Yale in 1954, and returned to Tübingen in 1960. Most Indologists in Germany have been, and still are, polyglot, address an international academic public, and have never united in any association or political-administrative institution striving for common goals. Given this, it would be better for one to speak of Indologists working and living in Germany. Much of the second part does not just concern this group that lacks a corporate identity. For the sake of simplicity, however, I will also use the common term 'German Indology' in what follows.

Sheldon Pollock's Analysis of 'German Indology' in the Nazi Period

In 1993, Sheldon Pollock, Professor of Sanskrit and Indian Studies at Columbia University, published his well-known article 'Deep Orientalism? Notes on Sanskrit and Power Beyond the Raj'.

[4] *Cf.* Grünendahl 2012, 189–190 and Adluri and Bagchee 2014, 7–10, who do not confine 'German Indology' to Germany, but believe that it has 'a sense of uniqueness [...] founded on the consciousness of possessing a unique (and superior) method' (Adluri and Bagchee 2014, 7), so that for them, American Indologists like E. W. Hopkins also become German Indologists; the term 'Indology' is, of course, likewise questionable: *cf.* Slaje 2003.

In this article, he argues that German Indology during the Nazi period

- has to be understood as a special variation of Edward Said's orientalism, since unlike orientalism in England or France, it was not directed at dominating and colonialising the global South, but 'inward—toward the colonization and domination of Europe' (Pollock 1993, 77);
- facilitated the setting up of an Indo-German 'counter-identity' to the Semite (ibid., 83), thus preparing the 'scientific' basis for racial anti-Semitism (Grünendahl 2012, 2); in other words, it is rooted in the idea of a racially and linguistically construed superiority that consequently helped to legitimise the Holocaust: 'German Indology of the NS era, a largely nonscholarly mystical nativism deriving ultimately from a mixture of romanticism and protonationalism merged with that objectivism of Wissenschaft earlier described, and together they fostered the ultimate "orientalist" project, the legitimation of genocide' (Pollock 1993, 96);
- posed as 'one local point of Indological work during the NS period ... the question of the *Urheimat* (the original home of the Aryans)' (ibid., 91); the related discipline 'Indogermanistik', especially, was much more interested in '*völkisches Gedankengut*' focusing on the *Urheimat* of the Aryans;
- interpreted 'Indian "caste law" as an expression of racial "hygiene" and adducing India a warning of the dangers of "blood chaos" that national socialism prevented at the eleventh hour. The ratio *ārya*: *caṇḍāla* (outcast, untouchable) :: German: Jew had already been proposed by Nietzsche, cited in Alsdorf 1942: 85' (ibid., 120, fn. 18). (Alsdorf distanced himself from this view);
- [and] misinterpreted the *Bhagavadgītā* to justify its Führer principle based on Jakob Wilhelm Hauer (*cf.* Malinar 2007, 25).

Pollock substantiated his theses by supplying some historical evidence. He shows that a number of Indologists in Germany had either been members of the NSDAP or had been actively involved in Nazi activities. As early as 1933, the names of Walther Schubring, Emil Sieg, Johannes Nobel, Johannes Hertel, and Friedrich Weller appeared in a famous declaration of 'Allegiance of German Professors and High-School Teachers to Adolf Hitler' (*Bekenntnis der deutschen Professoren zu Adolf Hitler*). But Pollock was not so much interested in the NS careers of Indologists in Nazi Germany as he was in the Indological contribution to NS thought. His analyses of Nazi Indologists had little to do with their party activities and involvement in politics; rather, he wanted to find out how certain Indologists contributed to the Nazi mindset *as Indologists*. And in the course of this, he mostly charged Ludwig Alsdorf, Bernhard Breloer, Erich Frauwallner, Jakob Wilhelm Hauer, Hermann Lommel, Richard Schmidt, and above all, Walther Wüst, for displaying Nazi thinking in their publications.

Pollock's ideas have been accepted, supported, extended, and defended. But they have also been criticised and rejected,[5] most notably by Reinhold Grünendahl (2006) and Jürgen Hanneder (2001). Grünendahl, especially, has argued that historical facts cannot account for Pollock's theory. He even goes so far as to admonish Pollock, stating that 'scientific and moral integrity count among the valuable goods one can lose once' (2006, 233). Grünendahl's *ad hominem* attacks must not be further explored here. But some of his factual criticism, though limited in its historical scope, probably holds true.

As Grünendahl rightly mentions, between 1933 and 1945, about twenty-five German Indologists had been employed at German universities, but only five or six can be counted as overt sympathisers of Nazi propaganda. Among them is Walther Wüst (*cf.* Marchand 2010; Pringle 2006), president of Heinrich Himmler's research institute *Ahnenerbe*, who became Vice-Chancellor of Munich University (1941–1945) and who, in this capacity, was personally involved in the imprisonment and subsequent execution of Hans and Sophie Scholl as well as Kurt Huber, all three of whom were prominent figures of the humanist Nazi resistance movement. Some of Wüst's writings undoubtedly reflect the worst racialist Nazi ideology, but Grünendahl argues that probably only few of his *Indological* publications had any direct influence on the Nazi leaders.[6] The same holds true for

---

5 See the debate on the Indology list; also see Larivière (1994), McGetchin (2009, 180), and Sengupta (2005, 5–6).

6 This probably does not apply for Wüst's *Indogermanisches Bekenntnis. Sechs Reden* (Berlin: Ahnenerbe-Stiftung Verlag, 1942), in which he wrote:

Hauer's and Frauwallner's publications.[7] In a list of publications considered influential for the Nazi *Weltanschauung* and published by the Nazis themselves in 1935, there is not a single work of any (German) Indologist.

Grünendahl further argues that between 1933 and 1945, the *Zeitschrift der Deutschen Morgenländischen Gesellschaft* (ZDMG) (*cf.* Houben 1996) did not contain any discriminatory article about the notion of '*Rassenreinheit*' (purity of race). However, according to the constitution of the German Oriental Society of 1938, 'People from the Orient, Jews, and others who could not receive the "Reichsbürgerschaft" (The *Reich*'s citizenship)' (Bericht über die Mitgliederversammlung der Deutschen Morgenländischen Gesellschaft 1994, 8) lost their membership. Moreover, in a longer historical perspective, racist Indological thinking has directly influenced Nazi ideology.[8]

If one considers those Indologists (or semi-Indologists) who had been involved in the Nazi regime, one should, likewise, not forget the Indologists who opposed the Nazi regime and ideology and thus had to leave Germany; or those who committed suicide because they were Jews (McGetchin 2009, 180–181): Wilhelm Geiger, Betty Heimann, Heinrich Lüders, Walter Neisser, Walter Ruben, Isidor Scheftelowitz, Hilko Wiarda Schomerus, Richard Simon, Moritz Spitzer, Otto Stein, Otto Straus, Hermann Weller, Moritz Winternitz, and Heinrich Zimmer. One could also recollect those German Indologists who were imprisoned by the British in India, for instance, Wilhelm Rau or Paul Thieme.

There are other Indological scholars who are less known, for example, the communist activist Philipp Schaeffer, author of a Tibetological work on Nāgārjuna's *Yuktiṣaṣṭikā*, perhaps the first

'*Heute wissen wir, dass Religion eigentlich eine geistig-körperliche Aktivität ist und dass sie daher rassisch ist*' ('Today we know that religion is a spiritual-physical activity and therefore it is racial'; p. 68).

7 *Cf.* Stuchlik (2009), Slaje (2010), and Stuchlik's reply (2011) to Slaje.

8 See, for instance, Houston Stewart Chamberlain, *Die Grundlagen des 19. Jahrhunderts—I and II* (2 vols, 1912), a very influential work for Hitler and Nazi propaganda, in which the Indologist Leopold von Schroeder's racist view on India is quoted several times.

Ph.D. student of Sinology in Heidelberg.[9] In Heidelberg, he became a close friend of the writer Anna Seghers. In 1927, he worked as a librarian at the Central Library Berlin-Mitte (which today is named after him). Due to his political activities, he was dismissed in 1932. He was imprisoned together with the socialist and political scientist Wolfgang Abendroth in 1935. In 1940, he was released, but was severely injured in 1942 when he tried to prevent the suicide of the Jewish couple Richard and Mathilde Hohenemserin, and could barely walk after that. Despite these injuries, he was imprisoned once again, sentenced to death, and decapitated in Plötzensee on 13 May 1943, on the alleged charge of high treason.

Following from this, one can argue that not all Indologists in Germany had been Nazis. Even those who held membership of the NSDAP did not necessarily subscribe to the Nazi ideology. On the contrary, Pollock's theory of a special and direct relationship between Indology and racialist theories is difficult to establish for mainstream 'German Indology'. The theory of the supremacy of the Aryan race is an apt example to prove this point. For the Nazis, belonging to the Nordic race was much more important than being of Indo-Iranian origin. As is well-known, they polemicised against the dark-skinned Europeans; likewise, they did not accept Indians as equal to the Nordic race, the 'real Aryans'.

We—as Germans—can thus say that, despite some shameful exceptions, 'German Indology' was not substantially involved in the production of Nazi ideology and propaganda. This does not mean that 'German Indologists' did not help to prepare the ground for disrespectful and despicable remarks about Indians, pointing out their intellectual inferiority, formlessness, otherworldliness, degenerate religiosity, monstrous literatures, lack of historical consciousness, etc. All of this added to a still existing subconscious prejudice against India. When I took my first Indological position at Münster University, one of the professors there told me how harmful it is for an Indologist to go to India and how proud he was that he had never been there. 'This will only spoil you,' he said. This view reflects the tradition of blaming British Indologists for being 'too close' to India: 'We know the Hindu less well than our [British] colleagues who live in this country and

[9] *Cf.* https://www.uni-heidelberg.de/de/universitaet/heidelberger-profile/historische-portraets/weiss-und-rot (accessed January 2022).

breathe this air. But to us is given, I hold, the possibility of knowing the Aryan of old India better than these [colleagues]' (Oldenberg 1906 [1967], 1518).

In other words, during the Nazi period, 'German Indology' was not a key player that justifies Pollock's idea of a German *Sonderweg* (separate path) of orientalism, even though Indological scholarship indirectly influenced Nazi ideology, for example, through occultism or the Theosophical Society (Goodrick-Clarke 2003; Treitel 2004). Indology was not, and is not, politically important enough to play such a prominent role. However, it must also be said—as far as I know and with the exceptions mentioned earlier—that 'German Indologists' in the Nazi period had not been members of any resistance movement. Moreover, they did not offer any resistance in intellectual fields where they could probably have done so (at least in the beginning of the Nazi period) without facing major dangers.[10] Only lately has German Indology begun to reflect upon its history during the Nazi period, and it was, after all, a 'foreigner', Sheldon Pollock, who initiated this debate on the history of 'German Indology'. Only after his intervention did several publications on the topic appear (see Brückner, et al. 2003; Junginger 1999; among others).

To sum up my first point: apparently, 'German Indologists' were neither better nor worse than most other scholars in Nazi Germany. They were, with some extreme and repellent exceptions, tacit collaborators. However, this also means that indologists working in Germany are part of the debate around the guilt that still rests on them. I personally believe that we have to acknowledge this collective guilt as Germans and Indologists, even though, individually, we may be free from any personal guilt.

The problem with the critics of Pollock, especially Grünendahl, is that they try to limit the Indologists to their indological writings and thus to exculpate Indology as an academic discipline. Even if it

---

10 One such exception is Paul Thieme, whose *Fremdling im Ṛgveda* was not opportunistic at all, but an indirect critique of Nazi ideology. Another exception is Hermann Weller (1878–1956), who published in 1937 his *Elegie Y*, a hidden criticism of Nazism clothed in Latin: see Dubielzig 2002 and Brückner, et al. 2006. However, it seems that even after the end of World War II, Weller never admitted that the 'anti-Nazism' reading of his *Elegie Y* was intended.

is true that 'German Indologists' did not substantially contribute to Nazi ideology, it remains a fact that the vast majority of scholars at German universities during the Nazi regime were guilty, from 1933 onwards. In 1935, many of them became members of the *Reichs-Dozentenbund* (the Nazi organisation of academic teachers). 'Already in 1936 (ZDMG vol. 90),' says Jan Houben (1996, Postscript 1),

> the participants of the 8th Orientalists' Day sent a special telegram to the 'Leader' and *Reichskanzler* in which they express their 'gratitude' and promise to engage themselves to reveal the value of foreign cultures in order to make them 'usable' for the German people. I am not aware of any exceptions let alone protests to this at that time apparently still 'voluntary' statement.

Together with the *NS-Studentenbund* (the Nazi student organisation), these Nazi academics represented the NSDAP, the National Socialist German Workers' Party, at the universities that frightened or even terrorised other scholars, especially Jewish colleagues, without being significantly hindered from doing so. For Jewish and many other university teachers, academic life became unbearable. They were either expelled or left 'voluntarily'. Heinrich Zimmer's fate in Heidelberg is telling on this count.

THE FATE OF HEINRICH ZIMMER

Zimmer[11] began his career studying Sanskrit and linguistics at the University of Berlin, where he graduated in 1913 with a dissertation on the history of the *gotras*. From 1914–1918, he participated in World War I. Between 1920–1922, he lectured at the University of Greifswald and worked on the Turfan manuscripts, but this work was never published. In 1922, he moved to Heidelberg, where he filled the extraordinary Chair of Indian Philology and Mythology. There

11 The following is based on Michaels 2010 and some unpublished documents in the possession of the late Lukas Rauch, son of Heinrich Zimmer, and his sister Maya Rauch (now kept in Deutsches Literaturarchiv Marbach). I am grateful to both for having sent me copies of some relevant documents. *Cf.* Rauch n.d.; Südkamp 2008; and Zimmer 1953.

he met Mila Esslinger, who was married to a rich Jewish artist. From this relationship, three 'illegitimate' children were born. Mila and her husband left for the USA in 1927.

One year later, Heinrich Zimmer met Christiane von Hofmannsthal, daughter of the famous Jewish novelist and poet, Hugo von Hofmannsthal (1874–1929), who was the author of the libretti of many operas of Richard Strauss, among them *Der Rosenkavalier* (*The Knight of the Rose*). Heinrich Zimmer soon fell in love with Christiane, who came to study Sanskrit. They married in 1928, after Zimmer had told her about his relationship with Mila. Four children were born to Zimmer and Christiane. In 1928, Mila Esslinger returned with her children to Heidelberg, while her husband remained a librarian at Michigan (Ann Arbor) and later settled in Switzerland. Zimmer and Mila continued their intimate relationship, apparently with the consent of Christiane.

In 1938, the Nazis dismissed Heinrich Zimmer, so he was not allowed to teach any more. Apparently, his marriage to Christiane von Hofmannsthal was the decisive factor in this step. In a note to the Rectorate, the then *Kanzler* (Registrar) of Heidelberg University declared him as racially impure ('*nicht-arisch versippt*').[12] This compelled him to leave Germany because he depended on the tuition fees that German professors used to get. Zimmer went via Zurich to England. Before leaving, he confessed to the *Reichssippenamt* (the racial office of the Third Reich) that he was the biological father of the aforementioned children of Mila Esslinger, so that they could be declared to be of pure Aryan race. Between 1939 and 1940, he taught at Balliol College, Oxford. In 1940, he moved to New York, where he eventually accepted the position of a Visiting Lecturer in Philosophy at Columbia University. One of his students during this period was Joseph Campbell, who later edited most of his English books. He died there, of pneumonia, the following year (1943).

Zimmer's pitiful situation is also expressed in a letter that Karl Jaspers wrote to him on 28 April 1938:

> The entire private hardship and the symbolism of this hardship for a reality that touches the heart of the German genius cannot be separated. With regard to you the nuisance is to be added that, despite

[12] Jahrbuch der Österr. Karl-Jaspers-Gesellschaft 6, 1993, 12.

> the acknowledged high rank of your work, you did not experience those sociological phenomena that are related to civil service, title and the official.[13]

As this example demonstrates, the entrapment of scholars and students during the Nazi regime cannot be reduced to publications. It was a silent agreement to the great injustice. But again, Indology was no different in this respect from other disciplines. The special guilt lies in having kept silent vis-à-vis certain racist ideas that could have been challenged, especially by Indologists. For instance, no German Indologist criticised Alfred Rosenberg's crude ideas on race (Pollock 1993: 94); no German Indologist objected to the theories of Aryan superiority or to the absurd ideas of *svastikā* heroism, of the *Führer* principle being derived from the *Bhagavadgītā*, etc. Indology remained silent on all these questions. This brings me to the second part.

The Silence of Indology in Germany

We have seen that, apart from very few exceptions, Indology did not play the politically influential role in the Nazi period that Pollock suggested. Despite the political influence of Walther Wüst, especially, it basically remained silent on political or societal issues. German Indology certainly did not manage to get Germans to sign up for Nazism and genocide. Despite the rather favourable political situation for them,[14] Indologists remained in an academic niche and continued their philological work on history and Sanskrit texts. With some exceptions, they—as Indologists—rarely got involved in any social and political debate.

13 *Die ganze private Not und das Symbolsein dieser Not für eine Wirklichkeit, die an das Herz des deutschen Genius greift, lässt sich nicht trennen. Bei Ihnen kommt hinzu all das zufällig Ärgerliche, daß Sie bei dem anerkannten, hohen Rang Ihrer Leistungen nicht einmal jene sociologischen Phänomene erfahren, die mit dem Beamtendasein, Titel, und dem Officiellen verknüpft sind. So gleichgültig das auf die Dauer gesehen sein mag, es ist doch jetzt wie eine Groteske* (ibid.).

14 See Erich Frauwallner's letter to Wüst applying, on ideological grounds, for the establishment of the Vienna Indological Institute: *cf.* Adluri 2011.

This aversion to theories and to socio-political debates continues even today. Indology in Germany still by and large keeps silent when it comes to public discussions. It rarely initiates critical debates or participates in them. Indology in Germany kept silent when India appeared on the front pages of newspapers, when the conflicts and problems would have needed at least some Indological expertise and comments, for example, in the context of Ayodhya as the birthplace of the god Rāma, the Aryan invasion debate, or when Indological colleagues were attacked for their writings: Wendy Doniger for her psychoanalyst approach, Michael Witzel in the California School Book debate, James Laine for his book on Shivaji, etc. The situation in the German Democratic Republic was equally depressing. And there is no reaction to the upcoming racist ideas and high veneration of Hitler in some right-wing circles in India. Instead, for quite some time, classical Indology in Germany has objected to chairs for modern Indian languages and studies on contemporary India. It has struggled over the division of classical and modern Indology to such an extent that almost two cultures of Indian studies developed: philological and cultural studies.

I believe that the dominance of Classical Indology with its focus on Sanskrit philology comes at the cost of cultural studies on India, and that its absence in theoretical debates ultimately contributes to a decline of Indology in Germany (*cf.* Michaels 2015). Even though the chairs at Cologne, Halle, and Mainz are presently endangered, the situation is still quite comfortable, given that there are still a number of universities with one or two Indological chairs: Bonn, Göttingen, Hamburg, Heidelberg, Leipzig, Marburg, Munich, Tübingen, and Würzburg. Germany thus has many more Indological chairs than England, France, or any other European country, and perhaps even the USA. But the decline of Indology in Germany is evident. At several traditional universities, Classical Indology is not taught any more, such as Berlin, Münster, Freiburg, and Kiel. The chairs in Cologne and Bonn have shifted their focus to Tamil and Modern South Asian Studies, respectively. If this development continues, Indology in Germany might become more and more marginalised.

Certainly, it is not only Indology that has caused this decline; other factors have also contributed to it, and the situation in India is not much better, as Sheldon Pollock (2009, 935) warns: 'In India (too), it (Sanskrit philology) is perilously close to the point of no return, and whether coming generations will even be able to read the texts of their traditions is now all too real a question.' He adds, 'systematic philological knowledge (in India) is fast becoming extinct' (ibid., 941).

However, like the debatable decline or death of Sanskrit in India that Pollock analysed for certain regions (in Kashmir, in sixteenth-century Vijayanagara, in the short-lived moment of modernity of Sanskrit at the Mughal court in mid-seventeenth-century Delhi, on the eve of colonialism in Bengal), German Indology—or at least, German armchair Classical Indology—might decline more if it claims a monopoly on the production of knowledge of India and reduces itself to a certain form of philology. Therefore, it is time to discuss the future of Indology, and this also means the future of (Sanskrit) philology.

The Future of Indological Philology

Fortunately, the renowned Indologist Walter Slaje from Halle University has recently initiated such a debate in Germany. In his well-written article, 'Was ist und welchem Zwecke dient Indologie? Tractatus irae' ('What is and what for is Indology? Tractatus irae', 2003), he defends philological Indology against Indology as a cultural studies discipline. He criticises those who look for '1001 attributes of relevance for the present day, economic-political benefit, orientation towards job market and professions [...] in order to save Indology from the alleged threat of its extinction'.[15]

Instead, Slaje defends the intrinsic value and elementary fundaments of scientific research, the methodical striving for knowledge ('*Erkenntnis*') as the highest good of humans endowed with reason. He is, of course, not alone in his grief about the Indological acclimatisation to the *Zeitgeist* (spirit of the age): 'It is much easier to

15 '*[...] 1001 Attributen von Gegenwartsrelevanz, ökonomisch-politischem Nutzen, Arbeitsmarkt- und Berufsorientiertheit [...], um es [...] vor dem vermeintlich drohenden Untergang zu retten. Wer will schon ein Nichts-Nutz sein?*' (Slaje 2003, 312).

begin to theorize, to make conclusions about classical society without having to do this tedious work of editing texts,' says Richard Larivière (1994, 17; as quoted in Slaje 2003, 313). Slaje suggests that a discipline must only follow 'its inner necessities as they emerge directly from its own dynamics of research'. And this is basically philology; he considers everything else as introduced from the outside. He then speaks of a tendency, especially among German-speaking professors ('Germanophone Professoren') to uncritically accept centralised or *Zeitgeist*-influenced themes and sees in them a '*Bereitschaft zur freiwilligen Integration in das Stechschrittkollektiv des Geistes. Mal war es die Rasse gewesen, mal die Klasse. ZurZeit ist es die Kasse*' ('Deliberate readiness to goose-step with the Zeitgeist. First it was race, then class, now it is cash' [Slaje 2002, 316]).

By this, Slaje suggests that Indology is only on safe grounds if it remains at a certain distance from fashionable contemporary cultural theories.

Instead, Slaje proposes a 'pure' Indology unspoiled by what he considers the *Zeitgeist*. One should study the 'specific nature and otherness of India in its authenticity' ('*die Eigenart und Fremdheit Indiens in seiner Ursprünglichkeit*' [Slaje 2003, 320]). The primary method to study this is philology, which only enables fundamental research and 'comparative reflections and abstractions':

> Indology diagnoses and analyses. This gives it the character of a pure *Wissenschaft*. It neither offers therapies, nor heals nor prognoses. The first is done by doctors, the last by meteorologists, pollsters or prophets—all with familiarly changing success and always unsafe results.[16]

In other words, Slaje follows the Weberian approach of the valorisation of science as 'value-free'.

This debate situates us in the *Zukunftsphilologie* (future philology) dispute, which was initiated in 1872 by the classicist Ulrich von Wilamowitz-Möllendorf when he criticised Friedrich Nietzsche

---

16 '*Indologie diagnostiziert also, und analysiert. Darin liegt ihr Charakter einer reinen Wissenschaft. Sie therapiert nicht, heilt und prognostiziert auch nicht. Ersteres tun Ärzte, letzteres Meteorologen, Meinungsforscher und Propheten—alle mit bekannt wechselndem Erfolg und stets unsicherem Ausgang*' (Slaje 2003, 321).

on his just published *The Birth of Tragedy*. At that time, philology had become the leading discipline in the humanities and social sciences.

> For Wilamowitz, true knowledge of any social or cultural phenomenon of the past could only be acquired by examining every feature of its historical context, and by doing so completely abstracting it from present-day perspectives. For Nietzsche, the approach of the newly professionalized (and only recently named) discipline of philology had completely deadened antiquity and perverted the true aim of its study; the philologists themselves had 'absolutely no feeling for what should be justified, what defended'. (Pollock 2009, 932)

Slaje continues this debate since he accepts not only the method of the classicists, but also their 'abstraction from present-day perspectives' that Nietzsche had criticised.

Already in his book *Deep Orientalism*, Pollock had emphasised that a critical philology has to recognise that

> disinterested scholarship in the human sciences, like any other social act, takes place within the realm of interests; that its objectivity is bounded by subjectivity; and that the only form of it that can appear value-free is the one that conforms fully to the dominant ideology, which alone remains, in the absence of critique, invisible as ideology. (1993, 96)

In his article 'Future Philology? The Fate of a Soft Science in a Hard World' (2009), Pollock, following Vico, even propagates philology as 'the language of the book of humanity' (ibid., 934). This is a clear turn —or return—to philology, which Hanneder (2001) would probably still characterise as opportunistic and trendy. But philology—the 'art of reading slowly', as Nietzsche defined it—must periodically come under critical review, and the present crisis of the discipline, eloquently captured by Sheldon Pollock, makes such a review all the more pressing.

CONCLUSION

Walter Slaje's defence of philology and propagation of a distance from the *Zeitgeist* reflects a widespread intellectual attitude in 'German

Indology' (and beyond), as most Indologists refrain from any involvement in politics and public debates. They distance themselves by diminishing non-German Indology as less pure, because these forms of production of Indological knowledge sacrifice philology either to the *Zeitgeist* (USA) or to religious aspirations (India). And sometimes they even see themselves as 'martyrs', defending Sanskrit philology against its alleged critics. On the other hand, they regard 'Future Philology' as just another fashionable turn.

I believe that this attitude has to do with Germany's Nazi period and India's image in Germany. The traumatic experience of the NS regime has created scepticism and even disgust of *Zeitgeist* theories, and has facilitated a view of such people who work on India's culture in Germany as esoteric and quixotic.

Is the reduction of Indology to philology responsible for the threat of a decline of this discipline in German universities? Or is it, as Pollock diagnoses, a

> hypertrophy of theory over the two past decades, which often wound up displacing its object of analysis; the devaluation of the strictly textual in favour of the oral and the visual; the growing indifference to and incapacity in foreign languages, especially in the historical languages worldwide; and the shallow presentism of scholarship and even antipathy to the past as such? (Pollock 2009, 934f)

I must admit that I do not have a clear answer to these pertinent questions. But instead of attacking each other, we Indologists should start a debate on such issues and not keep silent on them (as, for instance, the German *Indologie* e-discussion list). To be sure, in Indology philology must remain the primary method. But it perhaps needs more (theory, fieldwork, empirical or literary studies). 'Pure' philology cannot be the only future of Indology. It is not an innocent method. Slaje's definition of Indology as a 'purely European science [...] completely anchored in the context of European thinking' (Slaje 2003, 317) does not consider the extent to which 'European thinking' depends on distancing from other ways of thinking, which then have to be declared non-scientific—similar (but, of course, without its anti-Semitic undertones) to Frauwallner's dictum: 'Wissenschaft in the strict sense of the word is something that could be created only by Nordic Indo-Germans' (Pollock 1993, 93f.).[17] Pollock has demonstrated how other and premodern philological disciplines can contribute to a better understanding of the textuality of cultures. The dichotomy of the scientific West and the spiritual East does not hold any longer.

The belief that Germany is the best or purest place to study Indology and, from a certain perspective, better even than India, is still widespread and shared by many Indians. Such an alliance between German Indologists and Indian pandits comes at the cost of ignoring other productions of 'modern' *and* 'traditional' knowledge, which are still widely neglected at German Indological institutes. Through its focus on Sanskrit, Indology in Germany inevitably fosters analyses of India which maintain the idea that Brahmanic norms are the rules of Indian society, or that India is dominated by religion. Indology will be partly responsible for the metaphysical imaginary of India if it continues to downplay or ignore other approaches.

What does that mean? Scholarly attention has to be given not only to 'pure' philological studies, but also to the textuality and historicity of texts (*cf.* Michaels 2004). Context matters as much as texts do. Experiencing and observing cultural, social, and religious practices should be methodologically regarded to be as valuable as reading. The house and the streets are as important as the temple, the palace, or the ashram. The everyday is no longer to be considered only the sphere of life of small chores, but as the counter-world of the underprivileged and subaltern, women, farmers, or artisans. As Bourdieu puts it, diversity is no longer epiphenomenal and thus peripheral, but central. The private has become just as important as the public, sensibility as valuable as sense and reason. Understanding all this needs theory. For renouncing theories would mean using truisms, commonplaces, or, as Ernest Gellner (1988, 12) puts it in the German edition, '*Binsenwahrheiten*' (bromide). These theories must have to do with the *Zeitgeist*, that is, with what interests people now, and if necessary, academic disciplines, even philology, have to get involved in political and societal questions in order to evade irrational developments. This is what Plato said in his *Politeia*, and what Karl

17 This, however, was not said by Frauwallner, but by the Semitist and Altorientalist Wolfram von Soden (Grünendahl 2012, 231).

Jaspers reiterated in a famous publication ('Zur geistigen Situation der Zeit') written two years before Hitler's takeover. Philology without theory has no future, just as theory without philology is empty. Only at the confluence of philology and theory can Indology survive and blossom (*cf.* Michaels 2020).

REFERENCES

Adluri, Vishwa P. 2011. 'Pride and Prejudice: Orientalism and German Indology'. *International Journal of Hindu Studies* 15 (3), 253–292.

Adluri, Vishwa P., and Joydeep Bagchee. 2014. *The Nay Science: A History of German Indology*. Oxford and New York: Oxford University Press.

Bekenntnis der deutschen Professoren zu Adolf Hitler. Available at https://archive.org/details/bekenntnisderpro00natiuoft (accessed August 2021).

Bronner, Yigal, Whitney Cox, and Lawrence McCrea (eds). 2011. *South Asian Texts in History: Critical Engagements with Sheldon Pollock*. Ann Arbor: Association for Asian Studies.

Brückner, Heidrun, et al. 2003. *Indienforschung im Zeitenwandel. Analysen und Dokumente zur Indologie und Religionswissenschaft in Tübingen*. Tübingen.

Brückner, Heidrun, Uwe Dubielzig, and Konrad Plieninger. 2006. *Weite Horizonte: Hermann Weller 1878—1956, klassischer Indologe, lateinischer Dichter, christlicher Humanist*. Schwäbisch-Gmünd: Einhorn-Verlag.

Chamberlain, Houston Stewart. 1912. *Die Grundlagen des 19. Jahrhunderts—I and II* (2 vols). Munich.

Dubielzig, Uwe. 2002. 'Die neue Königin der Elegien: Hermann Wellers Gedicht, Y'. In Eckhard Keßler and Heinrich C. Kuhn, *Germania Latina—Latinitas Teutonica* 2, 855–878. Available at http://www.phil-hum-ren.uni-muenchen.de/GermLat/Acta/Dubielzig.htm (accessed August 2021).

Gellner, Ernest. 1988. *Plough, Sword, and Book*. Chicago: University of Chicago Press.

Goodrick-Clarke, Nicholas. 2003. *Occult Roots of Nazism: Secret Aryan Cults and their Influence on Nazi Ideology*. New York: New York University Press.

Grünendahl, Reinhold. 2006. 'Von der Indologie zum Völkermord: Die Kontinuitatskonstrukte Sheldon Pollocks und seiner Epigonen im Lichte ihrer Beweisführung'. In Ute Hüsken, Petra Kieffer-Pülz, and

Anne Peters (eds), *Jaina-Itihāsa-Ratna: Festschrift für Gustav Roth zum 90. Geburtstag*, 209–36. Marburg: Indica et Tibetica.

Grünendahl, Reinhold. 2012. 'History in the Making: On Sheldon Pollock's "NS Indology" and Vishwa Adluri's "Pride and Prejudice"'. *International Journal of Hindu Studies* 16, 189-257.

Hanneder, Jürgen. 2001. 'Review of Eli Franco and Karin Preisendanz (eds), *Beyond Orientalism: The Work of Wilhelm Halbfass and its Impact on Indian and Cross-Cultural Studies*'. *Zeitschrift der Deutschen Morgenländischen Gesellschaft* 151 (1), 238–239.

Houben, Jan E. M. 1996. 'Promising Continuity with a Discontinuous Past'. Report of a conference, (1995); two Postscripts (2014); two Further Postscripts, including a brief review, The Nay Science (2018). Available at https://www.academia.edu/7378413/Promising_continuity_with_a_discontinuous_past_report_of_a_conference_1995_two_Postscripts_2014_two_Further_Postscripts_incl_brief_review_The_Nay_Science_2018 (accessed October 2021).

Jaspers, Karl. 1931. *Die geistige Situation der Zeit*. Berlin: Walter de Gruyter.

Junginger, Horst. 1999. *Von der philologischen zur völkischen Religionswissenschaft. Das Fach Religionswissenschaft an der Universität Tübingen von der Mitte des 19. Jahrhunderts bis zum Ende des Dritten Reiches* (Contubernium, 51). Stuttgart: Franz Steiner.

Larivière, Richard W. 1994. 'Protestants, Orientalists, and Brahmanas: Reconstructing Indian Social History'. Second Gonda Lecture, Royal Netherlands Academy of Arts and Sciences, Amsterdam, 4 November.

Malinar, Angelika. 2007. *The Bhagavad Gītā: Doctrines and Contexts*. Cambridge: Cambridge University Press.

Marchand, Suzanne. 2010. *German Orientalism in the Age of Empire: Religion, Race, and Scholarship*. Cambridge and New York: Cambridge University Press.

McGetchin, Douglas T. 2009. *Indology, Indomania, and Orientalism: Ancient India's Rebirth in Modern Germany*. Madison: Fairleigh Dickinson University Press.

Michaels, Axel. 2004. 'Indology and the Cultural Turn'. In Angelika Malinar, Johannes Beltz, and Heiko Frese (eds), *Text and Context in the History, Literature and Religion of Orissa*, Studies in Orissan Society, Culture and History 3, 457–481. New Delhi: Manohar.

———. 2010. 'Friedrich Max Mueller, Heinrich Zimmer and the Purification of Religions.' Unpublished paper presented at the conference 'Cross-cultural Conversation: On India—Self-Image and Counter-Image', Indira

Gandhi National Centre for the Arts, New Delhi, 29 December; also at the Max Mueller Memorial Lecture 2009, Goethe-Institut Mumbai, in collaboration with Chhatrapati Shivaji Maharaj Vastu Sangrahalaya, 22 December 2009.

———. 2015. 'Perspektiven und Probleme der deutschsprachigen Indologie'. In Dieter Lamping (ed.), *Geisteswissenschaft heute: die Sicht der Fächer*, 282–306. Stuttgart: Kröner Verlag.

———. 2020. '"At the Point of Confluence of Sociology and Indology": Louis Dumont's Postulate Reconsidered'. *Contributions to Indian Sociology* 53 (3), 1–31 (with comments by Arjun Appadurai, Johannes Bronkhorst, Veena Das, Pratap Bhanu Mehta, Jonathan Parry, Thomas Trautmann, Ananya Vajpeyi, and a Postscript).

Oldenberg, Hermann. 1906 [1967]. 'Indische und klassische Philologie'. In Klaus L. Janert (ed.), *Kleine Schriften*, Vol. 2, 1515–1523. Wiesbaden: Fritz Steiner Verlag.

Pollock, Sheldon. 1993. 'Deep Orientalism? Notes on Sanskrit and Power Beyond the Raj'. In Carol A. Breckenridge and Peter van der Veer (eds), *Orientalism and the Postcolonial Predicament: Perspectives on South Asia*, 76–133, South Asia seminar series. New Cultural Studies. Philadelphia: University of Pennsylvania Press.

———. 2001. 'The Death of Sanskrit'. *Comparative Studies in Society and History* 43 (2), 392–426.

———. 2006. *The Language of the Gods in the World of Men: Sanskrit, Culture, and Power in Premodern India*. Berkeley: University of California Press.

———. 2009. 'Future Philology? The Fate of a Soft Science in a Hard World'. In James Chandler and Arnold Davidson (eds), *The Fate of the Disciplines*, Special issue, *Critical Inquiry* 35 (4), 931–961.

Pringle, Heather Anne. 2006. *The Master Plan: Himmler's Scholars and the Holocaust*. New York: Hyperion.

Rauch, Maya. 'Heinrich Zimmer 1890–1943. Ein Beitrag zu seiner Biographie'. Unpublished typescript, H. Z. Biog 6: IIX. 06, 9.

Sengupta, Indra. 2005. *From Salon to Discipline: State, University and Indology in Germany, 1821–1914*. Würzburg: Ergon Verlag.

Slaje, Walter. 2003. 'Was ist und welchem Zwecke dient Indologie?' *Zeitschrift der Deutschen Morgenländischen Gesellschaft* 153 (2), 311–331.

———. 2006. 'Stuchlik, Jakob: Der arische Ansatz. Erich Frauwallner und der Nationalsozialismus', *Asiatische Studien* 64, 447–463.

———. 2014. 'Review of Broner, et al., *South Asian Texts in History. Critical Engagements with Sheldon Pollock*'. *Zeitschrift der Deutschen Morgenländischen Gesellschaft* 164 (2), 574–578.

Stuchlik, Jakob. 2009. *Erich Frauwallner und der Nationalsozialismus*. Vienna: Verlag der Österreichischen Akademie der Wissenschaften.

——. 2011. 'Replik auf Walter Slajes Rezension meines Buches "Der Arische Ansatz. Erich Fauwallner und der Nationalsozialismus"'. *Asiatische Studien* 65 (1), 287–308.

Südkamp, Elisabeth. 2008. 'Heinrich Zimmer (1890–1943)'. *Heidelberg. Jahrbuch zur Geschichte der Stadt*, 12, 88–106.

Treitel, Corinna. 2004. *A Science for the Soul: Occultism and the Genesis of the German Modern*. Baltimore: John Hopkins University Press.

Windisch, Ernst. 1919–1920. *Geschichte der Sanskrit-Philologie und indischen Altertumskunde*. Berlin: Walter de Gruyter (Grundriss der Indo-Arischen Philologie und Altertumskunde, I, I B).

ZDMG. 1940. 'Bericht über die Mitgliederversammlung der Deutschen Morgenländischen Gesellschaft'. *Zeitschrift der Deutschen Morgenländischen Gesellschaft* 94, 7–8.

Zimmer, Heinrich. 1953. 'Notizen zu meinem Lebenslauf'. *Merkur* 7 (1), 49–54.

Six

Falling into a Brown Study

*Völkisch Nationalism, Indo-Nazism, and Historical Translations**

BENJAMIN ZACHARIAH

This chapter addresses the extent and nature of the closeness of Indian and German thought in relation to *völkisch* nationalism and National Socialism. In writing this chapter, I can be accused of presentism. After all, a study of *völkisch* and pro- or proto-National Socialist tendencies in Indian political thinking has immediate resonances with the rise and subsequent rule in India of a political party whose roots in the fascism(s) of the first half of the twentieth century are undeniable, even if the nature and extent of those roots are still the subject of some controversy. However, this chapter does not try and draw out a linear continuity from early twentieth-century organisations to the present day, staying in and before fascism's 'core' period—although it is of course tempting to note in passing that the Rashtriya Swayamsevak Sangh (RSS) is by now probably the world's longest-surviving fascist paramilitary organisation, or at any rate the only one with a(n almost) continuous legal existence.

Can a non-'European' fascism be the 'real thing'? Or is it a pale imitation that bears certain superficial resemblances to its (misunderstood) European 'originals'? I have written about a number of these points at length elsewhere; here, I shall summarise what I require from those earlier publications for the purposes of the current argument, and try to proceed from there (see Zachariah 2010, 2013a, 2014a, 2015a, 2015b, 2016). It is necessary, first, to abandon the idea that fascism is something uniquely European, an assumption that is remarkably resilient despite an emerging awareness of the

* This chapter is dedicated to the memory of Dirk Lass (1963–2016), philosopher, bookseller, and anti-fascist, without whose expertise and advice over the last few years much of my recent work could not have been written.

resonances of fascist and Nazi ideas elsewhere in the world (and here I treat Nazism as a form of fascism, if a more extreme form).[1] The emergence of fascism in the 1920s and 1930s depended to a large extent on what I call a 'voluntary *Gleichschaltung*' of ideas, movements, and institutions that recognised each other as members of a family, but took on more of the characteristics of the successful sibling on purpose. A number of these ideas had existed in earlier versions from the previous century, in which race and *Volk* were operative categories. (The similarities were often disavowed for public purposes, since the peculiar genius of each 'nation', 'race' or '*Volk*' was supposed to be unique and therefore necessary to preserve against dilution, disappearance, miscegenation, etc.) These ideas lent themselves to a *fascist repertoire* that found its conjuncture between the two World Wars. But the idea that 'Europe' and the rest of the world were somehow separate makes no sense: these ideas, movements, and institutions were not necessarily derivative of one another, emerging contemporaneously but not imitatively, even as they were often aware of each other's existence and were able to learn from one another. European empires, various national liberation movements, and many academic and popular ideas were in constant contact, and were part of the same public domain even if communication and transmission were not always smooth.

Second, this of course suggests that we need to approach the history of worldwide fascism in terms of how far it was part of the *Zeitgeist*—and not an aberration. This is an uneasy conclusion, given that it has been associated in some circles with the 'relativisation' of fascism. But it makes more sense as an approach than drawing a strong line between fascists and non-fascists on the basis of some retrospective identification of characteristics of fascism, many of which may have been common to more than fascist groups. It is further necessary to point out that India was very much a part of the world and of that *Zeitgeist*. Here, of course, it is important to look across the classificatory lines of fascist and non-fascist and to understand longer genealogies of engagement with ideas of race and *Volk*, which of course requires a deeper time-frame than merely looking at fascism's

[1] The reasoning behind this choice is provided at length in Zachariah (2014a).

core period between the two World Wars and until the conclusion of World War II. In addition, it requires us to look at *völkisch* ideas in their own right and not merely as 'precursors' to fascism, rather in the manner in which the widespread faith in forms of eugenics has now been acknowledged and not merely been assimilated to fascist or Nazi thinking, although it became an important part of it.

This leads us to a third point: that while a particular set of movements might have provided the language in which politics expressed itself (in this case, the language of Nazi or *völkisch* nationalism in Germany), it does not suggest that the ideas expressed in that language were somehow 'foreign' to India. The closeness that was recognised by Indian ideologues and intellectuals with Germany, or by Germans with India, was precisely because they were recognisable. The translators, linguistic as well as ideological, who made this recognition possible are to a large extent the subject of this chapter, and this loops us back to the first of the three points: that fascism was not uniquely European, even when it was *in* Europe; the Nazis' fascination with things Indian (and therefore 'Aryan') is a useful example here (Goodrick-Clarke 1992; Kurlander 2013). This is the case even if we want to suggest that the Nazis' Aryan India was an invention or an appropriation, because the sources from which these inventions or appropriations were possible, highlighted perhaps by both British and German 'Orientalists' or 'Indologists', were part of the same debates and discursive fields the world over, and therefore in 'India' as well as in 'Germany'.

The Indo-German ideological or 'cultural' exchanges have of course long been the subject of a somewhat celebratory historiography. In the manner in which States have usually celebrated their linkages with an invented genealogy of creative communication among their 'nations' since time immemorial, or at least from the earliest times to which they can reach back, the (two and then one) post-war German State(s) and the Indian State have contrived to write a celebratory set of histories. Their teleologies of statism have been ventriloquised politely through official or semi-official histories, facilitated by official bodies and diplomatic exchanges.[2]

[2] More specifically, the celebratory mode of writing Indo-German connections into the history books is a government-to-government project,

A more recent tendency has been to invoke some sort of celebratory globalism in attributing to Germany a special place in Indian intellectual development, or a parallelism that appears to be somewhat too neat, within the framework of the new 'global' histories. These, again, seem to be rather contrived, expressing their claim to newness in a show of surprise in the fact that 'Indian' and 'German' alike seemed to be able to communicate outside the boxes of 'Indian' and 'German' (Manjapra 2014; Sartori 2007). What these attempts have in common is an undifferentiated, and almost non-ideological, description of 'Germany' and 'India' through selected incidents and individuals. The idea that many of these connections were aligned with racist, *völkisch*, or Nazi thinking has had less takers in a context in which 'cosmopolitanism', 'transculturalism', 'transnationalism', and 'global' engagements or 'entanglements' are the buzzwords of our late capitalist mode of historical production. The fact that the world was not a disconnected and discrete set of places (who would speak of 'disconnected' or 'disentangled' histories?) (Subrahmanyam 1997) is so obvious as to be banal: Are we paying now for the hegemony of national histories and the exceptionalism of the postcolonial moment by realising that the world's interconnections had not vanished while historians were looking elsewhere, before being suddenly rediscovered as a late by-product of 'globalisation'? But before we waste too much effort in examining why historians' limited historiographical perspectives were projected onto historical actors whose limitations were at the least different ones, let us proceed to outline the argument.

A working definition of fascism is required here, and we shall work with the idea of a 'fascist repertoire', which is a repertoire to which

meant to cement inter-State relations, and much of it does not belong in the realms of critical scholarship, although it would pay to recognise that we have gathered together more than once to discuss this problem pretty much because it pays to do so (and we have been paid to do so). There has been a 'Year of Germany in India' and a 'Year of India in Germany'; and it was the 150th birth anniversary of Swami Vivekananda that provided the occasion for the Indian Council for Cultural Relations-funded conference at Heidelberg University in 2013 in which this chapter made its first appearance.

India(ns) contributed independently rather than imitatively. A 'fascist minimum' argument relies on an agreed-upon set of attributes without which a political movement is not yet, or not quite, fascism, whereas a 'fascist repertoire' argument is less concerned with a checklist of elements, all of which have to be present in order for the movement to meet the minimum qualification as properly fascist (and if we use this approach, we cannot properly distinguish between a fascist movement in search of State power and one that has already captured State power). We are concerned here with a wider repertoire from which ideologues have the agency to choose. The repertoire tends to include an organic and primordial nationalism; a(n aspiration towards a) controlling statism that disciplines the members of the organic nation to act as, for, and in that organic (or *völkisch*) nation. That nation must therefore be duly purified and preserved, in the service of which a tendency towards national discipline is invoked, very often taking the form of paramilitary mobilisation; and the coherence of the repertoire is maintained by invoking a sense of continuous crisis and the potential for decay of the organic nation if that discipline and purity are not preserved.

The idea of the *Volk* has its origins, of course, in romanticist imaginings of the German nation in an era of European nationalisms: organicist, anti-rationalist, ethnic, racialised, and anti-Semitic, it glorified all things it could claim as 'Germanic'. The extent of its commitment to paganism, or to religion at all, remains open to debate (Arvidsson 2006). The glorification of an 'Aryan' past in India, or a connection with sacred soil and sacred space, hardly needed a (later) Nazi affiliation, but it had been a part of the same building blocks of romantic nationalism across the world. Groups like the Arya Samaj, various social reformers and anti-Muslim campaigners, the Ramakrishna Mission, or the Theosophists and their splinter groups did not substantially disagree that there was an authentic Hindu or Aryan past, present, and future that was there to be recovered and preserved, even if they might have disagreed on some of the details. Many of the debates on the nature of the national self to be invented were semi-contemporaneous with European—Italian or German—debates on the same theme, and Indians were listening to and assimilating these debates, which makes their familiarity with their terms, and the fact that they were equating and collating their own debates with them, unsurprising.[3]

This chapter uses the figure of Benoy Kumar Sarkar, educationist, pioneering sociologist, economist, historian, and an important member of the National Council of Education formed in Calcutta around the time of the Bengali 'Swadeshi' ('of our own country') movement, of which he was an activist, as somewhat of a stalking horse to track this closeness, and in so doing, attributes to him a pre-eminence as 'translator' of Indian ideas into German. Benoy Kumar Sarkar, who made an attempt to create a whole language of the social sciences based on an 'indigenous', Indian set of concepts (Sanskrit-derived and therefore not exactly in contemporaneous use), was a polyglot with a sound understanding of the German language and German political and philosophical ideas, which he mobilised exceptionally well.[4] Sarkar became a spokesman for, and a link figure in, several networks of scholars, ideologues, and political activists, whose engagements ranged from the conservative to the radical Right. His work resonated with a larger public that sought an anti-colonial voice of authority to speak for a colonised people. His is the voice, and pen, that linked a religious reform movement of middle-class political nationalism in the Ramakrishna Mission and the founder of the Mission, Swami Vivekananda (recalling, if you will, the idea of a 'political religion' that some theorists on fascism have taken as central; see Gentile 1996), with Indian imperialist fantasies of the Greater India Society; and, one might add, he represented the project of a 'Swadeshi' intellectualism that sought to present, and to

---

3 See Chandra (1966) on economic nationalism and Friedrich List, and Bayly's chapter on nationalism in *The Birth of the Modern World* (2004) on the simultaneity of the rise of nationalisms, in opposition to a Europe-first model.

4 Benoy Kumar Sarkar's revival is only just beginning: see Goswami (2012); Manjapra (2014, esp. 143–160); and Sen (2015). Of these, only Satadru Sen has succeeded in bringing in something of a critical reading, for in the ambiguous aftermath of the 'postcolonial' moment, to be 'international' or 'cosmopolitan' or 'transnational' is apparently to be worthy of celebration in and of itself.

perform, a glorious precolonial and predominantly 'Hindu' past for the Indian nation-State-to-be.[5]

INDO-NAZI LINKS: WHAT THEY MIGHT MEAN (AND WHAT THEY DO NOT)[6]

That there were strong institutional links between Indians and (future) Nazis is not in question. When, in 1933, Benoy Kumar Sarkar welcomed the coming of Adolf Hitler to power in Germany in a pamphlet entitled *The Hitler State*, he was not exhibiting a new-found enthusiasm (see Sarkar 1933). Sarkar had long been a part of an extended circle of excited intellectuals who saw in German history the unfolding of events that should be replicated in India.

From the other side, as early as 1923, the 'Bavarian extremist leader Hitler', as British intelligence reports referred to him, was attempting to mobilise various intellectuals from Turkey, Egypt, and India behind him; a meeting at Hitler's house in Schwabing in Munich was due to be attended, among others, by Maulvi Mohammad Barkatullah, former Hindustani lecturer at Tokyo University, subversive member of the Ghadar network, and former Prime Minister of a Government of Free India set up under German patronage in Kabul during World War I (in the end, Barkatullah did not make it to the meeting).[7] These early attempts were not particularly successful, with Mussolini's Italian fascists winning more recruits among Indians, perhaps by virtue of being the first fascists past the post (Banaji 2013; Casolari 2002; Delfs 2008). Both ideological and organisational Indo-German Nazi connections were, however, formed reasonably early.

In 1928, the Deutsche Akademie founded its 'Indischer Ausschuß'; the parent organisation had been founded in 1925 (today's Goethe-

5 The classic work on the Swadeshi movement remains Sarkar (1973).

6 The events and details presented in this section are partly based on material presented in Zachariah (2013a and 2014a), in which more details and the wider contexts are presented.

7 India Office Records, British Library, London [IOR]: L/PJ/12/102, 1923, f. 2.

Institut started off as a branch of the Deutsche Akademie, whose language-teaching branch even bore the same name).[8] The co-founders of the 'Indischer Ausschuß' were Karl Haushofer, a specialist in 'geopolitics' and one of the pioneers and popularisers of the theory of '*Lebensraum*' so beloved of the National Socialists, and the Bengali nationalist Tarak Nath Das.[9] Tarak Nath Das had been, along with Benoy Kumar Sarkar, a member of the National Council of Education in Bengal, which had debated a 'Swadeshi' curriculum for an Indian education that would be free of the domination of colonial models of education and acculturation which the Swadeshi intellectuals believed had provided the ideological underpinnings to colonial domination. Das had moved to the United States as a fugitive from British 'justice' in connection with the Swadeshi Movement. There, he associated himself with organising Indian immigrant labour in the US and Canada, and with the beginnings of the Ghadar Party which had mobilised Indian immigrant labour during World War I and attempted to send bands of immigrants back home to foment rebellion from within India (Puri 1983; Ramnath 2011; Sohi 2014). Das had acquired his US citizenship as early as 1913, had been a member of the wartime Independence for India Committee in Germany based in Berlin, and had spent a number of years in Fascist Italy before returning to Germany.[10]

The membership of the Berlin India Committee, which had sought to help Wilhelmine Germany's war effort in the hope that a successful war waged by the Central Powers would end British imperial rule in India, included a number of persons whose politics were quite diverse, including the future communist Virendranath Chattopadhyay and Bhupendranath Dutta, the brother of India's first successful international spiritual export, Swami Vivekananda (whose real name was Narendranath Dutta) (Oesterheld 2004). Another difficult member

8 Bundesarchiv, Berlin: R51/1-16 & 144.

9 This was acknowledged in the official history of the institute, available at *Indien-Institut e.V. München*, http://www.indien-institut.de/cms/en/chronik/ (accessed December 2021). There is a sudden jump for the Nazi period: nothing is said for the time between 1932 and 1946.

10 IOR: L/PJ/12/166.

of that committee was Har Dayal, often regarded as the founder of the Ghadar Movement, although his political jumps were numerous and difficult to classify; but Har Dayal, Viren Chattopadhyay, and Vinayak Damodar Savarkar, the pre-eminent ideologue of Hindu nationalism, had once been colleagues and fellow-writers for the journals of the Indian émigré activist and political organiser, Shyamji Krishnavarma, in London in the early years of the twentieth century (Zachariah 2013b).

The Deutsche Akademie's India Institute awarded scholarships to about 100 Indian students between 1929 and 1938. From 1937, it was headed by the Indologist and member of the SS, Professor Walther Wüst (Sailer 2008), displacing Franz Thierfelder, who had also switched his allegiance easily to the Nazis in 1933, signing his letters '*mit deutschem Gruß und Heil Hitler*'.[11] The Institute also became active in pro-German propaganda during the Nazi period, was integrated into the NSDAP's Auslands-Organisation (NSDAP-AO), and was instrumental in starting Nazi cells in various firms in India which were under German control. It also funded German *Lektoren* who taught German to Indian students who wished to come to Germany; one such person taught German at the Calcutta Young Men's Christian Association (YMCA). Horst Pohle, the Nazi agent who was the German *Lektor* at Calcutta University, was said to be very close to the Arya Samaj, whose members were singled out as desirable students for the Munich-based India Institute.[12] Among the Indians to be closely associated with the Institute were Benoy Kumar Sarkar and Ashok Bose, son of the Bengali nationalist Sarat Bose

[11] Bundesarchiv, Berlin, R51/16, R51/8. Thierfelder was responsible for the document written in 1945 that claimed the Deutsche Akademie to be a non-Nazi institution, and he cited Tarak Nath Das' membership of the Indische Ausschuß as grounds to claim its non-Nazi nature, seeking to blame all its Nazi activities on Wüst: see Bundesarchiv, Berlin, R51/8, ff. 0203054–0203067, written in 1945. Thierfelder was back in charge of the institute from 1946, alongside Tarak Nath Das.

[12] IOR: Indian Political Intelligence (IPI) file L/PJ/12/505, ff. 80–81. From printed report: 'Strictly Secret: An Examination of the Activities of the Auslands Organization of the National Socialistische Deutsche Arbeiter Partei [sic], Part II: In India'.

and nephew of Subhas Chandra Bose, who went on to collaborate with Nazism.[13]

Tarak Nath Das and Benoy Kumar Sarkar continued to be associated with an extended circle of Nazis in the new Reich, not least through the Deutsche Akademie.[14] Benoy Sarkar was also a regular contributor to Haushofer's journal *Geopolitik*. A stream of Indian students continued to pass through German universities and polytechnics throughout the 1930s, many of whom were to a greater or lesser extent impressed by the Nazis; and the Indischer Ausschuß of the Deutsche Akademie continued to fund a number of these, and to provide back-up support.[15] Not all of these students acquired a long-lasting fascination with German Nazism, although some at least returned to a home university with a tradition of support for National Socialism, such as Calcutta University, where Benoy Kumar Sarkar was the leading light of its 'German Club'.[16] In Aligarh, Dr Spies [*sic*], the German professor, ran the Aligarh University Nazi cell from 1935, along with Professor Abdur Sattar Kheiri, formerly associated with the World War I Berlin India Committee; in 1937, Kheiri led a Brown Shirts' march at his university in honour of the Prophet's birthday.[17]

---

13 Publicity materials for the India Institute, Munich, distributed on the occasion of their seventy-fifth anniversary in 2003, do not mention the names of Ashok Bose and Benoy Kumar Sarkar. An earlier version of the Indien-Institut's website listed their names: http://www.indien-institut.de (accessed May 2010), but this has been relatively recently replaced by the version cited above. Leonard Gordon (1990, 256–257) mentions Ashok Bose's presence in Munich from 1931 as a student of applied chemistry.

14 'Akademie zur wissenschaftlichen Erforschung und zur Pflege des Deutschtums'. Bundesarchiv, Berlin, R51/1, rules of the association, 1925, end of file, no page numbers.

15 Bundesarchiv, Berlin, R51/16. Records of students are few and far between, and it is unclear whether they were destroyed by the vicissitudes of war or were deliberately destroyed.

16 Maharashtra State Archives (MSA), Bombay, Home Department (Special), files 830A, 1939 and 830(i), 1939.

17 NAI: Home Department, Government of India, File No. 21/65/39 Poll. (Int.). 'Consideration of steps to be taken to combat Nazi activity in the Aligarh University', 1–7. Copy in Jawaharlal Nehru University (JNU), Archives on Contemporary History (ACH), PC Joshi Archive, File 11–1939.

Kheiri's German wife was in charge of publishing and circulating the Nazi journal, *Spirit of the Times*, whose German version, *Geist der Zeit*, was the official Nazi paper abroad.[18]

This brief institutional history, a far longer telling of which could easily be provided here, is already disruptive of the rather misleading view we have hitherto held about the relatively insignificant impact of Nazism in India. But it does not imply that the institutional connections were necessarily the driving force of Indo-Nazi collaboration. There were Hindu ideologues as well as Muslim and 'secular' ones with avowed closeness and institutional connections with the Nazis; another example can be provided here, again from a 'Muslim' group: Inayatullah Khan, or Allama Mashriqi, the founder and leader of the Khaksar movement, which was also called fascist in its own time, claimed to have met Hitler in 1926 and even claimed later that Hitler had learned from him.[19] Although connections among proponents of a militant Hindu nationalism (now simply referred to as the Sangh Parivar or *Hindutvavādī*) as a *völkisch* nationalism with fascism and Nazism, not to mention with its leaders, are often highlighted,[20] it is doubtful how much of the appeal that Hindu ideologues, such as M. S. Golwalkar, K. B. Hedgewar or V. D. Savarkar, had for their Indian followers *depended* upon the borrowings of their ideas from fascists or Nazis. It is more productive to see the similarities that they recognised with, and perhaps reformulated in the language of, fascism or Nazism (Golwalkar 1939; Savarkar 1928). The greater power of Germany, or Italy before it, to enforce the 'national' will and to purify the national body of outsiders was fascinating to them, but the project to enforce something of a quasi-Rousseauesque 'general will' was also in varying degrees fascinating to those who did not identify with a project to exclude particular people from a future nation-State (Zachariah 2005).

18 Ibid.

19 See Daechsel (2006, 453) on Mashriqi's account of his meeting with Hitler.

20 For example, see Banaji (2013); Casolari (2002); Delfs (2008); and Sarkar (1993). By contrast, Christophe Jaffrelot (1996) specifically avoids the fascism question.

The exclusionary project is clearly readable in this oft-quoted passage from M. S. Golwalkar's *We or Our Nationhood Defined*:

> To keep up the purity of the Race and its culture, Germany shocked the world by her purging the country of the Semitic races—the Jews. Race pride at its highest has been manifested here. Germany has also shown how well-nigh impossible it is for Races and cultures, having differences going to the root, to be assimilated into one united whole, a good lesson for us in Hindusthan to learn and profit by.[21] (1939, 35)

The Sangh Parivar, and especially those who organised its paramilitary wings and wrote its ideological treatises, were familiar with European fascism, in particular its most successful Italian and German variants, and found them worthwhile and useful models to emulate. They were, however, not the only ones, and dreams of mass mobilisation without loss of control drove many fantasies of nationhood, national discipline, and nation-building in India (Zachariah 2005), as well as many organisational and paramilitary groupings (Raza and Roy 2015). This is not to suggest that all of their ideas were merely imitations; and the establishing of their closeness to European fascism, or specifically to German Nazism, although working in today's discursive framework to discredit them to some extent, does not exhaust our responsibility of analysis.

There are plenty of indications that Indian ideologues were well aware of the need to find an 'authentic' nation by finding ways to exclude the foreign elements within. The first version of Vinayak Damodar Savarkar's text defining 'Hindutva', *Essentials of Hindutva*, was published in 1923, barely a year after the Fascist March on Rome and seizure of power in Italy. In many respects, it is clearly part of a set of ideas that belong in the fascist repertoire. Savarkar's claiming of the unity of the 'race' that is to make up the 'nation' is quite clearly based on a family of blood-and-soil arguments, but not quite in as literal-minded a fashion as might be expected. Savarkar speculated on Orientalist research on the origins of the Aryans, but stopped short of claiming the Aryans as altogether indigenous to India. Instead, he postulated that Aryans and non-Aryans, who had inhabited India

21 A passing reference in the text from which it is taken, but a shared view among many of the Sangh Parivar's ideologues.

before the coming of the Aryan outsiders, 'knitting themselves into a people were born as a nation' at the time of 'the glorious reign of Lord Rama as described in the Ramayana' (Savarkar 2003 [1923], 12).[22] Savarkar rejected the idea of Hindu*ism*, which to him is a 'spiritual or religious dogma or system' (ibid., 4), and propagated instead the idea of *Hindutva* as 'nationality' (translated from his original '*rāṣṭra*') and *Arya* as 'race' (translated from '*jāti*')—and a 'race' need not *actually* be of pure blood, but must '*feel*' it is one, 'a *jāti*, a born brotherhood' that consequently possesses a common '*sanskriti*', civilisation (ibid., 32–33, 38–39, 84, 89, 116). The outsiders, from whom the nation must be purified, are those with foreign loyalties, Muslims or Christians whose holy lands are elsewhere, in 'Arabia or Palestine' (ibid., 113).

For those inclined to see Savarkar in the light of his later fascist or proto-fascist period, it might be worth a quick glimpse at an earlier text. Savarkar's *The Indian War of Independence* was written around 1908: Indians in Europe, America, or Bengal had not yet clearly differentiated into Left and Right, and this was epitomised by the diversity of the circles that grew up around Shyamji Krishnavarma and his journal, the *Indian Sociologist*, in Europe, or around Lala Lajpat Rai in his American years.[23] Here, Savarkar struggled with what to do with Muslims in his narrative, while at the same time using the rhetoric of the sacred and holy war of Hindus to purify themselves and their nation.[24] But we are getting ahead of, or behind, the story.

Translations: Benoy Kumar Sarkar's Indo-Germanic and Germano-Indic History[25]

Ten years after the publication of Savarkar's *Essentials of Hindutva* (1923), Benoy Sarkar's views on the desirability of the fascist State were expressed with unembarrassed clarity: Sarkar celebrated Hitler's

22 First published as *Essentials of Hindutva* (1923).

23 For a sense of this milieu, see Agnes Smedley's novel *Daughter of Earth* (1977 [1929]); see also Barooah (2004, 1–61), and Fischer-Tiné (2007).

24 For a fuller treatment of this text, see Zachariah (2014b, 95–100).

25 For a fuller treatment of this theme, see Zachariah (2015a).

accession, describing him as 'Vivekananda multiplied by Bismarck'. 'Hitler is the greatest of Germany's teachers and inspirers since Fichte' (Sarkar 1933, 4). 'What Young Germany needed badly was the moral idealism of a Vivekananda multiplied by the iron strenuousness of a Bismarck. And that has been furnished by Hitler, armed as he is with two among other spiritual slogans, namely, self-sacrifice and fatherland' (ibid., 13). (Vivekananda has often been seen as a nation-builder in India, with his exhortations to physical and moral self-improvement in search of the collective greater good winning him many followers, in particular among the Bengali middle class [see Sarkar 1993b].) Benoy Sarkar saw the Jewish question in Germany as a *Kulturkampf* in the manner of the Catholic confrontation with the Bismarckian State, 'which no one hears of any more today'. In a similar manner, he wrote, 'The Jewish question [. . . will] be liquidated in Nazi Germany in a few years' (Sarkar 1933, 31). The need for Nazi action against Jews came allegedly from the 'over-Judaization of the public institutions in Berlin as well as in other cities', which made it necessary to 'purge the public institutions of the Jews and ordain for them a legitimate proportion of the services not exceeding the demographic percentage' (ibid.).

Fundamentally sympathetic towards a Germany humiliated and dispossessed of its colonies after the Versailles peace settlement, Sarkar had stated that Germany would be a hope for the liberation of the colonies of other powers since the country was now a non-possessor of colonies:

> It now remains for Germany to speak out and act in the manner in which the Orient expects that a great race bent on the revindication of its claims should act both for its own honour and national self-assertion as well as for opening out new vistas in international relations and world-culture. The infiniteward energism of the 'Fausts' of Young Asia as well as their Siegfried-like *sadhana (Streben)* for freedom will supply the *Volksseele* of Germania not only with its spiritual nourishment but will also furnish for it a bracing milieu of hopefulness and the perennial springs of creative youth. (Sarkar 1922b, 37)

Much of the driving force in his writing is an almost postcolonialist insistence that India could provide, or had provided, the world with great and worthwhile intellectual products. He extended this argument to whatever would hold it, on one occasion reminding readers that Nietzsche, whose idea of the Will to Power he greatly admired, had learned his philosophy from the *Manusmṛti* and his politics from the *Arthaśāstra* (Sarkar 1918–1919).[26]

'In the reconstruction of Indian history, modern scholarship has to be devoted more and more to the exposition of the influence that the masses of the country have ever exerted in the making of its civilization,' Benoy Sarkar (1917, Preface, vii) programmatically declared. To understand this 'folk element', one must have undergone an 'initiation amongst the folk' (ibid., ix).[27] The caste system had 'never been a disintegrating factor in Hindu communal existence', he stated, and was 'most probably a very recent institution'. And 'Hinduism' was 'an eclectic and ever-expansive socio-religious system built up through the assimilation of diverse ethnic, natural and spiritual forces during the successive ages of Indian history' (ibid., x). Sarkar provided a glorification of instinctive folk wisdom that was more authentic than all the cultural sophistication of supposed higher forms. Culturally, Sarkar further declared, there could be discerned a continuity across Asia of folk forms of religion, which meant that distinctions made between Buddhist, Shaiva, and Vaishnava traditions did not hold (ibid., xvi).[28] This was more or less a corollary to the 'Greater India' arguments made by some of his colleagues, whom he cited approvingly in his books and who likewise cited him approvingly in theirs,[29] and who argued from the presence of Hindu and Buddhist monuments in Southeast Asia that a 'Greater India'[30] of a cultural and economic

26 Originally, this was an address given at Columbia University, New York, in April 1918.

27 Quoting Professor R. R. Marrett's paper, 'Folklore and Psychology', read before the London Folklore Society.

28 See also Sarkar (1916), from which he quotes at length in the 'Preface' to *The Folk-Element in Hindu Culture* (1917).

29 See Mookerji, *Indian Shipping* (1999 [1912]); Mukherji (1925); and author's 'Preface' in Sarkar (1917). It should be noted that they do not merely cite each other's works in a few footnotes: they declare their intellectual debts and allegiances strongly.

30 On the Greater India Society, see Bayly (2004) and also Zabarskaite (2017).

expansionist sort could be discerned in the history of those countries, by which means a sort of spiritual *Lebensraum* thus opened out for Greater India. The connections among the scholars of the 'Greater India Society', based in Calcutta, Visva Bharati, Allahabad or Benares Hindu University, should be noted; and for their popularisers, notably the Hindu Mahasabha supporter and publisher-journalist Ramananda Chatterjee, there was a territorially bounded India that was 'Hindu' and eternal, but the 'culture' of India was entitled to move freely and colonise other parts of the world.

The 'folk element' argument solved another problem of inventing a nation: upper-caste Hindu textual or scriptural traditions would yield nothing of the numbers required in a nation-building game. Meanwhile, non-caste Hinduism, if appropriated through this idea of folk practices, could provide an idea of the organicist unity of the community that was to become the nation. And the fantasy of mobilising the masses from above without losing control was greatly enabled by the hope of an organic national discipline of the *Volk*.

On its own, the 'folk element' was therefore not to be given autonomy without leadership being exercised strongly on its behalf, and upon it. Benoy Sarkar's appreciation of the movement of the holy man Ramakrishna Paramhansa and his educated middle-class disciple Vivekananda, already invoked as an aspect of the German Führer's avatar, is worth looking at again in this connection: Vivekananda's importance to India was Sarkar's comparative yardstick for the importance of Hitler to Germany. In a pamphlet derived from a speech and published in 1936, Benoy Sarkar's Ramakrishna is presented as a *völkisch* hero and his Vivekananda as a Germanic romantic (Sarkar 1936). Ramakrishna, for Benoy Sarkar, epitomised the 'folk'. His was a 'folk-language', his wisdom was 'folk-wisdom', his logic 'folk-logic' (ibid., 4). His message of the equality of faiths, of heterogenous roads to freedom, laid deeper foundations for 'inter-racial' harmony. But Ramakrishna was also somewhat akin to Fichte.

Fichte's attitudes are well-known. Writing in 1808 for Young Germany, he said: '*Euch ist das groessere Geschickzuieil* [sic] *geworden, uberhaupt* [sic] *das Reich des Geistes und der Vernunft zu begruenden* [To you has been assigned the greater destiny, namely that you have to establish the Empire of the spirit and reason], *und die rohe koerperliche Gewalt insgesamt als beherrschendes der Welt zu vernichten* [and that you have to annihilate raw physical power as a determinant of the world]. It is this supremacy of the spirit and reason, and the emancipation of the mind from matter, or rather, the mind's dominion over the world, that constitutes the *leitmotif* of Ramakrishna's sayings (Sarkar 1936, 9):

> In this synthesis of the transcendental and the positive he is but a chip of the old Hindu block coming down from the Vedic, and perhaps still earlier times.... And it is on the strength of this synthesis, again, that his Narendra, the Vivekananda thundered a Young India into being, the India of economic energism as well as of spiritual creativeness, of material science and technocracy as well as of self-control and social service.[31] (ibid., 11–12)

The 'moral and spiritual values' of Ramakrishna and Vivekananda 'were destined to constitute the living religion of our country, of our masses and classes, during the present century' (Sarkar 1936, 12–13).[32] In those contexts, Vivekananda was described as 'the Carlyle of Young India' and credited with 'the gospel of Napoleonic energism and triumphant defiance of the Western chauvinists' (ibid., 12). Vivekananda was 'an *Avatar* of youth-force', a socialist (but not like Marx; he was rather a romantic socialist like St Simon), a nationalist, and an internationalist, who 'served to establish the universalistic, cosmopolitan and humane basis of all religious and social values'. He was, 'like Fichte, the father of the German youth-movement, an exponent of nationalism and socialism', preaching the 'gospel [...] of energism, of mastery over the world, over the conditions surrounding life, of human freedom, of individual liberty, of courage trampling down cowardice, of world-conquest', just as the West was 'groping in the dark' for a solution along those lines. Nietzsche's *Also sprach Zarathustra* 'had awakened mankind to the need for a more positive, humane and joyous life's philosophy than that of the *New Testament*'. Vivekananda was a 'pioneer of a revolution' and 'the positive and

---

31 Sarkar cited himself often, referring here to his *Positive Background of Hindu Sociology* (1914, 1921, 1926), and *The Political Institutions of the Hindus* (1922a).

32 Again, citing himself, he says that he had anticipated this more than two decades ago in his *Vishwa-Shakti* (*World Forces*) (1914 [1913]).

constructive counterpart' to Nietzsche's 'destructive criticism'. The doctrine of 'energism, moral freedom, individual liberty, and man's mastery over the circumstances of life' was promulgated by Immanuel Kant, and later by Robert Browning. The ancients already had the Upanishads and the Gita (ibid., 15–17). Oswald Spengler, in his *Untergang des Abendlandes* (1918), had been interested in the transformation of epochs, in what the Hindus would call *Yugantara*, in the 'cultures yet to be'. Insofar as Spengler was looking for the 'new element of inwardness' such as could sponsor the regeneration of life for the 'world-historical phase of several centuries upon which we ourselves are entering', he was echoing the Vivekanandist doctrine of Man-born-to-conquer-Naturism (Sarkar 1936, 17–18).

Sarkar's parallels between Indian and German history are strained—he cites Karl Haushofer in connection with being superior to many, inferior to a few, but not among the last (ibid., 24)[33]—and in his summary of Vivekananda's message to the Bengali people, Sarkar quotes an 1897 speech 'seven or eight years before the Bengali "ideas of 1905" take a definite shape'. Vivekananda's speech in Benoy Sarkar's summary goes like this:

> 'We have to conquer the world', he declares, 'That we have to! India must conquer the world and nothing less than that is my ideal. It may be very big, it may astonish many of you, but it is so. We must conquer the world or die. There is no other alternative. The sign of life is expansion; we must go out, expand, show life or degrade, fester and die. There is no other alternative.' (Sarkar 1936, 25)

In this context, citing Haushofer begins to make sense. Sarkar celebrates the fact that the Ramakrishna Mission has begun to expand all over the world: Britain, Spain, Czechoslovakia, Poland, France, and Germany, all have editions of Ramakrishna and Vivekananda's works.

> It is but the six thousand year old Indian tradition of *digvijaya*, World-conquest, and elevation of the most diverse races and classes to soul-enfranchising ideals and activities that Vivekananda and after him the

33 Here there is a citation of Karl Haushofer, *Jenseits der Großmächte* (1932, 489).

> Swamis of the Ramakrishna Order have been pursuing under modern conditions, thereby exhibiting the virility and strenuousness of Hindu humanism and spirituality.[34] (Sarkar 1936, 28)

Trajectories and Models of Indo-Germania

The idea of Nazism as an Indian choice has attracted much ridicule, as it did in its own time from Indian contemporaries of the Indo-Nazis. But it is evident that the wider interest in finding the authentic *Volk* was a prerequisite and an impetus to working towards the Nazis, in the sense of seeing Indian historical and contemporary developments in the light of a teleology of the Nazi State. The example I have selected here is not a commentary on a set of eccentric or fringe elements: Ramakrishna and Vivekananda were central figures in the Bengali moral imagination, and in the 'ideas of 1905' that Benoy Sarkar refers to, and which he and others sought to project onto all of India, even as he imagined that the energies of 'Germania' ought to merge with those of Young Asia. Sarkar's palimpsest of Indo-Germania merits further attention than it has received, and the wider world to which it refers effortlessly needs to be recognised as part of the political imagination of Indian public life. This of course requires us to reopen our engagement with the Swadeshi-era oeuvre, and to examine in more detail the imperatives to identifying those who belonged to the nation-to-be and finding them an indigenous history.

That such a quest is a fraught one goes without saying. It is only where fascism was identified and discredited as fascism that a clear separation between a participatory-democratic socialist imagination and a populist-*völkisch* organicist nation has been upheld, both politically and historiographically. The historiography of South Asia, with its tendency towards undifferentiated studies of 'freedom fighters', has so far been ill-equipped to do this; and the distinction is also difficult to sustain if one is looking at the ideological swamp at

34 Citations on this point inevitably include himself: *The Futurism of Young Asia* (1922b), as well as P. T. Hoffmann (1915) and Helmuth von Glasenapp (1930).

the turn of the century, from which we in retrospect might learn to distinctively label tendencies as Left or Right. The trouble is that a claim to the 'indigenous' is in South Asia one that often goes unchallenged as a political claim in itself. Sarkar himself often rejected the charge of Indian thinking as derived from or subservient to European thinking, and is credited with being the founder of various 'Indian' schools of various disciplines: sociology, political science, international relations. His rejection of the 'derivative' charge is justified, but a necessary corollary to the recognition of the centrality of that rejection must be a recognition of the problematic claims of the indigenous. Sarkar's palimpsest of Indo-Germania is indication enough of the closeness of *völkisch* thinking across the specificities of claimed 'national genius': analogies that make us feel at home in another set of histories. If Ramakrishna–Fichte set the ball rolling, a Vivekananda could only be Führer when multiplied by an as-yet-absent Bismarck. The National Socialist present was the promised Indic future.

REFERENCES

Arvidsson, Stefan. 2006. *Aryan Idols: Indo-European Mythology as Ideology and Science*. Chicago: Chicago University Press.

Banaji, Jairus (ed.). 2013. *Fascism: Essays on Europe and India*. New Delhi: Three Essays Press.

Barooah, Nirode K. 2004. *Chatto: The Life and Times of an Indian Anti-Imperialist in Europe*. New Delhi: Oxford University Press.

Bayly, C. A. 2004. *The Birth of the Modern World, 1780–1914: Global Connections and Comparisons*. Maiden, MA: Blackwell Publishing.

Bayly, Susan. 2004. 'Imagining "Greater India": French and Indian Visions of Colonialism in the Indic Mode'. *Modern Asian Studies* 38 (3), 703–744.

Casolari, Marzia. 2002. 'Hindutva's Foreign Tie-Up in the 1930s. Archival Evidence'. *Economic and Political Weekly* 22 January, 218–228.

Chandra, Bipan. 1966. *The Rise and Growth of Economic Nationalism in India: Economic Policies of Indian National Leadership, 1880–1905*. New Delhi: People's Publishing House.

Daechsel, Markus. 2006. 'Scientism and its Discontents: The Indo-Muslim "Fascism" of Inayatullah Khan al-Mashriqi'. *Modern Intellectual History* 3 (3), 443–472.

Delfs, Tobias. 2008. *Hindu-Nationalismus und Europäischer Faschismus: Vergleich, Transfer- und Beziehungsgeschichte*. Hamburg: EB-Verlag.

Fischer-Tiné, Harald. 2007. '"Indian Nationalism and the World Forces": Transnational and Diasporic Dimensions of the Indian Freedom Movement on the Eve of the First World War'. *Journal of Global History* 2 (3), 325–344.

Gentile, Emilio. 1996. *The Sacralization of Politics in Fascist Italy*. Cambridge, MA: Harvard University Press.

Glasenapp, Helmuth von. 1930. *Indien in der Dichtung und Forschung des deutschen Ostens*. Königsberg: Gräfe und Unzer.

Golwalkar, M. S. 1939. *We or Our Nationhood Defined*. Nagpur: Bharat Publications.

Goodrick-Clarke, Nicholas. 1992. *The Occult Roots of Nazism: Secret Aryan Cults and their Influence on Nazi Ideology*. New York: New York University Press.

Gordon, Leonard. 1990. *Brothers Against the Raj: A Biography of Indian Nationalists Sarat and Subhas Chandra Bose*. New York: Columbia University Press.

Goswami, Manu. 2012. 'AHR Forum: Imaginary Futures and Colonial Internationalisms'. *American Historical Review* 117 (5), 1461–1485.

Haushofer, Karl. 1932. *Jenseits der Großmächte*. Leipzig: B. G. Teubner.

Hoffmann, P. T. 1915. *Der indische und der deutsche Geist von Herder bis zur Romantik*. Tuebingen: Laupp.

Jaffrelot, Christophe. 1996. *The Hindu Nationalist Movement and Indian Politics, 1925 to the 1990s: Strategies of Identity-Building, Implantation and Mobilisation*. London: Hurst.

Kurlander, Eric. 2013. 'The Orientalist Roots of National Socialism? Nazism, Occultism, and South Asian Spirituality, 1919-1945'. In Joanne Miyang Cho, Eric Kurlander, and Douglas T. McGetchin (eds), *Transcultural Encounters between Germany and India: Kindred Spirits in the 19th and 20th Centuries*, Routledge Studies in the Modern History of Asia, 155–169. London: Routledge.

Manjapra, Kris. 2014. *Age of Entanglement: German and Indian Intellectuals Across Empire*. Cambridge, MA: Harvard University Press.

Mookerji, R. K. 1999 [1912]. *Indian Shipping: A History of Sea Borne Trade and Maritime Activities of the Indians from Earliest Times*. New Delhi: Munshiram Manoharlal [originally published by Longman Green].

Mukherji, Radhakamal. 1925. *Borderlands of Economics*. London: George Allen & Unwin Ltd.

Oesterheld, Frank. 2004. '"Der Feind meines Feindes ist mein Freund": Zur Tätigkeit des Indian Independence Committee (IIC) während des Ersten Weltkrieges in Berlin", unpublished *Magister* thesis, Humboldt University, Berlin.

Puri, Harish K. 1983. *Ghadar Movement: Ideology, Organisation and Strategy*. Amritsar: Guru Nanak Dev University Press.

Ramnath, Maia. 2011. *Haj to Utopia: How the Ghadar Movement Charted Global Radicalism and Attempted to Overthrow the British Empire*. Berkeley: University of California Press.

Raza, Ali, and Franziska Roy. 2015. 'Paramilitary Organisations in Interwar India'. In *Völkisch and Fascist Movements in South Asia*, Special issue of *South Asia* (December).

Sailer, Anna. 2008. 'Der Indologe Walther Wüst und das NS-Regime, 1933–1945', unpublished *Magisterarbeit*, Humboldt-Universität zu Berlin.

Sarkar, Benoy Kumar. 1914 [1913]. *Vishwa-Shakti* (*World Forces*). First published in *Grihastha*, Calcutta.

———. 1916. *Chinese Religion Through Hindu Eyes: A Study in the Tendencies of Asiatic Mentality*. Shanghai: The Commercial Press.

———. 1917. *The Folk-Element in Hindu Culture: A Contribution to Socio-Religious Studies in Hindu Folk-Institutions*. London: Longman, Green & Co.

———. 1918–1919. 'The Influence of India on Western Civilisation'. *Journal of Race Development* 9, 101–102.

———. 1914, 1921, 1926. *The Positive Background of Hindu Sociology*, 2 vols. Allahabad.

———. 1922a. *The Political Institutions and Theories of the Hindus*. Leipzig.

———. 1922b. *The Futurism of Young Asia and Other Essays on the Relations between the East and the West*. Berlin: Julius Springer.

———. 1933. *The Hitler State: A Landmark in the Political, Economic and Social Remaking of the German People*. Calcutta: Insurance and Finance Review.

———. 1936. *The Might of Man in the Social Philosophy of Ramakrishna and Vivekananda*. Mylapore, Madras: Sri Ramakrishna Math [Printed at the Commercial Gazette Press by J. Lahiri, 6, Parsi Bagan Lane, Calcutta].

Sarkar, Sumit. 1973. *The Swadeshi Movement in 1903–1908*. New Delhi: People's Publishing House.

———. 1993a. 'The Fascism of the Sangh Parivar'. *Economic and Political Weekly* 28 (5), 163–167.

———. 1993b. *An Exploration of the Ramakrishna Vivekananda Tradition.* Shimla: Indian Institute of Advanced Study.

Sartori, Andrew. 2007. 'Beyond Culture-Contact and Colonial Discourse: "Germanism" in Colonial Bengal'. *Modern Intellectual History* 4 (1), 77–93.

Savarkar, V. D. 2003 [1923]. *Hindutva.* New Delhi: Hindi Sahitya Sadan.

———. 1928. *Hindutva: Who Is a Hindu?* Nagpur: Bharat Publications.

Sen, Satadru. 2015. *Benoy Kumar Sarkar: Restoring the Nation to the World.* New Delhi: Routledge.

Smedley, Agnes. 1977 [1929]. *Daughter of Earth.* New York: Coward-McCann; new edn London: Virago.

Sohi, Seema. 2014. *Echoes of Mutiny: Race, Surveillance and Indian Anticolonialism in North America.* Oxford: Oxford University Press.

Subrahmanyam, Sanjay. 1997. 'Connected Histories: Notes towards a Reconfiguration of Early Modern Eurasia'. *Modern Asian Studies* 31 (3), 735–762.

Zabarskaite, Jolita. 2017. '"Greater India" in Indian Scholarship and in the Public Domain: Origins of an Expansionist Imagination, c. 1890–1921'. *Zeitschrift für Indologie und Südasienstudien* 34, 259–288.

Zachariah, Benjamin. 2005. *Developing India: An Intellectual and Social History, c. 1930–1950.* New Delhi: Oxford University Press.

———. 2010. 'Rethinking (the Absence of) Fascism in India, c. 1922–1945'. In Sugata Bose and Kris Manjapra (eds), *Cosmopolitan Thought Zones: South Asia and the Global Circulation of Ideas*, 178–209. New York: Palgrave Macmillan.

———. 2013a. 'Indian Political Activities in Germany, 1914–1945'. In Joanne Miyang Cho, Eric Kurlander, and Douglas T. McGetchin (eds), *Transcultural Encounters Between Germany and India: Kindred Spirits in the 19th and 20th Centuries*, 141–54. New York: Routledge.

———. 2013b. 'A Long, Strange Trip: The Lives in Exile of Har Dayal'. *South Asian History and Culture* 4 (4), 574–592.

———. 2014a. 'A Voluntary *Gleichschaltung*? Perspectives from India towards a non-Eurocentric Understanding of Fascism'. *Transcultural Studies* December, 63–100.

———. 2014b. 'Histories and National Memory: 1857'. In Crispin Bates (ed.), *Mutiny at the Margins*, Vol. 6, 84–112. New Delhi: Sage.

———. 2015a. 'At the Fuzzy Edges of Fascism: Framing the *Volk* in India'. *Völkisch and Fascist Movements in South Asia*, Special Issue, *South Asia* December.

Zachariah, Benjamin. 2015b. 'Global Fascisms and the *Volk*: The Framing of Narratives and the Crossing of Lines'. *Völkisch and Fascist Movements in South Asia*, Special Issue, *South Asia* December.

——. 2016. 'Nazi-Hunting and Intelligence-Gathering in India on the Eve of the Second World War'. In Ashley Jackson, Yasmin Khan, and Gajendra Singh (eds), *An Imperial World At War*. Aldershot: Ashgate.

Seven

Ideas of Indian Philosophy in Nineteenth-century Germany

Vivekananda, Deussen, and Garbe

Angelika Malinar

Debates about the interpretation of 'Indian Philosophy' in the late nineteenth and early twentieth century mirrored not only the philosophical standpoints of the debaters, but also the entangled history of the interpretation of Indian culture and of 'Eastern' and 'Western' values in this period. In the last quarter of the nineteenth century, Oriental studies thrived as more sources became available and new positions were created. The reasons for this development were manifold and led to the emergence of a complex historical constellation that defies any monolithic depiction of attitudes. While the individuals entering the expanding discipline of 'Indology' were moving in a historical-cultural context marked by the German Kaiserreich's engagement with the 'colonial race', there was a relativisation of the leading role of classical studies and Christian theology and the spread of comparativist, diffusionist, and racial taxonomies in the study of cultures, exhibiting quite different ideas, attitudes, and intentions. This historical constellation was also reflected in the conflicting constructions of the 'essence' of Indian philosophy and in the comments on the state and purpose of Sanskrit studies in Germany. In fin-de-siècle ideas of 'Indian philosophy', a bifurcation of attitudes towards Indian culture resurfaced, which was established at the beginning of the nineteenth century. At that time, the initial romantic German enthusiasm for India was countered by a criticism of the 'value' of Indian culture and a reassertion of Western philosophical and religious superiority. This bifurcation meant either an emphasis on the value of India's spiritual and metaphysical traditions, or an acknowledgement of its rationalistic and scientific achievements as being on par with the (Greek) classics and/or modern science.

In the field of philosophy, the first was regarded as being represented by Indian monism, Advaita-Vedānta, and the second by Sāṃkhya philosophy and other schools of Indian rationalism. The controversial assessment of these philosophies can be seen in the works of philosopher and Sanskritist Paul Deussen (1845–1919), who championed Advaita, and of Sanskritist Richard Garbe (1857–1927), who preferred Sāṃkhya. While the controversy around these points is rooted in differing philosophical inclinations, it is also intrinsically connected to larger debates on the value of Indian philosophy and the relevance of Sanskrit studies. Despite their different philosophical positions, Deussen and Garbe found common ground as they both aimed at promoting and institutionalising the study of Indian philosophy in Germany. The promotion of Indian philosophy in the West, in particular Advaita-Vedānta, was also a major goal of Swami Vivekananda (1863–1902) when he travelled and lectured in the United States and Europe. In 1896, he famously met Paul Deussen in Kiel and afterwards wrote an article on him ('On Dr. Paul Deussen', 1896), in which he narrated how the study of Sanskrit influenced Deussen's life and provided a brief account of the development of Sanskrit studies in Germany. This account is turned into an appeal to his Indian audience to emulate the new type of Sanskrit scholar that Vivekananda saw emerging in Europe, embodied by Deussen and Friedrich Max Müller (1823–1900), Professor of Comparative Philology in Oxford. Müller also supported Advaita-Vedānta as the essence of Indian religion and was in contact with Vivekananda, but neither he nor Vivekananda shared Deussen's rejection of Sāṃkhya philosophy. Like Vivekananda, Müller was an important voice in the contemporary debate on Indian philosophy in general and the interpretation of Vedānta in particular.[1] Vivekananda's text on Deussen is an interesting document regarding the larger intercultural and international contexts in which he propagated the study of Indian philosophy. Therefore, this text shall be analysed first, before dealing with the ideas and attitudes of Deussen and Garbe.

[1] The role of Müller in the debates discussed in the following would need separate treatment; for the interactions between Müller and Vivekananda, see Green (2016, 2017).

VIVEKANANDA ON DEUSSEN AND SANSKRIT STUDIES IN GERMANY

In September 1896, after having met Friedrich Max Müller in Oxford and travelling to Switzerland, Swami Vivekananda met Paul Deussen in Kiel, where the latter was Professor of Philosophy. Shortly afterwards the two met again in Bremen, and Deussen accompanied Vivekananda and his companions to Amsterdam and England. In England, they continued to meet each other and also spent time with Friedrich Max Müller. The two protagonists commented upon their encounter in quite different ways, and thus the interpretation varies according to the source texts used.[2] The encounter with Deussen forms the background

---

2 Apart from Vivekananda's article on Deussen, the meeting is mentioned in some of his letters. Deussen reports on the visit and the journey to Amsterdam and London in his autobiography *Mein Leben* (1922, 305–307), which he finished in 1914, about twenty years after the event, and which was published posthumously in 1922 in an abridged form. In 1912, the account of Mrs. Sevier who, together with her husband, had accompanied Vivekananda to Kiel, was published in a volume titled *The Life of Swami Vivekananda by his Eastern and Western Disciples* (1912, 426–427). This account (as well as extracts from Vivekananda's article on Deussen) was republished in Romain Rolland's article on Vivekananda and Deussen in the 1928 *Schopenhauer-Jahrbuch* (Rolland 1928), and it is also the source of the depiction of the visit in the biography of Vivekananda by Swami Nikhilananda (1953). Those who refer to Sevier's account tend to depict Deussen as if he were a disciple of Vivekananda. Those who also draw on Deussen's account of the meeting point out that Deussen neither recognised Vivekananda's importance nor had any of the veneration that the Swami had for him (see Rolland 1928, 158). Feldhoff (2008, 172–174) also notices this difference in attitudes and explains that Deussen had an aversion to any 'cult of saints'. He further maintains that Deussen presented Vivekananda with a copy of the lecture he gave in Bombay in 1893, titled 'On the Philosophy of the Vedānta in its Relations to the Occidental Metaphysics', which became the basis for Vivekananda's interpretation of Advaita-Vedānta as 'practical philosophy'. This statement seems to be based on Indologist Paul Hacker's study of the influence of Schopenhauer and Deussen on what he called 'Neo-Hinduism', in which he claimed that Vivekananda adopted Deussen's exposition of

of the article mentioned above, which Vivekananda wrote in 1896 for his journal *Brahmavādin*, titled 'On Dr. Paul Deussen'.[3] While this article is often referred to by scholars studying the meeting between Deussen and Vivekananda, it has to my knowledge not been analysed in greater detail as an early evaluation of the development of Sanskrit studies in 'the West' by a prominent Indian intellectual.

Vivekananda begins his text on Deussen with a biography-style narrative—apparently based on first-hand biographical information, perhaps offered by Deussen during the visit—which introduces Deussen as 'a young German student', son of 'a not very well-to-do clergyman', who attended lectures about Sanskrit, a language at that time 'new to European scholars'. These lectures were given by Christian

so-called '*tat tvam asi*' ethics as the basis of his 'practical Vedānta' (Hacker 1961). Hacker's claims are critically discussed by Halbfass (1995), and are rejected by Beckerlegge (2006, 2013), who points out that the root of Vivekananda's ideas about 'practical Vedānta' as social service was more a response to his Western audiences than the basis of his concept of 'devotional service' (*sevā*). His concept of *sevā* seems more connected to the teachings of Ramakrishna and the emergence of 'social services' in Britain and the US during the colonial period, and was in place even before he learned about Deussen's exposition.

While the question of whether Vivekananda developed his idea of practical Vedānta independently of Deussen (and the 'West') is still an issue (see, for instance, Maharaj 2020; Patil 2016), the academic debate now focuses also on the entangled history of ideas in the colonial period. This includes closer studies of the influence of the larger discussion on the relationship between science, religion, philosophy, and (esoteric) spirituality, as well as on the role of Ramakrishna, Max Müller, and theosophy in shaping Vivekananda's exposition of Vedānta (Beckerlegge 2006; Green 2016, 2017). In his study of Vivekananda and Müller, Green, for instance, suggests:

> The adoption of Vedanta as the religion best fitted for their apparently secular age by Vivekananda and Müller, was not a result of borrowing from East by West, or *vice versa*; rather it was the product of a rich and complex interaction between Europeans, Americans and Indians as they sought to shape and comprehend the future of religion in a secularizing world. (Green 2016, 173)

The interpretation of Indian philosophy, discussed in the following, plays an important role in this interaction.

3 Vivekananda, *Complete Works* (henceforth CW) IV, 272–277.

Lassen[4] for free, as Vivekananda stresses, because 'it is impossible for any one in any European University to make a living by teaching Sanskrit, unless indeed the University backs him' (CW IV, 272).[5] For Vivekananda, Lassen belongs to the 'heroic band of German scholars, the pioneers of Sanskrit scholarship in Germany'. They were 'heroic' since they turned to Sanskrit because of 'their pure and unselfish love of knowledge'. Like Lassen, young Deussen chose knowledge, and with it an uphill struggle instead of a promising career which would have been open to him; but 'then there was this Sanskrit!' (ibid., 273). Vivekananda depicts in considerable—and in certain respects exoticising[6]—detail the fascination that the 'strange' Sanskrit exerted on Deussen, which is interpreted as being indicative of his strong desire for knowledge.

At this point Vivekananda interrupts his account and turns to his Indian readers, pointing out that it has become hard 'for us modern Indians' to understand 'this kind of thirst for knowledge for its own sake'. However, this attitude can still be found among Pandits and, in particular, Saṃnyāsins in places like Varanasi or Nadia (ibid.). The sacrifices they made in order to study the manuscripts are favourably contrasted with the luxury at the disposal of the 'modern Europeanised Hindu', and the meagre output of the modern Indian universities. Vivekananda pleads that Indians must again develop the qualities of ancient Indian scholarship which he observes as being at work in Germany:

---

[4] Christian Lassen (1800–1876) was, since 1840, Professor of Old Indian Language and Literature at Bonn University.

[5] Deussen himself reports that he attended in 1865 Sanskrit classes held by Lassen and his disciple Gildemeister, although it appeared to him as '*völlig brotlose Kunst*' (an art that leaves you unemployed; Deussen 1922, 87–88). This reflects the fact that the study of Sanskrit and other forms of 'Orientalistik' were still mostly included in theological and classical seminars, and separate disciplines like Indology or Sinology had not yet been established (see Marchand 2009). Deussen could attend the Sanskrit classes for free because Lassen was one of the few Sanskritists holding a salaried position.

[6] '... the strange language, the strange sounds of which, although uttered with all those difficult peculiarities that Sanskrit consonants are subjected to in the mouths of unaccustomed Europeans, had strange fascination ...' (CW IV, 272).

> Unselfish and genuine zeal for real scholarship and honest earnest thought must again become dominant in the life of our countrymen if they are ever to rise to occupy among nations a rank worthy of their own historic past. It is this kind of desire for knowledge which has made Germany what she is now—one of the foremost, if not the foremost, among the nations of the world. (CW IV, 273)

The non-worldly attitude that Vivekananda ascribed here to the German scholars is turned into a criticism of the forms and purposes of education imposed by the British colonial government in India, as well as its Indian supporters. This criticism intensifies at the end of the article.

Resuming what he calls the 'world-old story of successful scholars and their hard work', he informs the readers that in the case of the struggling young student as well, this path was crowned with success: 'Now—not only Europe, but all India knows this man, Paul Deussen, who is the Professor of Philosophy in the University of Kiel.' Still, there is more to this story, since Deussen and Müller stand out from other Sanskritists in the West because of their friendly attitude towards India: 'Paul Deussen—or as he prefers to be called in Sanskrit, Deva-Sena[7]—and the veteran Max Müller have impressed me as being the truest friends of India and Indian thought.' Here, Vivekananda refers to their personal encounter in Deussen's house, where he met 'this ardent Vedantist' and made a pleasing experience.[8] In explaining what makes Deussen und Müller the 'truest' friends of India, Vivekananda turns to the academic dimension of the matter and provides the following account of the development of Sanskrit Studies in Europe:

> The earliest school of Sanskritists in Europe entered into the study of Sanskrit with more imagination than critical ability. They knew a little,

[7] In his travelogue, Deussen explains that 'Devasena' is the result of a Sanskritised rendering of his name in letters he received from India (Deussen 1904, 3).

[8] 'It will always be among the most pleasing episodes in my life—my first visit to this ardent Vedantist at Kiel, his gentle wife who travelled with him in India, and his little daughter, the darling of his heart—and our travelling together through Germany and Holland to London, and the pleasant meetings we had in and about London' (CW IV, 274).

> expected much from that little, and often tried to make too much of what little they knew [....] These were naturally followed by a reactionary band of superficial critics, more than real scholars of any kind, who knew little or nothing of Sanskrit, expected nothing from Sanskrit studies, and ridiculed everything from the East [....] What a medley of results from such critical scholarship! [...] After a feverish period of such treading-on-each-other's-toes of original research, a better state of things has dawned. It has now been found out that mere adventure without some amount of the capital of real and ripe scholarship produces nothing but ridiculous failure even in the business of Oriental research, and that the traditions in India are not to be rejected with supercilious contempt, as there is really more in them than most people ever dream of [....] There is now happily coming into existence in Europe a new type of Sanskrit scholars [*sic*], reverential, sympathetic, and learned—reverential because they are a better stamp of men, and sympathetic because they are learned [....] (CW IV, 274–275)

In declaring both earlier romantic enthusiasm for Sanskrit and its reactionary rejection a matter of the past, Vivekananda welcomes a 'new type' of Sanskrit scholar. He speaks of a 'new movement' of which Max Müller is the 'old pioneer' and Paul Deussen 'one of its younger advance-guard' (CW IV, 176). This 'new type' of Sanskritist is characterised by three attributes that Vivekananda explains by entwining the character of a scholar with the quality of research. The first quality he observed in these scholars is that they are 'reverential', because they are a 'better' type of men. The taxonomy employed here is based on Vivekananda's depiction of an almost dialectical evolution of Sanskrit scholarship. This evolution starts with heroic pioneers and some enthusiasts, who are being 'naturally' followed by 'reactionaries' questioning the value of such studies. The two extremes have now made room, Vivekananda observes, for a 'better state of things'. Better scholars are available who represent an advanced stage of Oriental research, in which both naïve enthusiasm and contempt for Indian culture among earlier scholars have vanished. The taxonomy of a dialectical progress is also evident in Vivekananda's entwining of sympathy and erudition that characterises the new scholars, who 'are sympathetic because they are learned'. The reason for this lies in their ability to be 'reverential', an adjective apparently understood by

Vivekananda as a somehow moral quality that makes them a 'better stamp of men'.

This new form of erudition entails not only having more knowledge of the subject matter, but also following a better approach. Vivekananda explains this approach on two levels. First—as we have seen—he emphasises the biographical dimension when he talks about the hardships Deussen had endured to learn Sanskrit in contemporary Germany. This connects him with the traditional forms of Indian scholarship connected with an ascetic lifestyle. Second, the 'new type' employs a different method. The new scholars are not only philologists sitting over manuscripts, but are also champions of the truth and knowledge they find in the Indian texts. This distinguishes them from earlier scholars because their work does not result in expropriating Indians of their cultural achievements. The latter occurred when earlier scholars had combined philological methods with historical criticism in order to trace the origin of texts and ideas. Says Vivekananda:

> Suddenly, on one fine morning, the poor Hindu woke up to find that everything that was his was gone; one strange race had snatched away from him his arts, another his architecture, and a third, whatever there was of his ancient sciences; why, even his religion was not his own! Yes—that too had migrated into India in the wake of a Pehlevi cross of stone! (CW IV, 275)

But now, Vivekananda continues, a 'better state of things had dawned' (ibid.).

Scholars like Müller and Deussen represent this 'dawn' since they are able to bring to the light what 'philological interest had hidden long from view', namely 'the gems of thought and spirituality to be found in the mine of our ancient scriptures' (ibid., 276). While philological interest has, in the case of Müller, reaped admirable results with respect to 'the preservation, spreading, and appreciation of the literature of our forefathers', he also found a few gems which he 'exhibited [...] to the public gaze, compelling attention to them by means of his authority as the foremost philologist'. What distinguishes Müller from the earlier generation is the fact that his philological studies are no longer 'disinterested',[9] confined to the circles of academics and playing only a marginal role in the canon of the sciences. Rather, he aims to popularise his findings and strives to make room for 'the East' and its 'gems' in both the academia and the larger public. Yet, Deussen is credited with a more far-reaching and deeper understanding that surpasses the mere showcasing of findings because he publicly championed Vedānta:

> Deussen, unhampered by any philological leanings and possessing the training of a philosopher singularly well versed in the speculations of ancient Greece and modern Germany, took up the cue and plunged boldly into the metaphysical depths of the Upanishads, found them to be fully safe and satisfying, and then—equally boldly declared that fact before the whole world. Deussen is certainly the freest among scholars in the expression of his opinion about the Vedanta. (ibid.)

In Vivekananda's view, philology is valuable for retrieving texts, but of limited use in the understanding of the 'gems' that philologists unearth in the 'mines'. Vivekananda is concerned that philology 'hides' what is actually contained in the texts. The metaphors used by Vivekananda express his taxonomy well. While philologists work in the mines, they usually defy any showcasing, and it is left to philosophers and other interpreters to evaluate the gems and make them shine. Vivekananda sees Deussen at the head of 'the new movement' of Sanskrit studies because he is not 'hampered by philological leanings' when he philosophically analyses Indian texts. This approach allows him to champion certain philosophical positions and become publicly an 'ardent Vedāntist' (ibid., 274). Vivekananda praises Deussen for his bold disregard for the opinions of the academic establishment and the larger German public. He stresses that such boldness is badly needed, both in Germany and in India.

Here, Vivekananda juxtaposes philology and philosophy in a way that resonates with tensions not only between disciplines and their respective claims to authority, but also within the thriving field of 'Indology'. He notices a change in the Western study of the East

---

9 On the self-perception of German Orientalists as being 'distinterested', that is, without any connection to actual colonial rule and devoid of any commercial or ideological interest, see Marchand (2009, 42–43).

which he depicts as a story of 'progress' in knowledge and attitude. An initial scholarly enthusiasm based on a limited number of sources has now turned into a more critical, yet sympathetic approach that overcomes Eurocentric prejudice and the professional commitment of most academics to pure philology and academic positivism. At the end of the article, he recommends this combination of criticism and sympathy in dealing with Indian texts and traditions to his Indian readers. He expresses the hope that Max Müller and Paul Deussen will be not only 'reverential', but also bold 'in showing to us our defects, the later corruptions in our thought-systems in India', and concludes:

> Just now we very much require the help of such genuine friends as these to check the growing virulence of the disease, very prevalent in India, of running either to the one extreme of slavish panegyrists who cling to every village superstition as the innermost essence of the Shāstras, or to the other extreme of demoniacal denouncers who see no good in us and in our history, and will, if they can, at once dynamite all the social and spiritual organizations of our ancient land of religion and philosophy. (CW IV, 277)

In certain respects, Vivekananda's view finds an echo in contemporary criticism of 'Orientalist', hegemonic philology and the hermeneutics of textual and literary criticism. Recent postcolonial criticism stresses that these methods superimpose alien modes of interpretation on texts that were dealt with quite differently in the textual communities in which they were transmitted. However, while the thrust of Vivekananda's observations is similar, their context and intention are different since he is interested in forging strategic alliances for his mission of national and spiritual uplift in India. Therefore, his praise of Deussen's unselfish quest for knowledge serves as a reference point for his depiction of the deplorable state of scholarship in India, and for appeals to his Indian readers. Thus, his text contains not only a critical evaluation of Sanskrit studies in Germany, but is also an example of how such evaluation was used by Vivekananda to assert his own position of authority which he, in this case, uses to criticise the situation in India. This criticism is combined with turning Germany into an example for India when it sets out to obtain a (or the) top position among the nations of the world. This also entails that 'knowledge for its own sake' must no longer be confined to exclusive circles transmitting age-old truths, but should go public and be made relevant and put to practical use in the building of the Indian nation.

Vivekananda's depiction of the development of Sanskrit scholarship in Germany in some respects seems to anticipate the recent historical studies of the reception of Indian texts and ideas in Germany, in particular with respect to what has been analysed as German 'romanticism' and 'orientalism'.[10] Vivekananda's article is an important comment that should be taken into account as being part of that discourse as it highlights that Sanskrit studies in Germany were connected to certain academic and national agendas not just in Germany, but in India as well.[11] Vivekananda's comments demonstrate the complex, entangled history of the study of Sanskrit in the late nineteenth century. Recent studies have demonstrated that the 'new type' of scholar is not Vivekananda's creation as it lends support to

---

10 Some studies on this history of Indology in Germany in the nineteenth and early twentieth centuries connect it to the rise of fascism in Germany. It is argued that the initial 'romanticism' turned into a peculiar form of 'German orientalism' that helped to prepare the ground for Nazi ideology in Germany. While Sanskrit studies in Germany can be seen as being part of the larger colonialist and imperialist endeavour of Western Orientalism, its specific 'German' dimension is spotted in its transporting of ideas of cultural superiority connected to constructions of the 'Aryan' race that were adopted in Nazi ideology; see Pollock (1993, 80ff.) and Kontje (2004) who classify 'German Orientalisms' according to a binary model: On the one hand, there is a German orientalism that lays the 'groundwork' for the Holocaust (Kontje 2004, 8), and on the other hand, there is an another that has 'a degree of openness toward the foreign' and is motivated by a critique of contemporary Germany (ibid., 10). This construction of 'German' attitudes has been criticised and partly rejected as being too monolithic and de-contextualised. Recent studies on the history and structure of German Indology, and also more generally on German *Orientalistik* have revealed a rather broad spectrum of views and positions taken by scholars, intellectuals, and the literati. See, for instance, the essays in Brückner, et al. (2001) and the studies by Sengupta (2005), Marchand (2009), and Myers (2013); see also Chapter 5, this volume.

11 This interconnectedness is emphasised in Halbfass' (1988) study on India-Europe encounters.

his interest in spreading his idea of Hinduism and Indian philosophy, but is indeed indicative of larger cultural and political transformations in post-1860 Germany. In her comprehensive transdisciplinary study on the development of 'Orientalistik' in nineteenth-century Germany, Suzanne Marchand speaks of a 'Second Oriental Renaissance' as a result of a post-1850 intensification of European imperialism, in the course of which Germany entered the colonial race as well: 'It was a product of new access to sources, of the declining cultural power of the established churches, of the waning of neohumanist forms of *Bildung*, and of new forms of patronage made possible by German unification and the Reich's increasing economic dynamism' (Marchand 2009, 158). The thriving of *Orientalistik* in general, and Indology in particular, resulted in the emergence of a generation of scholars claiming a general relevance of their field (ibid., 213). In some cases, this led to a criticism of the positivistic attitude of younger scholars aiming at the 'larger picture' when interpreting religious and cultural history in a synthesising way:

> These younger scholars also often denounced their *Doktorväter* for their narrow source usage and old-fashioned chronologies; many began to incorporate material culture, psychological, or ethnological insights, and oral and folkloric traditions into their work. Confident that Germans needed and wanted cultural and spiritual overhaul, they were willing to challenge the methods and norms of their positivist 'fathers'. (ibid.)

This also entailed 'seizing humanist and theological territory' (Marchand 2018, 216). Furthermore, it meant not just establishing a further specialisation in discipline, but also addressing the larger debates about the relationship between religion, philosophy, and science. Both Paul Deussen and Richard Garbe represent certain aspects of this constellation in their differing attempts to seize philosophical 'territory' in the humanities and address a larger public. The differences between them did not only concern their conflicting evaluation of the philosophical schools of India, but also their attitude towards British colonialism and the employment of a comparative and diffusionist perspective in the study of Indian culture. While differences between them were reflected in mutual criticism, this took place on common ground: the shared goal of establishing Indian philosophy as a field of study in both Sanskrit Studies and Philosophy departments. Since the controversy between them unfolds also against the background of the earlier reception of Indian philosophy and a bifurcation in attitudes towards India in Germany, this shall be delineated briefly before turning to Deussen and Garbe.

INDIAN PHILOSOPHY IN NINETEENTH-CENTURY GERMANY

As is well-known, the source-based study of Indian philosophy in Germany began at the end of the eighteenth century with the first translations of the *Bhagavadgītā* and the first source-based description of Indian philosophical texts and tenets by Henry T. Colebrooke in a series of essays titled *On the Philosophy of the Hindus* (1823). The latter became the source for early inclusions of India in histories of philosophy (see Cousin 2018 [1829]; Hegel 1974b [1830–1833]). By the 1820s, the German enthusiasm for a more or less 'imagined' India had extended to Indian philosophy. At that time, however, the interest in India already differed from the earlier Romanticism—famously exemplified by Friedrich Schlegel—as it had already taken a distinct philological note in the study and translation of original sources. This is illustrated in the debate about the translation and interpretation of the *Bhagavadgītā*, which resulted in different views on the value of Indian thought. Wilhelm v. Humboldt and August Wilhelm Schlegel voiced their conviction about the intrinsic and even indispensable value of Indian philosophy as expressed in this text. Georg Friedrich Hegel opposed them and doubted such value, and generally ranked the 'Indian spirit' with the lower objectifications of the 'world-spirit'.[12] However, Hegel later stated that Indian philosophy 'very well deserves to be called philosophy' (Hegel 1979a, 144) and the texts of the two schools he was dealing with—Sāṃkhya and Nyāya—were 'real philosophical works' (Hegel 1979b).[13] This statement was largely

12 On this debate, see Malinar (2007). Deussen and Garbe also treated the *Bhagavadgītā* as a philosophical text in their respective translations and interpretations of the text (see ibid.).

13 This positive evaluation in Hegel's interpretation of Indian philosophy is stressed by Halbfass (1988, 84–99).

ignored, while Hegel's view that philosophy in the fullest sense existed only in Greece and not in India gained popularity. This view fostered exclusions of India from general histories of philosophy later in the century. Although Hegel's exclusion of India from the history of philosophy proper became highly influential, other philosophers and intellectuals continued to emphasise its importance. It gained prominence when Arthur Schopenhauer favoured the foundational texts of the school of Advaita-Vedānta (monism). He rejected Hegel's philosophy and welcomed Indian philosophy as an indispensable element in his own philosophy, believing that it could be important for Europe at large.[14] Thus, from the 1830s, Indian philosophy was by and large assessed following the divide between Hegelian and anti-Hegelian philosophers, the latter camp being most prominently represented by Schopenhauer and Nietzsche.

The interpretations of Indian philosophy by prominent philosophers of the nineteenth century were paradigmatic with respect to the terms of its further study in the academic disciplines of Sanskrit studies and philosophy. Apart from the inevitability of superimposing one's own understanding on the thoughts of others, implied in any hermeneutic situation, the uncritical manner in which this was done and the larger colonial contexts connect the interpretation of Indian philosophical texts to some of the appropriative and judgemental traits ingrained in hegemonic claims to Western supremacy ('Orientalism').[15] Indicative of this is the fact that the terms of debate were fixed, so that transposing Indian terms into Western referential frameworks became standard procedure, both in Europe and India.[16] This was done either by trying to find equivalents for Indian terms and doctrines in European positions or by detecting deficiencies in Indian philosophy, or both. The application of these taxonomies was neither monothetic nor uncontested; there is not just *the* 'orientalist'

14 For further analysis of Schopenhauer's reception of Indian philosophy, see Halbfass (1988, 105–120).

15 For a discussion of the tension between hermeneutics and 'orientalism', see Halbfass (1997).

16 For the reception of Western philosophy by nineteenth-century Indian thinkers, see Halbfass (1988).

or 'Eurocentric' reification of Indian philosophy.[17] Indian philosophy was seen as deficient or preliminary when compared with the European tradition, or as instructive or even indispensable in that it could accentuate issues neglected and forgotten in the West, or it was simply ignored. This constellation occasioned choices with respect to which philosophical schools were regarded as forming the 'core' of Indian philosophy. Those emphasising the 'rationalist-logical' schools (Nyāya, Sāṃkhya, Buddhism) opposed those preferring the 'monistic-idealistic' ones (Advaita-Vedānta). These developments are mirrored in the works of Deussen and Garbe and in their attempts to champion Indian philosophy as a field of study.

In their engagement with Indian philosophy, Garbe and Deussen did not only pursue disciplinary interests, but also felt that Indian philosophy deserves to be taken seriously as a way of thinking that is no less important than the European tradition. Therefore, it should be firmly established in the curricula of German universities. In order to achieve this, a primary concern was to make a greater number of philosophical texts available through editions and translations based on philological principles. They thereby opened up a new field of research within Sanskrit studies, which had mainly focused on Vedic literature, Dharmaśāstra, and Buddhism.[18] Furthermore, Deussen and Garbe sought to explain and evaluate Indian philosophy in monographic treatments of individual philosophical schools, thereby recommending it to trained academic philosophers. This endeavour of critical advertisement implied establishing the authoritative knowledge of Indian thought vis-à-vis academic peers, and explaining its relevance to patrons in the political and cultural establishment.

17 This point is also emphasised by Marchand in her criticism of Said's view of German orientalism at large (Marchand 2009, xix–xxvii).

18 This is corroborated by the fact that the first large-scale translation of a corpus of Indian texts, Max Müller's *Sacred Books of the East,* only included one philosophical text, namely the *Brahmasūtra* with the commentaries of Śaṃkara and Rāmānuja (Thibaut 1890–1904). Apart from this, there was another volume with texts that were, at least by some scholars, classified as 'philosophical', namely *Bhagavadgītā*, *Sānatsujātīya*, and *Anugītā* (Telang 1882); on the context and aims of Müller's project, see Girardot (2002).

In doing so, Deussen and Garbe entertained a double discourse of academic authority and popularising justification, which distinguishes them from earlier scholarship (see above). While their research was based on philology, they also applied their ideas of what constitutes 'philosophy' to the texts, and drew on larger theoretical frameworks in the explanation of history and culture. While Deussen and Garbe agreed that there is philosophy in India[19] which deserves to be taken seriously, they disagreed with respect to its history and 'essence' and its relationship with religion. While Deussen propagated Advaita-Vedānta, Garbe voiced his sympathies for Sāṃkhya.

Deussen and Garbe: Biographies and Taxonomies

Paul Deussen (1845–1919) is known to the larger academic public primarily as a more or less distant friend of Friedrich Nietzsche, and his work is sometimes referred to in Nietzsche studies.[20] He viewed himself as a philosopher, following Kant as well as Schopenhauer, and with a passion for Sanskrit and Advaita-Vedānta philosophy. He studied Protestant theology and philosophy and took Sanskrit classes with Christian Lassen in Bonn—a fact stressed by Vivekananda in his depiction of Deussen. Deussen's academic life had many twists and turns, as he reports in his memoirs (*Mein Leben*, 1922). After completing his studies, he first became a schoolteacher and then the private tutor of the son of a rich Russian family. The latter position enabled him to pursue his academic career, which resulted in his habilitation and obtaining the title of *Privatdozent* at the University of Geneva, where he then initiated the study of Sanskrit. After a controversial intermezzo

---

19 By the end of the nineteenth century, it was generally acknowledged that India had 'philosophy', but it was largely ignored. The debate on the question of whether there is an equivalent for philosophy in Sanskrit and, if not, whether India can have 'philosophy' in its true sense set in after World War II (see Halbfass 1988).

20 An important source for Deussen is his autobiography, which was published posthumously in an abridged version (*Mein Leben*, 1922); see also the biography by Feldhoff (2008).

as a lecturer at the University of Aachen (see below), he moved to Berlin. There he taught for ten years as a Professor of Philosophy without a regular salary, but hoping for promotion to full professor after being appointed as *Extraordinarius* in 1887.[21] Eventually, in 1889—at the age of fifty-four—he was appointed as full Professor of Philosophy, not in Berlin, but at the less prestigious University of Kiel, where he taught until his death in 1919. Since the usual career ladder would have been the other way round, taking him from a 'provincial' university to Berlin or some other high-ranked university, Deussen at first hesitated to accept the offer from Kiel.[22] The difficulties he faced in obtaining a salaried position reflect, on the one hand, the increasing number of Orientalists seeking positions, and on the other, were also the result of his particular blend of philosophy and Sanskrit, especially his championing of Schopenhauer and Advaita-Vedānta. While the combination of expertise in philosophy and Sanskrit allowed him to bridge the chasm between the disciplines, he was perceived as being 'between the disciplines', a *Grenzgänger*, and thus potentially belonging nowhere.[23] However, in the universities, disciplinary boundaries were well in place, as can be seen in the fact that in the same year that Deussen was appointed Professor of Philosophy, the University of Kiel appointed Hermann Oldenberg

---

21 Among his supporters in Berlin was Albrecht Weber, who held the Chair for Sanskrit and provided Deussen with a scholarship (Feldhoff 2008, 123).

22 On the internal hierarchy of German universities at that time, see Baumgarten (1997, 211ff); for Deussen's doubts about moving to the 'province' of Kiel and the reasons for accepting the offer, see Deussen (1922, 262ff), Feldhoff (2008, 100ff), and Delfs (2017, 115). Marchand (2009, 99f) cites Deussen's appointment in Kiel as an example of the fact that in several cases, positions were created not by the general approbation of the faculties, but by 'royal fiat' or the lobbying of influential individuals. In the case of Deussen, the influential lobbyist was ministry director Friedrich Althoff (1839–1908). On the politics of the 'System Althoff', see the contributions in vom Brocke (1991).

23 See Heimann's (1931) article on Deussen and Indology, where she stresses his achievements, but also finds problematic his tendency to give his philosophical views priority over philological concerns.

as full Professor of Sanskrit (he later moved 'up' to Göttingen University).[24]

Deussen was a very productive writer and earned himself a reputation as a solid academic philosopher and Sanskritist. In 1883 he published *Das System des Vedānta*, a comprehensive monographic treatment of the *Brahmasūtra* based on the commentary of Śaṅkara, which was followed by a translation of these texts (Deussen 1887). In 1892 he travelled to India and narrated his experiences in a travelogue titled *Erinnerungen an Indien* (1904). In 1897, he published the first complete German translation of the Upaniṣads, which is still acknowledged as a seminal achievement and was also translated into English.[25] At about the same time he started his ambitious, multi-volume *Allgemeine Geschichte der Philosophie mit besonderer Berücksichtigung der Religionen*, in which India played a prominent role. In 1902 he founded the *Schopenhauer-Gesellschaft* and also prepared a complete edition of Schopenhauer's writings. The publication series of the *Schopenhauer-Gesellschaft*, the *Jahrbücher der Schopenhauer-Gesellschaft*, became an important forum not only for philosophical studies on Schopenhauer, but also for Indian philosophy.[26]

Richard Garbe (1857–1927) had to also endure a period of insecurity and straitened economic means, but he embarked on his established career track in Sanskrit studies without being torn between philosophy and Sanskrit, as had been the case with Deussen. He studied Sanskrit and General History of Religion (*Allgemeine Religionsgeschichte*) with Rudolph von Roth in Tübingen. This is an example of the strong

24 It is thus problematic when Deussen is regarded as an 'Indologist'; see, for instance, Myers (2013, 177) and Bagchi (2003, 282).

25 *Cf. The Philosophy of the Upanishads.* Authorised English translation by A. S. Geden, Edinburgh, 1908. Other books were translated as well: *The Elements of Metaphysics Being a Guide for Lectures and Private Use*, London, 1894; *Outline of the Vedanta System of Philosophy According to Shankara*, Cambridge, 1906; and also his travelogue, *My Indian Reminiscences*, Madras, 1912.

26 According to the information provided by the *Jahrbücher*, the *Schopenhauer-Gesellschaft* has also an Indian branch; on the history of the *Schopenhauer-Gesellschaft* and Deussen's role in it, see Hansert (2010).

connection between Sanskrit studies and the study of religion(s) after the early romantic enthusiasm faded away, and historical debates about the origins and diffusion of languages, religions, and artefacts dominated the field (Marchand 2009, 191; see also the essays in Brückner, et al. 2003). For Garbe, this meant studying the Veda as the 'oldest' form of Sanskrit and Indian religion, and thus his dissertation and habilitation were on Vedic ritual texts, which he edited and translated. From 1878 to 1894, he taught at the University of Königsberg, for the first two years as *Privatdozent*, then for almost fifteen years as *Extraordinarius* on a very low salary before he was, in 1894, appointed as full professor. The time in Königsberg was a period of financial instability and thus, in 1885, Garbe happily accepted a one-year scholarship for India granted by Emperor Wilhelm I. It was a prestigious stipend, which Garbe saw as helping him promote his academic career. His aim was to work on the translation of major Sāṃkhya texts with Indian scholars in Varanasi, and he therefore did not just travel to India, but actually stayed and worked there. Furthermore, he was given the task of acquiring Sanskrit manuscripts for the libraries in Tübingen and Berlin.[27] His account of his stay in India was published in 1889 under the title *Indische Reiseskizzen*. His strained financial situation was one reason why this book and other articles were published in non-academic journals. At this point in his life, he had turned away from Vedic studies (and Rudolph Roth's appraisal of the Veda) and made Indian philosophy his field of specialisation. He thus illustrates the previously mentioned generational change that surfaced in the 1870s, as Garbe sought to expand the relevance and scope of Sanskrit studies. In 1895 he accepted the offer from the University of Tübingen and held the chair for Sanskrit until his death in 1927.[28] In contrast to Deussen, Garbe moved 'up' from a provincial to a high-profile university.

Like Deussen, Garbe was a very productive scholar who published translations of major texts of the Sāṃkhya school, namely the *Sāṃkhyakārikā* with the commentary of Vacaspatimiśra (1891) and

[27] On the collection of manuscripts and its role in the institutionalisation of Indology, as well as for the academic career, see Sengupta (2005).

[28] For further biographical details, see Malinar (2003); on the travelogue, see note 38.

the *Sāṃkhyasūtras* with the commentaries of Aniruddha (1892) and Vijñānabhikṣu (1889), as well as monographs on the same titled *Die Sāṃkhya-Philosophie, eine Darstellung des indischen Rationalismus* (*Sāṃkhya: An Account of Indian Rationalism*, 1894), *Sāṃkhya und Yoga* (1896), and a general survey of Indian philosophy, *The Philosophy of Ancient India* (1897).

Although neither Deussen nor Garbe published any programmatic statement on the scope and method of their discipline,[29] statements in their publications allow for a characterisation of their academic agenda. The programmatic implications of these statements throw light on an aspect often neglected in studies of Indology in Germany, which mostly focus on its being part of a general discourse of colonial hegemony and nationalist supremacy, namely the need to justify the study of Sanskrit and Indian philosophy as a state-funded academic discipline.[30] This is especially true in the case of Garbe. Although Deussen did not view himself as an expert in Indian affairs as Garbe did, he felt that his philosophical positions were strengthened through the corroborative evidence of Indian metaphysics. Deussen—who held, after all, a chair for philosophy and not for Sanskrit—was more concerned with championing a particular philosophy. According to Deussen, Schopenhauer's metaphysics is the culmination of the philosophical ideas developed already by Plato and Śaṃkara and perfected by Kant, as well as of the religious and ethical principles formulated in ancient India and in the New Testament. These traditions represent the pinnacle of human thought in their teaching of monistic idealism, which provides the necessary antidote to what Deussen calls the 'perverted' materialistic rationality of the modern age (for instance, in the lecture on Vedānta that he gave in Bombay in 1893). Deussen's commitment to Schopenhauer, Kant, and Śaṅkara was based on his belief that they incorporated the highest philosophical truth and the highest cultural achievements of the European and Indian mind, respectively. In continuation of

29 For an example of such a programmatic statement, see Rhys-Davids (1903–04).

30 The necessity of bringing these aspects together is stressed by Marchand (2009); see also Sengupta's (2005) foundational study of the process of institutionalisation of Indology as an academic discipline in Germany.

Schopenhauer's appreciation of the upaniṣadic-vedāntic strand of Indian philosophy, Deussen saw in 'monistic idealism' the origin and essence of Indian philosophy.

This commitment hindered not only his career—as indicated by his being a professor in Kiel and not in Berlin—but also his becoming as influential in contemporary (academic) philosophy as he had hoped. For instance, when Deussen taught at the University (*Polytechnikum*) of Aachen in 1875, conservative Catholics (ultra-Montanists) accused him of being an agent of the Prussian-Protestant *Kulturkampf* against Catholicism. They complained about his lectures on Schopenhauer and Indian thought, in which Christianity was allegedly belittled. As a consequence, Deussen was ordered by the ministry to stop his lectures on the subject and only teach the history of philosophy from Plato to Kant.[31] Furthermore, in his teaching of Schopenhauerian metaphysics as the pinnacle of philosophy and theology, Deussen also parted company with Hegel (and his followers), who had already proclaimed the end of philosophy (and thus also of metaphysics) in the age of science.[32] With this position, Deussen alienated himself from non-Hegelian philosophers as well, such as his former school friend Friedrich Nietzsche. The latter saw him as arguing in favour of philosophies that ought to be rejected and overcome. In a letter to Deussen, Nietzsche explained that where Vedānta and Schopenhauer (as well as Deussen) say 'No', he says 'Yes'.[33]

---

[31] Deussen reports this in his autobiography (1922, 177–186), see also Feldhoff (2008, 98ff). This situation reflects the so-called *Kulturkampf* that was waged between Bismarck and German Catholics in the 1870s and 1880s, triggered by a series of anti-Catholic laws. Although he deals with the impact of the 'Kulturkampf' on German 'visions' of India, Myers (2013, 178–184) does not mention these events in his chapter on Deussen (see, however, Marchand 2009, 304).

[32] See also Deussen (1922, 176), where he speaks of his 'having broken off all bridges' connecting him with mainstream philosophy in Germany when he published in 1877 his *Elemente der Metaphysik*.

[33] After praising, in a letter to Deussen, the monograph on Vedānta philosophy (Deussen 1883), Nietzsche states:

> It is of great pleasure to me to once get to know the classical expression of the thought-form foreign to me. Your book achieves this. Everything that

Garbe's commitment to Indian philosophy had a different background, as he was a trained Sanskritist (whereas Deussen studied Theology) without a personal philosophical agenda. Furthermore, for him, it meant a turning away from Vedic literature and religion, in which he saw no intrinsic value. He criticised the romantic idea that truth is only complete in the beginnings of history and is best preserved in the oldest texts. Instead, he employed a different, similarly Eurocentric taxonomy in his attempt to provide more 'realistic' accounts of India and Indians. In doing so, he employed a taxonomy of national and sometimes racial characteristics that revealed his Anglophilia and anti-clerical (in particular, anti-Catholic) ressentiment (see Malinar 2003). His intention to claim greater relevance for Sanskrit studies and widen its scope was marked by his focus on Indian philosophy and the use of anthropological and comparativist approaches. In fact, the exclusive focus on the oldest texts as being the most original and pure would confine Sanskrit studies to one or two areas, as the rest of Indian culture and literature could, because of its diminished truth, only be of limited interest. Such limitations were certainly not helping Sanskritists to gain the status of an expert in Indian affairs before a wider public. Garbe sought to establish his authority and expert status, as well as the claim of general relevance for the study of Indian culture, by stressing not its exceptionality, but its exemplariness when viewed from comparative and historical perspectives. In doing so, he occasionally also dealt with contemporary issues and post-classical developments in India, for instance with the Mughal emperor Akbar.[34] Garbe quite often used a classificatory scheme developed by the

I already suspected in regard to this type of thinking comes to light in it in the most naive manner. Accident wills it that at the moment a manifesto of mine is printed which says approximately with the same eloquence Yes! where your book says No!' (Letter to Deussen, 16 March 1883, cited according to the English translation by Rollmann 1978, 128)

34 In 1909, Garbe gave a talk on Akbar on the occasion of the birthday of Emperor Wilhelm II, which was translated into English in the same year. The choice of this topic reveals Garbe's sympathies for Indian Muslims and the achievements of the Mughal period, which are also expressed in his travelogue.

anthropologist Edward B. Tylor (1832–1917).[35] In his taxonomy of cultural achievements, Tylor arranges cultures on what he calls 'the scale of civilization':

> The educated world of Europe and America practically settles a standard by placing its own nations at one end of the social series and savage tribes at the other, arranging the rest of mankind between these limits according as they correspond more closely to savage or to cultured life. The principle criteria of classification are the absence or presence, high or low development, of the industrial arts, [...] the extent of scientific knowledge, the definiteness of moral principles, the condition of religious belief and ceremony, the degree of social and political organization, and so forth. (Tylor 1871, Vol. I, 23–24)

This taxonomy allows for a global mapping of not only the plurality of cultures, but also of cultural differences within one culture. It implies a shift away from the humanistic idea of assigning an intrinsic educational value to certain cultures to a practice of measuring the achievements of peoples and nations in the different segments of civilisation. This also means that one finds multiple cultural stages within a particular culture, rather than an essence. Furthermore, and in contrast to Deussen's taxonomy, Garbe believes that cultural contacts and the diffusion of ideas and texts do not 'contaminate' the originality of a religion or philosophy. Borrowing does not hinder either originality or improvement.[36] Garbe drew on Tylor's

---

35 Garbe thus corroborates Marchand's (2009, 213) observation that the new generation of Sanskritists used concepts from other disciplines in order to embed their findings in general theoretical frameworks. Furthermore, his use of Tylor testifies to his general Anglophilia in his theoretical preferences as well. They lie, in contrast to many German scholars' emphasis on 'Ur-Monotheism', with a Frazerian evolutionary model, according to which the original religion was animism (see ibid., 229). This is another reason for the conflict with Deussen, who entertains anti-British sentiments and follows a degeneration model of history that places the 'highest truth' in the older sources, to be sustained by modern scientific philosophy (see also below).

36 This is made clear, for instance, in his overview of ancient Indian philosophy, when he states that a possible influence of India and borrowing by Greek philosophers do not diminish the latter's achievements (Garbe 1897, 39).

taxonomy and his anti-romantic and anti-clerical stance, which served as yardsticks in his attempts to establish 'order' in the manifold Indian culture. While the deployment of these yardsticks entails condescending judgements about the 'typical' national traits of Indians, it results in neither a generalising or essentialising image of India, nor in a general deprecation. In contrast to Hegel, Garbe does not use this scheme to place all of India on the lower rungs on the evolutionary ladder of world civilisations. Rather, Garbe aimed to delineate cultural differences within India and detect those segments that were particularly worthy of academic study. He explained the simultaneous presence of cultural phenomena belonging to different historical periods; therefore, phenomena that might arouse doubts in Germany about the value of Indian culture as a whole (for example, widow-burning; see Garbe 1903) and, as a consequence, of the necessity of funding Indology, were normalised (de-exoticised) through their classification as 'remnants' of a barbaric stage of cultural evolution, which can be detected in many cultures.[37]

Garbe employed the same taxonomy in his opposition to the 'neo-romantic' attitude that he saw developing in Germany at the end of the nineteenth century. He considered it his professional duty to correct the image of India as the land of dreams and monistic harmony that was resuscitated by Deussen and others. Garbe criticised Deussen for propagating what the former considered a 'wrong' image of India.[38]

---

37 For more details on Garbe's application of this taxonomy to Indian culture, see Malinar (2003, 128ff).

38 This can be seen in the comments they make about each other in their travelogues, which exemplify what Pfister (1993) calls 'dialogical intertext', that is, an intertextuality imbued with criticism or corrections of another text of the same genre. Deussen misses, for example, the snakes, which 'Freund Garbe' saw in Elephanta (Deussen 1904, 35), and refuses to share Garbe's enthusiasm for the Taj Mahal (ibid., 76). Garbe is also present when Deussen declares that his empathy for Vedānta philosophy is the ideal precondition for understanding India (ibid., 3). Conversely, in the second edition of his travelogue, Garbe claims authority over Deussen by pointing out that the latter never stayed in India during the hot season and was anyway carried away by his Vedantic inclinations (Garbe 1925). Garbe also refuses to stay in Esplanade hotel in Bombay, calling it too exclusively European, and thus too far away from 'real Indian life' (ibid., 28), whereas Deussen claims that

Confronted with the problem of legitimising the general relevance of Indian culture as an object worthy of publicly funded academic treatment, Garbe was fighting both the neo-romantic imagination of India and scandalising reports about Indian 'horrors'. At the same time, he was stressing India's cultural achievements and complained about the lack of interest in India among the larger academic public, and thus did not entirely conform to the disinterested, positivistic self-representation entertained by the majority of pre-war Indologists, who rejected any 'Schopenhauerian India'.[39]

SĀṂKHYA VERSUS ADVAITA-VEDĀNTA

Garbe's ranking of cultural achievements resulted in his regarding Sāṃkhya and Nyāya, due to their advocating 'rationalism', as the pinnacle of Indian philosophy and the source of Buddhism and later Vedānta. According to him, all these schools were based in the Kshatriya circles of Indian society and signalled the development of rational, moral, and scientific principles in Indian culture. Thus, the emergence of rationalism in India implied a critique of Brahmanical ritualism as well as of 'clergical' Brahmanical hegemony which Garbe regarded as belonging to a lower stage of cultural development and as an element of Indian culture that continues to hamper its development. The influence of Brahmanical thinking is also mirrored in the history of Indian philosophy, which resulted from a criticism of Brahmanical ritualism among the warrior class. This is argued in a chapter in his overview of Indian philosophy, titled 'Hindu Monism: Who Were its Authors, Priests or Warriors?' (Garbe 1897, 57). After castigating both

the hotel is the 'ideal surrounding to study the Veda and the Upanishads' (Deussen 1904, 34). Both texts show typical features of colonial-orientalist travel-writing of the period, as studied by Pratt (1992). Bagchi (2003) deals with some of these features in Garbe's travelogue, but not with intertextual involvements and cultural-historical contexts; on Deussen's travelogue, see Delfs (2017).

39 On this rejection, see Marchand (2009, 299f.), who cites also the conflict between 'positivist' Heinrich Lüders (1869–1943), Professor of Sanskrit in Berlin between 1909 and 1935, and the more philosophically inclined Heinrich Zimmer (1890–1943).

the caste system for being as harmful as all forms of 'class government' and the greed of the Brahmanical priests, he rejects the idea that all of this could be forgotten because of the 'wisdom' of the Upaniṣads, which Garbe credits as constituting the beginning of philosophy in India. But the 'wise' were not priests, but kings and warriors:

> In later times, it is true, this philosophy [monism of the Upaniṣads] became in the fullest sense the property of the Brahmans, and has been cultivated by them for twentyfive centuries, down to the present day, so that it is still regarded as the orthodox doctrine of Brahmanism. But this does not alter the fact that it took its rise in the ranks of the warrior caste. To this caste belongs the credit of clearly recognising the hollowness of the sacrificial system and the absurdity of its symbolism, and, by opening a new world of ideas, of effecting the great revolution in the intellectual life of ancient India [. . . .] these things developed in ancient India just as they did in the rest of the world. Intellectual enlightenment is opposed by its natural enemy, the priesthood, until it has become too strong in the people to be successfully opposed any longer. Then the priest, too, professes the new ideas, and tries to harmonise them as far as possible with his hollow shams. (Garbe 1897, 78–79)

While the later Vedānta schools attached themselves to the authority of the Vedic texts, Sāṃkhya philosophers turned away from the Vedas and championed 'rationalism', the inquiry into ontological principles and cosmological structures by means of logic and syllogistic reasoning. Says Garbe: 'For the first time in the world has all the independence and freedom of the human intellect, the complete confidence in its own power appeared in Kapila's teaching.' The Sāṃkhya system can, 'more than any other product of the fertile Indian speculation claim the attention of those contemporaries, whose world-view is based on the results of the modern natural sciences' (Garbe 1917, 185; see also Garbe 1897, 30). This rationalism had practical and social consequences as well, since it resulted in a dissemination of knowledge in all social strata and thus opened up the chances of liberation for everyone and not just for the three upper castes, in particular the Brahmins, as is the case in Advaita-Vedānta. After quoting Deussen's explanation of the Vedānta view that excludes women and Śūdras from learning philosophy, Garbe states that Sāṃkhya never cultivated such religious, typically Brahmanical prejudices. The atmosphere of freedom also implied that the teaching of Sāṃkhya was based on competence, and not on caste: 'Whoever has obtained the discriminating knowledge [the goal of Sāṃkhya] is qualified to instruct others, any restriction to professional teachers is denied. Another unbrahmanical trait!' (Garbe 1917, 198). In his preference for Sāṃkhya as a 'rationalistic' philosophy and thus as the representative of rationalism, intellectual freedom, and social egalitarianism in India, he came in open conflict with earlier appraisals of the Veda (by his teacher Roth and others), as well as with Deussen's idea of what constitutes the core of Indian thought.[40]

In contrast to Garbe, Deussen deemed the 'rationality' of Sāṃkhya to be a later 'degeneration' of the original metaphysical idealism. In his depiction of Sāṃkhya, Deussen sometimes seems to indulge in his aversion to this 'unbearable' and 'horrid' philosophy.[41] For instance, in the chapter on Sāṃkhya included in *Allgemeine Geschichte der Philosophie*, Deussen's dislike of Sāṃkhya dualism is expressed as follows:

> [I]t is the nature of a philosophical principle to be a unity, through which the variety of worldly phenomena can be derived. Therefore, monism is for philosophy the natural position, and dualism, whenever it appeared in the history of philosophy, was always the result of previous, severe disorders and, so to speak, a symptom of an illness of the philosophizing mind. (Deussen 1894–1917, 1, 3, 220)

In India, dualism is the result of the self-undermining (*Selbstzersetzung*) of Upaniṣadic thought; it is a philosophical illness, the symptom of an intellectual and metaphysical fatigue. It appears when the original philosophical quest for truth ebbs away and philosophy becomes a mere medicine, an antidote against suffering, and thus ceases to be an end in itself. In its original 'healthy' state, however, philosophy is the idealistic and monistic quest for truth as an end in itself. Therefore,

40 For a discussion of Garbe's views on Indian religions and his strong emphasis on the divide between Brahmanical and Kshatriya traditions, see Malinar (2003).

41 Vivekananda seems to have noticed this trait as well when he characterises Deussen as follows: 'He is what I should call "a warring Advaitist". No compromise with anything else' (Letter to E. T. Sturdy, 10 September 1896; CW, VII, 388).

realism, empiricism, and materialism are, according to him, the opposite, if not the destroyer, of 'true philosophy'. In a paradigmatic lecture on 'Vedanta in its Relation to Occidental Philosophy' that he delivered in Bombay in 1893, Deussen stated that materialism is dangerously surging in Europe,

> metaphysics, the very centre and heart of serious philosophy, are only supported by a few ones [....] In India the influence of this perverted and perversive spirit of our age has not yet overthrown in religion and philosophy the good traditions [....] Vedānta is, now as in ancient times, living in the mind and heart of every thoughtful Hindu. (Deussen 1893 [1904], 243)

Rather unexcitedly, Garbe responded to Deussen's polemics in the second edition of his monograph on Sāṃkhya by pointing out that such statements are the result of his colleague's unjustified enthusiasm for Vedānta, which makes him grossly overrate the value of the Upanisads and voice false, outdated ideas about Sāṃkhya (Garbe 1917, 41–42).

The controversy saw no winner, except for the two philosophical schools themselves. For quite some time Sāṃkhya and Advaita-Vedānta seemed to pass for *the* philosophies of India. Something like a papal blessing for this situation was voiced shortly after the publication of Garbe and Deussen's seminal studies, when Max Müller proclaimed in his monograph *The Six Systems of Indian Philosophy* (1903) that Vedānta and Sāṃkhya are the two most important philosophical systems of ancient India:

> It is in that Walhalla of real philosophies that I claim a place of honour for the representatives of Vedānta and Sāṃkhya [....] if hitherto no one would have called himself a philosopher who had not read and studied the works of Plato and Aristotle, of Des Cartes and Spinoza, of Locke, Hume and Kant in the original, I hope that the time will come when no one will claim that name who is not acquainted at least with the two prominent systems of ancient India, the Vedānta and the Sāṃkhya. (Müller 1899, xvii)

However, the change that was hoped for did not really come—except that the study of Indian philosophy became a firmly established area of specialisation in Indology.

Championing Indian Philosophy

Despite these disagreements with respect to method, taxonomy, and attitude, there are certain commonalities between Garbe and Deussen. Both approach the Indian texts with a Western taxonomy and with a universalistic idea of philosophy that allows not only a reconstruction of a 'general' history of philosophy, but also invites comparative perspectives. As a consequence, philological scruples are set aside when they present Indian philosophy not only to specialists in the field, but also to academic philosophers and other philosophically interested readers. Despite being trained philologists, neither Deussen nor Garbe represent Indian philosophical tenets as they are formulated and treated in the original sources. Instead, they are explained by drawing on typically Western ideas of what philosophy is. In doing so, the notion that philosophy is articulated in the form of philosophical systems plays an important role. As a result, Indian philosophical teachings are re-organised according to the features deemed constitutive of a philosophical system, and by using the classifications of philosophical topics and sub-disciplines familiar in Western academic philosophy. One consequence of this procedure is that Garbe, for instance, treats all the texts of a philosophical school as being part of one and the same system, which may have had variants and been reformulated and transformed by later thinkers, but has basically remained the same. Therefore, philological and text-historical considerations are not particularly relevant for Garbe because he is convinced that true philosophy is always an 'integral whole' (Garbe 1917, 36). In his view, the Indian philosophical systems were not developed over centuries, but originally formulated as full-fledged, complete systems. While Deussen has a different, more evolutionistic view of the development of philosophical systems,[42] he—like Garbe—regards Indian philosophy as made up of systems, and in his presentation, employs Western categories. Exemplary in Deussen's

42 These differences become particularly apparent in the debate between Garbe and Deussen on the place of the epic *Mahābhārata* in the history of Indian philosophy, and whether it makes sense to speak of an 'epic philosophy'; see Malinar (2017).

method is the already mentioned lecture, 'On the Philosophy of the Vedānta in its Relations to Occidental Metaphysics'. Therein, Deussen organises the Vedānta system in

> four parts, which Śaṅkara's system contains, and every complete philosophical system must contain: (1) Theology, the doctrine of God or the philosophical principle; (2) Kosmology [*sic*], the doctrine of the world; (3) Psychology, the doctrine of the soul; (4) Eschatology, the doctrine of the last things, the things after death. (Deussen 1904, 244)

Another commonality between the two opponents is their goal to promote the study of Indian philosophy in Western philosophy departments. In doing so, Indian thought is presented as neither exotic nor other, nor even same, but rather as something (still) unfamiliar that should be explored, explained, and evaluated. They hoped that through their work, Indian philosophy would no longer be neglected or ignored, but rather would find a firm position in the general history of philosophy and thus also in the curricula of philosophy departments. This intention is one of the reasons for the monographic treatment that they accorded to philosophical systems. In the case of Deussen, this goal resulted in his ambitious, multi-volume *Allgemeine Geschichte der Philosophie mit besonderer Berücksichtigung der Religionen* ('General History of Philosophy with Special Consideration of the Religions'). The title indicates a departure from a conventional historiography of philosophy in its inclusion of 'religions'. Marchand (2009, 302) views this 'collapsing' of philosophy and religion as a strategy that allowed Deussen to include India in the general history of philosophy, and sees this as 'innovation'. But the reason that Deussen gives for this, namely that some religions hide their philosophy in a 'mythical garment', echoes an approach already employed by Schopenhauer in his praise of the 'wisdom' of ancient Indian thinkers, who were quite skillful in distinguishing knowledge from myth (*cf.* Schopenhauer 1844 [1819], § 63). Furthermore, Deussen is not the first to include India in a history of philosophy, and it is highly probable that he also intended to counter Hegel's form of making India part of his history of philosophy (see above). More remarkable is Deussen's treatment of India and Europe as autonomous, independent traditions, as is pointed out by Marchand, who then concentrates on his treatment of European philosophy. This postulate allowed him to avoid further engagement with the ongoing debate on the priority accorded to Greek philosophy by postulating the complete autonomy and independence of Indian thought.[43] As a consequence, his general history of philosophy consists of two independent histories, which, however, show remarkable parallels, and both of which need to be studied in order to get the complete picture. The two histories are dealt with in two volumes. The 'philosophy of the Indians', as Deussen tends to put it, is studied in Volume I, which comprises three parts dealing with the Veda, the Upaniṣads, and the post-Vedic period. Volume II covers—also in three parts—the philosophy of the Greeks, the Bible, and recent philosophy from Descartes to Schopenhauer.

Deussen justifies the room accorded to philosophy in India in the preface to Volume I by pointing out that Indian philosophy constitutes the only true parallel to 'Western-Asiatic' philosophy, as he called what is otherwise termed 'European' philosophy. In anticipation of the potential criticism that might be raised against such extensive treatment of India, Deussen states that Indian philosophical thinking is not only older than 'ours', but has also continued till date. In its intensity it can hardly be beaten by the Europeans, especially not the contemporary ones. In spite of its different interests, terms, and methods, the 'parallel universe' of Indian intellectual history has produced similar results with respect to philosophical positions and doctrines (Deussen 1894–1917, 1, 1, 7). Yet, Deussen also points out that any judgements about the intrinsic value of the Indian tradition have to be suspended for the time being, since more studies are necessary (ibid., ix). In any case, he claims that studying Indian philosophy could have a liberating effect on Europeans because it reveals the narrowness and limitations implied in the philosophical terminology and axioms that 'we' as Europeans apply to the world and to ourselves (ibid., x). Indian philosophy shows 'that there is a quite different way to understand things than that which Hegel has

43 In his book on ancient Indian philosophy, Garbe dedicated a whole chapter to this question and thought it probable that early Greek philosophy was indeed influenced by Indian philosophy (1897, 37).

construed as the only possible and reasonable one' (ibid., 36).[44] In this way, Deussen connects his plea to study the philosophy of the Indians with his criticism of the modern age, which Hegel had declared was the post-philosophical culmination of scientific reason.

However, this does not mean that he views science in opposition to philosophy and religion. Quite similar to other *fin-de-siècle* exponents of monistic positions, Vivekananda or Theosophy, for instance, he declares the 'truths' discovered in philosophy and religion to be in perfect harmony with scientific methods and proofs. According to him, Kant and Schopenhauer had perfected the earlier Indian and Greek systems by providing them with the true scientific basis they were lacking. While Plato and Śaṃkara had grasped the metaphysical truth by intuition, they were unable to prove it. One of the major points in the lecture he delivered in Bombay was that help for Plato and Śaṅkara had arrived with Kant. He states that his 'brothers in India' would be astonished 'to find in Germany the scientific substruction of their own philosophy, of the Advaita Vedānta! [...] The scientific proofs are not in Śaṅkara, not in Plato, but only in Kant' (Deussen 1904, 248). This is the message that Deussen sought to convey to his Indian audience: While they were always possessing and living the 'truth', the encounter with European thought is no threat but an affirmation, and most importantly, an encouragement to keep monistic Vedānta alive. Thus, for Deussen, there is nothing essentially 'new' in Kant's philosophy, but it is a milestone in the history of philosophy as it substantiates the old truths with new arguments and proofs. This is the achievement of Western thought in the modern period, while India had succeeded in keeping to the old and essential truths in the form of a living Advaita-Vedānta.

---

44 'Man würde vielleicht für naiv gehalten werden, wollte man unserm, in allen Stücken, "so herrlich weit"' fortgeschrittenen Zeitalter zumuten, von den alten Indern noch etwas zu lernen; aber einen Nutzen wird das allgemeinere Bekanntwerden der indischen Weltanschauung doch haben: diesen nämlich, uns zum Bewufstsein zu bringen, daß wir mit unserm gesamten religiösen und philosophischen Denken in einer kolossalen Einseitigkeit stecken, und daß es noch eine ganz andere Art, die Dinge anzufassen, geben kann, als die, welche Hegel als die allein mögliche und vernünftige konstruiert hat' (Deussen 1894–1917, 1, 1, 36).

The basis of the alliance between anti-materialist—and, by extension, anti-British—thinkers in India and Germany imagined by Deussen is certainly Eurocentric, in that it was based on the claim of superiority of Western scientific philosophy, providing Indians the means to better understand what they think and do.[45] Yet, the seriousness of the praise of a living Vedānta in India should not be downplayed since Deussen was indeed concerned—as were many of his contemporaries—about the practical consequences of the vanishing influence of religion and philosophy in the academy and society at large. He felt that Schopenhauer, Kant, and Advaita-Vedānta were badly needed during the cultural, even spiritual, crisis that contemporary Germany and Europe were currently undergoing. In her interpretation of this concern, Suzanne Marchand (2009, 300) calls Deussen a 'Schopenhauerian Christian' who ultimately wanted to prove the supremacy of Protestant Christianity. This is also mirrored in his history of philosophy when he depicts Western medieval philosophy as an unhappy mixture of Semitic and Christian elements, and claims that true philosophy can only unfold when purged of these 'Semitic' elements. Therefore, Deussen is not advocating a 'perennial philosophy' (as claimed by Heimann, for instance), and 'his history of philosophy is not only an "inclusive" one, it is also a racial one' (ibid., 306).[46] While this may certainly characterise some aspects of his

---

45 The acceptance of this claim lies at the core of the epistemic hegemony of 'Europe' implemented by colonial rule, as discussed by Chakrabarty (1992). The lecture was appraised in some quarters in India, and his interpretation was not accepted, endorsed, or adopted, not even by Vivekananda, although he found some of its aspects useful in lobbying his own agenda, in both India and the West.

46 Marchand explains:

> In some respects, his promotion of 'Aryan' ideas was a continuation of that anti-clerical, iconoclastic liberal tradition practiced by Voltaire or Max Müller—which [...] also already contained elements of racist thinking as well. Deussen hoped, above all, to use Schopenhauer and Indian philosophy to clean up Christianity, rather than to denigrate the Jews. (2009, 309)

Delfs stresses this point as well, although he detects racial stereotypes in Deussen's travel account and a mixture of religious and racist elements of anti-

treatment of Western philosophy in his *General History of Philosophy*, this does not apply to his depiction of the course that philosophy had taken in India. As discussed earlier, the low points of Indian thought, marked by a debasement of 'pure idealism', was not due to any mixture with 'alien' thoughts, but the result of the rise of realist Sāṃkhya philosophy brought on by a 'disease of the philosophical mind'. This setback has its parallels in the history of philosophy in the West, but with one difference—monistic idealism remained very much alive in India. The championing of a monistic Christianity is thus necessary in the West, but Deussen does not advocate any missionary activities in India (here, also following Schopenhauer's assessment).

Although on a smaller scale and with no intention of inscribing Indian thought into the general history of philosophy in the manner envisioned by Deussen, Garbe published his monograph on Sāṃkhya Philosophy (1894) with a similar thrust when he stated in the Preface: 'May this book help to remove the indifference of occidental philosophy towards her Indian sister' (Garbe 1895, v). In his general account of Indian philosophy, he ponders the reasons for the neglect:

> In the compendiums of the general history of philosophy the Indian systems are usually entirely omitted. lt now need not be proved that this is a mistake. An explanation of this indifference may be found in the fact that the Indian systems became known in Europe and America only in their roughest outlines in this century, and that even now only Buddhism and [...] Vedānta and Sāṃkhya, have been laid open to study by detailed works. (Garbe 1897, 55)

Twenty years later, not much seemed to have changed when Garbe noted: "The historical accounts of all philosophy used to leave the

Semitism (Delfs 2017, 124). Delfs states that it is difficult to decide whether his statements express his personal convictions, or if they are political tactics. On the one hand, Deussen was attacked by nationalist (*völkisch*) members of the Schopenhauer-Gesellschaft as '*verjudet*' because of his Jewish wife and his friendship with Henriette Hertz, also a Jew. On the other hand, he corresponded with Houston Chamberlain, one of the chief propagators of racist ideas of Aryan superiority (ibid., 125). See also Myers (2013, 178–184) on the reception of Deussen's 'prescriptive historical hermeneutics' in Chamberlain's texts.

Indian systems out of consideration [....] Generally the qualified specialists are facing Indian philosophy with unfounded indifference' (Garbe 1917, 135f.). He feels that change should now be underway, with all the editions, translations, and monographic treatments of Indian philosophical texts being made available.

Final Remarks

In their unique ways, both Garbe and Deussen had their own agenda in their academic engagement with Indian philosophy, which is in many respects 'Orientalist' and Eurocentric in the sense of subjecting Indian thought to Western philosophical categories and in applying taxonomies mirroring specific cultural-political agendas. However, they follow neither the 'romanticism-orientalism-Nazi ideology' pattern of constructing the history of German Indology, nor the distinction used by some scholars between German Sanskritists who show a sympathetic openness for India and those who advocate an 'Aryan superiority' (see note 10). In his depiction of Sanskrit Studies in Germany, Vivekananda spotted a 'new type' in which sympathies were combined with the ability to voice criticism and the philological approach was combined with an engagement with contents. In their engagement with Indian philosophy, Deussen and Garbe differed not only in their attitudes, but also in their methods, since they aimed to draw attention to what they viewed as valuable, perhaps even indispensable, modes and traditions of thought. Furthermore, the justification of a State-funded study of Sanskrit and Indian philosophy was an important aspect of their agendas. While their philosophical engagement cannot be separated from the cultural contexts in which India was hegemonically imagined and assessed in late nineteenth- and early twentieth-century Germany, their understanding of the relevance of Indian thought was not merely a historiographical and/or hegemonic exercise. Using their respective taxonomies, they claimed that Indian philosophy deserved to gain the attention of a larger academic public, in particular that of academic philosophers. In this way, they can be seen as representing a new generation of scholars who claimed greater relevance for their fields.

This constellation is not captured when scholarly perspectives are confined either to a monolithic or a binary classification of German attitudes towards India, such as being either 'open' (that is, a positive perception of India) or 'orientalist-national socialist' (that is, a negative perception, as it uses India to construe an 'Aryan race', in which the white Aryan takes the top position; see above). In their attempts to recommend the study of Indian philosophy to the larger academic public, Deussen and Garbe entertained a double-edged discourse of authority and justification, of advertising and criticising. Both based their translations, editions, and analyses of the terminology of Indian texts on philological methods, which they nonetheless set aside in their monographical treatment of the philosophical schools. In doing so, they presented Indian philosophy according to Western taxonomies, and by inserting them within contemporary models of the historiography of intellectual thought. The tension between philological methods and philosophical perspectives was clearly noticed by Vivekananda, and it is indeed an issue that concerns scholars working in this field even today. In employing his own taxonomies, Vivekananda applauded Deussen's overcoming of 'philological leanings', since it seemed to allow the latter to freely expose the philosophical truth of Vedānta philosophy. Like Vivekananda, Deussen and Garbe were quite aware that philological work in the mines of the texts (to use Vivekananda's metaphor) is not enough when dealing with Indian philosophy and attempting to draw attention to it. The classifications and interpretations that they launched in trying to seize philosophical territory brought them acclaim as well as criticism, the latter often connected to their alleged neglect of philological concerns. Since then, a great deal of work has been done by Indologists, but whether that has changed the lack of interest in Indian philosophy in the larger German (and European) academic context is another question. R.-P. Droit's take on the situation seems quite appropriate when he states that it is 'as if the attention philosophers give to Indian teachings is inversely proportional to the amount of erudition dedicated to them' (Droit 2004, 18; translation mine). Thus, while Deussen and Garbe, with their attempts to launch Indian philosophy as a subject of study, certainly helped to establish Indian philosophy as an area of specialisation in Indology, they failed by and large with respect to the philosophy department, where Indian philosophy has remained almost as marginal as it was in their time.

REFERENCES

Bagchi, Kaushik. 2003. 'An Orientalist in the Orient: Richard Garbe's Indian Journey, 1885–1886'. *Journal of World History* 14 (3), 281–325.

Baumgarten, M. 1997. *Professoren und Universitäten im 19. Jahrhundert. Zur Sozialgeschichte deutscher Geistes- und Naturwissenschaftler.* Göttingen: Vandenhoeck und Ruprecht.

Beckerlegge, Gwilym. 1998. 'Swami Vivekananda and *Sevā*: Taking "Social Service" Seriously'. In William Radice (ed.), *Swami Vivekananda and the Modernization of Hinduism*, 158–193. New Delhi: Oxford University Press.

———. 2000. *The Ramakrishna Mission. The Making of a Modern Hindu Movement.* Oxford: Oxford University Press.

———. 2006. *Swami Vivekananda's Legacy of Service: A Study of the Ramakrishna Math and Mission.* Oxford: Oxford University Press.

———. 2013. 'Swami Vivekananda (1863–1902) 150 Years On: Critical Studies of an Influential Hindu Guru'. *Religion Compass* 7 (10), 444–453.

Bruckner, Heidrun, et al. 2003. *Indienforschung im Zeitenwandel. Analysen und Dokumente zur Indologie und Religionswissenschaft in Tubingen.* Tubingen.

Chakrabarty, Dipesh. 1992. 'Postcoloniality and the Artifice of History: Who Speaks for "Indian" Pasts?' *Representations* 37, 1–16.

Colebrooke, H. T. 1828. *Essays on the Religion and Philosophy of the Hindus.* London: Williams and Norgate.

Cousin, Victor. 2018 [1829]. *Cours d'Histoire de la Philosophie Morale au Dix-Huitième Siècle.* France: Hachette Livre-BNF.

Delfs, Tobias. (2017). 'Devasena auf Reisen: Der Kieler Philosoph Paul Deussen, die Briten und der "Orient"'. In Oliver Auge and Martin Göllnitz (eds), *Mit Forscherdrang und Abenteuerlust: Expeditionen und Forschungsreisen Kieler Wissenschaftlerinnen und Wissenschaftler*, 107–145. Frankfurt am Main: Peter Lang.

Deussen, Paul. 1883. *Das System des Vedānta nach den Brahma-Sūtra's des Bādarāyaṇa und dem Commentare des Çaṅkara über dieselben als ein Kompendium der Dogmatik des Brahmanismus vom Standpunkte des Çaṅkara aus.* Leipzig.

Deussen, Paul. 1887. *Die Sûtra's des Vedânta oder die Çârîraka-Mîmâṅsa des Bādarāyaṇa: Nebst dem vollständigen Commentare des Çaṅkara aus dem Sanskrit übersetzt*. Leipzig.

———. 1890. *Die Elemente der Metaphysik: Als Leitfaden zum Gebrauche bei Vorlesungen sowie zum Selbststudium zusammengestellt*. Leipzig: Brockhaus.

———. 1894–1917. *Allgemeine Geschichte der Philosophie mit besonderer Berücksichtigung der Religionen*, Bd. 1, 1: *Allgemeine Einleitung und Philosophie des Veda bis auf die Upanishad*; Bd. 1, 2: *Die Philosophie der Upanishad's*; Bd. 1, 3: *Die Nachvedische Philosophie der Inder*; Bd. 2, 1: *Die Philosophie der Griechen*; Bd. 2, 2: *Die Philosophie der Bibel*; Bd. 2, 3: *Die Neuere Philosophie von Descartes bis Schopenhauer*. Leipzig: Brockhaus.

———. 1897. *Sechzig Upanishad's des Veda aus dem Sanskrit übersetzt und mit Eineitung und Anmerkungen versehen*. Leipzig: Brockhaus.

———. 1904. *Erinnerungen an Indien. Mit einer Karte, 16 Abbildungen und einem Anhange: On the Philosophy of the Vedānta in its Relations to Occidental Metaphysics*. Leipzig and Kiel: Lipsius & Tischer.

———. 1922. *Mein Leben*, Erika Rosenthal-Deussen (ed.). Leipzig: Brockhaus.

Droit, Roger-Pol. 2004. *L'oubli de l'Inde: Une amnésie philosophique*. Paris: PUF.

Feldhoff, H. 2008. *Nietzsches Freund. Die Lebensgeschichte des Paul Deussen*. Köln: Böhlau Verlag.

Garbe, Richard. 1888. *Sāṃkhya Sūtra Vṛtti or Aniruddha's Commentary and the Original Parts of Vedāntin Mahadeva's Commentary*. Bibliotheca Indica 122. Calcutta: Asiatic Society.

———. 1889a. *Sāṃkhya-pravacana-bhāṣya: Vijñānabhikṣu's Commentar zu den Sāṃkhyasūtras*. Leipzig: Brockhaus.

———. 1889b. *Indische Reiseskizzen*. Berlin: Paetel (2nd edn München, 1925).

———. 1891. *Der Mondschein der Sāṃkhya-Wahrheit*. Abhandlungen der Bayerischen Akademie der Wissenschaften 19 (3). München: K. Akademie.

———. 1891–1892. *Aniruddha's Commentary and the Original Parts of Vedântin Mahâdeva's Commentary on the Sâṃkhya Sûtras, Transl. with an Introduction on the Age and Origin of the Sâṃkhya System*. Calcutta: Baptist Mission Press.

———. 1892. *The Sāmkhya Sūtra Vṛitti or Aniruddha's Commentary and the Original Parts of Vedântin Mahâdeva's Commentary to the Sâṃkhya Sûtras/ Edited with Indices*. Bibliotheca Indica 131. Calcutta: Asiatic Society.

———. 1894a. *Die Sāṃkhya-Philosophie, eine Darstellung des indischen Rationalismus*. Leipzig: Haessel (2nd edn, Leipzig 1917).

———. 1894b. *The Philosophy of Ancient India*. Chicago: The Open Court Publishing House.

———. 1895. *The Sāṃkhya-pravacana-bhāṣya or Commentary on the Exposition of the Sānkhya Philosophy by Vijñānabhikṣu*, Harvard Oriental Series 2. Cambridge, MA: Harvard University Press.

———. 1903. 'Die Witwenverbrennung'. In *Beiträge zur indischen Kulturgeschichte*, 141–182. Berlin: Deutsche Rundschau.

Girardot, N. J. 2002. 'Max Müller's "Sacred Books" and the Nineteenth-Century Production of the Comparative Science of Religions'. *History of Religions* 41, 213–250.

Green, Thomas J. 2016. *Religion for a Secular Age: Max Müller, Swami Vivekananda and Vedanta*. London: Routledge.

———. 2017. '"The Spirit of the Vedānta": Occultism and Piety in Max Müller and Swami Vivekananda's Interpretation of Ramakrishna'. *Numen* 64, 229–257.

Hacker, Paul. 1961. 'Schopenhauer und die Ethik des Hinduismus'. *Saeculum* 12, 366–399.

Halbfass, Wilhelm. 1988. *India and Europe: An Essay in Understanding*. Albany: State University of New York Press.

———. 1995. 'Practical Vedānta'. In V. Dalmia and H. von Stietencron (eds), *Representing Hinduism: The Construction of Religious Traditions and National Identity*, 211–223. New Delhi: Sage.

———. 1997. 'Research and Reflection: Responses to my Respondents. II. Cross-Cultural Encounters and Dialogue'. *Poznań Studies in the Philosophy of the Sciences and the Humanities* 59, 141–159.

Hansert, Andreas. 2010. *Schopenhauer im 20. Jahrhundert. Geschichte der Schopenhauer-Gesellschaft*. Köln: Bohlau.

Hegel, G. W. F. 1979a. *Berliner Schriften*, Werke, Band 11, 1818–1831. Frankfurt am Main: Suhrkamp.

———. 1979b. *Vorlesungen über die Geschichte der Philosophie*, Werke, Band 18, 1830–1833. Frankfurt am Main: Suhrkamp.

Heimann, Betty. 1931. 'Paul Deussen und die heutige Indologie'. *Schopenhauer Jahrbuch* 18, 246–254.

Kontje, Todd. 2004. *German Orientalisms*. Ann Arbor: University of Michigan Press.

Maharaj, Ayon. 2020. 'Śivajñāne jīver sevā: Reexamining Swami Vivekananda's Practical Vedānta in the Light of Sri Ramakrishna'. *Journal of Dharma Studies* 2 (2), 175–187.

Malinar, Angelika. 2003. '"Kṣatriya-Glaube" und "Opferwesen": Richard Garbe und die indischen Religionen'. In H. Brückner, et al. (eds), *Indien-Forschung im Zeitenwandel: Analysen und Dokumente zur Indologie und Religionswissenschaft in Tübingen*, 121–141. Tübingen: Attempto.

Malinar, Angelika. 2007. *The Bhagavadgītā: Doctrines and Contexts*. Cambridge: Cambridge University Press.

——. 2017. 'Philosophy in the *Mahābhārata* and the History of Indian Philosophy'. *Journal of Indian Philosophy* 45 (4), 587–604.

Marchand, Suzanne. 2009. *German Orientalism in the Age of Empire: Religion, Race, and Scholarship*. New York: Cambridge University Press.

Müller, Friedrich Max. 1903. *The Six Systems of Indian Philosophy*. New York: Longmans & Green.

Myers, Perry. 2013. *German Visions of India 1871–1918: Commandeering the Ganges during the Kaiserreich*. London: Palgrave.

Patil, Vinutha S. 2016. 'Swami Vivekananda on Service'. *Pragmata: Journal of Human Sciences* 3 (1), 83–93.

Pfister, Manfred. 1993. 'Intertextuelles Reisen, oder: Der Reisebericht als Intertext'. In Herbert Foltinek, Wolfgang Riehle, and Waldemar Zacharasiewicz (eds), *Tales and 'their telling difference'*, 109–132. Heidelberg: Winter.

Pollock, Sheldon. 1993. 'Deep Orientalism? Notes on Sanskrit and Power beyond the Raj'. In C. A. Breckenridge and P. van der Veer (eds), *Orientalism and the Postcolonial Predicament: Perspectives on South Asia*, 76–133. Philadelphia: University of Pennsylvania Press.

Pratt, M. L. 1992. *Imperial Eyes: Travel Writing and Transculturation*. London, New York: Routledge.

Rhys-Davids, T. W. 1903–04. 'Oriental Studies in England and Abroad'. *Proceedings of the British Academy* 1, 183–197.

Rolland, Romain. 1928. 'Vivekananda et Paul Deussen'. *Schopenhauer Jahrbuch* 15, 153–165.

Rollmann, Hans. 1978. 'Deussen, Nietzsche, and Vedānta'. *Journal of the History of Ideas* 39 (1), 125–132.

Schopenhauer, Arthur. 1844 [1819]. *Die Welt als Wille und Vorstellung*. Erster Band, vier Bücher, nebst einem Anhange, der die Kritik der Kantischen Philosophie enthält. Leipzig: Brockhaus (2nd improved and extended edn).

Sengupta, Indra. 2005. *From Salon to Discipline: State, University and Indology in Germany (1821–1914)*. Würzburg: Ergon Verlag.

Swami Nikhilananda. 1953. *Vivekananda: A Biography*. New York: Ramakrishna Center.

Telang, K. T. 1882. *The Bhagavadgîtâ, Together with the Sanatsugâtîya and the Anugîtâ, Translated*, Sacred Books of the East, Vol. 8. Oxford: Clarendon.

The Life of Swami Vivekananda by his Eastern and Western Disciples. Calcutta: Advaita Ashrama, 1960 [1912], 6e.

Thibaut, G. 1890–1904. *The Vedanta-Sutras, with the Commentary of Saṅkarācarya and Rāmānuja Translated*, 3 vols, Sacred Books of the East 34, 38, 48. Oxford: Clarendon.

Tylor, E. B. 1871. *Primitive Culture: Researches into the Development of Mythology, Philosophy, Religion, Art, and Custom*, 2 vols. London: Murray.

Vivekananda. 1995. *The Complete Works of Swami Vivekananda*, Mayavati Memorial Edition, 8 vols. Calcutta: Advaita Ashram.

vom Brocke, Bernhard (ed.). 1991. *Wissenschaftsgeschichte und Wissenschaftspolitik im Industriezeitalter. Das 'System Althoff' in historischer Perspektive*. Hildesheim: Verlag A. Lax.

Eight

The Post-Historical Subject as Project

Some Communicological Reflections

RAJENDRA DENGLE

Engaging with the interface of literature and the new media philosophically is a relatively recent phenomenon in the academic curricula of German Studies in Indian universities. The theories of the new media (the 'Medial Turn') have not only taken forward the discourse of literature and culture in a creative manner by focussing on the new challenges posed to the Gutenberg galaxy, but they have also tried to re-map the history of culture by reflecting deeply on the relationship between the subject and the object of knowledge, the written word, the spoken word, and the visual image, and between philosophy, religion, science, and technology. That these reflections could perhaps throw a different light on Indo-German intellectual encounters is a challenge—and a promise—that needs to be fulfilled.

Courses such as the History of German Literature and *Landeskunde* (information on German-speaking countries), while reconstructing the context in which German literature needs to be studied, do touch upon the Indo-German intellectual encounters, but more in the manner of disseminating information—names, facts, and figures. The tacit desire to 'compare cultures', to 'understand the other in that one understood oneself' in the basic hermeneutic sense, which takes root in every learner of foreign languages in the beginning and blossoms as s/he becomes a student of literary or cultural studies, seldom evolves into a seriously self-reflective and critical research interest. And if it does evolve at an advanced stage to focus on travelogues, contemporary literary texts that have India as a theme, films, multilingualism, migrant literature, and so on, one finds that it is not just concepts from disciplines such as anthropology or ethnology that are used without deeper theoretical reflection or apperception, but that a hasty refuge is sought behind the protective façade of postcolonial theory, bringing the discourse to an end rather than allowing it to grow in openness. It is important that the interdisciplinary, intertextual, and intercultural approach does not remain a programmatic concept, but is institutionally encouraged, practised, and sustained in a creative, open-minded manner.

Dealing with the History of German Literature theoretically within the framework of philosophical debates around historicism reveals a methodological chasm between the positivistic, objective, and the 'scientific', and the phenomenological-hermeneutic perceptions of knowledge. Not only does the positivistic perception not consider the experience of the subject a reliable source of knowledge, but it also relegates the expression of this experience in various forms of art and literature to the peripheral realm of aesthetics. The hermeneutic perception, by contrast, does the very opposite: by shifting the focus to the subject of knowledge and its experience, along with the expression of this experience and its understanding, it moves away from the definition of the object of knowledge as a 'given' to one that is produced, constructed, and that owes its existence to the effect that it has on the recipient. Various forms of art and literature find that, through their ability to bring about a change in the perception of their recipient, they have become important sources of knowledge about the past, and since the reception is an action that takes place in the present, they can actually do justice to *aesthesis*, *poiesis*, *catharsis*, and *phronesis* together, and help the recipient to create meaning out of his existence and try and find answers to the three main questions that Kant formulated: 'What can I know? What ought I to do? And what can I hope?' (Kant 1998, 677). Can this knowledge give me a vision that lends my life a direction and a purpose, yielding meaning to each new day? Does this bring me in touch with my feelings and emotions, for my ability to deal with these sets me free in the true sense of the term? Or do I give in to the pressures of my compulsive thinking and hastily pack this knowledge up in thought and concept clusters and delude myself into believing that I have practised a most effective critique of culture and am emancipated?[1]

---

1 See Buber (1951, 8):

> My rationality, my rational power of thought is merely a part, a particular function of my nature; when however I 'believe', in either sense, my entire being is engaged, the totality of my nature enters into the process [....]

This tradition, which arguably begins with Vico and flows along Herder, Droysen, Schiller, the Schlegel brothers, Novalis, Dilthey, all the way to Schopenhauer and Nietzsche, opens itself up to the epistemological, metaphysical traditions of other cultures, resulting not merely in widening the horizons of knowledge, but in deepening its understanding of experience itself in a willingness to see things differently, which leads to a critique of its own cultural memory. While one branch of this tradition grows in the direction of Greenblatt's New Historicism and Poetics of Culture in our times, the other sustains its focus on the human subject and its relationship with language. While the relationship between these two is both obvious and fascinating, the latter will be of particular interest within the present context, for it is here that a dialogue between European and Indian philosophical thought appears to be exploring the possibilities of defining the human subject, its language, and its understanding of the culture of communication amongst subjects differently.

Two early twentieth-century examples from German literature may serve as cases in point to initiate this debate. The text of Fritz Mauthner's *Buddha* (1921) and Hugo von Hofmannsthal's *Ein Brief* ('The Letter of Lord Chandos') are both expressions of their reflections on the crisis of the modern European subject as a crisis of language and communication (see also Dengle 2001–2002, 2013; Kocher 2013).

Mauthner's Buddha 'recovers' his desire to live when he finds that Subhadda, an uninitiated listener (who has actually been sent to listen to his discourses with the intention of exposing the Buddha as a fraud), 'understands' his teaching of non-self as love (*maitri*), whereas Ananda, Buddha's star student, who has memorised the teaching accurately and is confident about taking the master's place after he has passed on, can only repeat the master's teachings word for word. While Ananda busies himself with the judicious distribution of the parts of the master's body after his death among the followers and orders the

---

To be sure we are not allowed to substitute 'feeling' for this personal totality; feeling is by no means 'everything' as Faust thinks, but is at best only an indication of the fact that the being of the man is about to unite and become whole, and in other cases it is an illusion of becoming a whole without its being actually effected.

uninitiated Hindu Subhadda to be chained and sent back to his master Kassapa, who would later order the 'traitor' Subhadda to be stoned to death, the reader finds the Buddha thanking Subhadda for the love that he brought him. His last teaching is to Subhadda alone, for he alone can understand him, asking him not to be of any institution, but be true to his own self. The Buddha confesses to Subhadda that he now has a new desire to live, to begin a new life. Subhadda is his true echo, not the efficient repetition of Ananda and the other initiated monks. In the unconditional love that Subhadda has for the Buddha lies the potential for survival of the Buddha's teaching. Although Mauthner seems to be in favour of 'a master narrative of salvation through faith'—or love—'replacing a master narrative of emancipation through enlightenment', his critique of language, or 'mysticism minus God', cannot have religion as a closed system, precluding the possibility of religious conflict. Mauthner's Buddha becomes in a sense Barlaam and Subhadda becomes Josaphat (see MacQueen 1998). Subhadda and the Buddha both bring each other out of their apparent separate selves and, in their difference to each other and their love for each other, make the *Gespräch* (dialogue/conversation) in the sense of Gadamer a real possibility, while showing, in the methodological sense, the possibility of realising Mauthner's utopia of aesthetic being, of regaining confidence in language and creating a society based on meaningful communication.

Hofmannsthal's Chandos 'recovers' his willingness to write, to communicate in spite of being aware that he has absolutely no power over the meaning that his reader/listener may find in what he has to say. This entails the realisation that intense engagement with one's own self may lead to isolation ('*selbstische Erstarrung*', that is, self-absorbed fossilisation, paralysis), whereas understanding it as such and overcoming it opens up a way of life with a different understanding of the self and the other: '*Der Weg zum Sozialen* [*ist*] *als Weg zum höheren Selbst: der nichtmystische Weg* [*zu verstehen*]' ('Turning to the Social is finding the way to the higher self: the non-mystical way'; translation mine)[2] (see Diersch 1977, 1981).

---

2 Excerpts from these articles of Diersch can be found under the title 'Selbstentfremdung und Depersonalisation der Wiener Dichter um die Jahrhundertwende' (von Hofmannsthal 1981, 34–38).

Manfred Diersch points to the constellation of Hugo von Hofmannsthal, Hermann Bahr (*Ichlosigkeit*—the 'I'-lessness), and Ernst Mach (*Das unrettbare Ich*—'the irretrievable I') while providing an insight into its relationship with the philosophy of Mauthner. He describes the latter as a self-reflective positivism, or, if we use a category of literary history in the sense of Hermann Broch, as an *erweiterter Naturalismus* (extended naturalism):

> Hofmannsthal and Bahr found a justification for this sensualistic subjectivism in Frits Mauthner's critique of language. Mauthner supported the impressionistic worldview with his philosophy of language: according to him 'no two human beings speak the same language; the standpoint of the individual determines the difference of all horizons. These different horizons are realized in the language and thus emerges the misery of loneliness ... from the language.' *Thinkers therefore have the task of finding a language which can recreate the 'play of associations' within the various subject-realities.*[3]

While talking about Ernst Mach's '*Das unrettbare Ich*' ('the irretrievable I') in his *Überwindung des Naturalismus* or 'Refutation of Naturalism', Hermann Bahr says: 'Sensations alone are the truth, the dependable and undisputable truth; the I has always been—and is—a construction.'[4]

References to their libraries with titles from the philosophies of India and the Far East and discussions on how these have influenced

---

[3] 'Die sprachphilosophische Begründung dieses sensualistischen Subjektivismus fanden Hofmannsthal und Bahr bei Fritz Mauthner in dessen Werk *Beiträge zu einer Kritik der Sprache.* Mauthner stützte die impressionistische Weltsicht mit sprachphilosophischer Argumentation: Nach ihm gibt es nicht zwei Menschen, die die gleiche Sprache reden. "Der Standpunkt des Einzelnen bedingt die Verschiedenheit aller Horizonte." Diese verschiedenen Horizonte seien in der Sprache realisiert, und so komme "alles Elend der Einsamkeit [...] von der Sprache. "*Aufgabe der Denker müsse es darum sein, eine Sprache zu finden, die 'das Spiel der Assoziationen' innerhalb der verschiedenen Subjektwirklichkeiten nachbildet*' (see Hofmannsthal 1981, 36, 37; translation and emphasis mine).

[4] 'Die Sensationen allein sind Wahrheit, zuverlässige und unwiderlegliche Wahrheit; das Ich ist immer schon Konstruktion' (see Beniston 1998, 9; translation mine).

their understanding of the human subject are most obviously present in the case of both Mauthner and Hofmannsthal (see, for Hofmannsthal, Mistry 1972). This is also true of Martin Buber, the 'forgotten classical philosopher of communication' (see Bidlo 2007), who was for many years Professor of Comparative History of Religion at the University of Frankfurt (see Friedman 1976). Buber's interaction with Rabindranath Tagore and his correspondence with Mahatma Gandhi are known, as is his piece on Sri Ramakrishna ('From his Life', based on the notes of his disciple Swami Vivekananda) in *Ecstatic Confessions: The Heart of Mysticism* (Buber 1996 [1909], 13–17)—which, according to Friedman, is perhaps the first mystical anthology. Friedman has explained the evolution of Buber's early Vedantist position into a 'mature philosophy' of 'I and Thou' with its focus on dialogicity and communicability of knowledge, in the sense that we spoke of earlier in the context of Mauthner and Hofmannsthal. Friedman quotes Buber thus:

> [...] only in the primitive word of India is the 'I' proclaimed that is one with the 'All' and with the 'One'. The unity which the mystic experiences when he has brought all his former multiplicity into Oneness is not a relative unity, for the ecstatic man no longer has outside of himself others with whom he has community. It is the absolute, unlimited Oneness which includes all others.[5] (Friedman 1976, 415)

Friedman points out that,

> [...] In *Ecstatic Confessions* [...] Buber speaks of the paradox that all mystics want to communicate, and [...] enter the reality of the *I and the Thou, the Many and the One. 'We turn inward and listen, and we do now know which sea it is that we hear.'* Buber was closer here to the qualified non-dualist position of *Ramanuja* than to *Sankara* [...] In the book *Daniel,* [...] Buber refers to the Vedanta unmistakably [...] *as one of the false paths that we can take on the way to the 'final teaching'.* [...] But the experience of this wrong path confirms that the unity that was

5 See also, among many of his other writings, Martin Buber's *Der Geist des Orients und das Judentum* for insights into the difference that Buber points out between the Occidental and the Oriental man, and the historically significant role that the Jew has to play in creating a bridge of dialogical understanding between the two in that he changes himself. In Buber, *Werkausgabe, 2.1 Mythos und Mystik—Frühe religionswissenschaftliche Schriften*, 187–203.

> found outside the world can be won again in the world. [...] (Friedman 1976, 414; emphasis mine)

In this sense, it is possible to interpret Vilém Flusser's experiments with the philosophies of India and the Far East. Even as a young man of seventeen or eighteen, Flusser was deeply impressed by Buber's thought and presence (Bidlo 2009). Flusser writes about this experience:

> He left an unbelievable impression on me. The great black beard, that strong figure and that look in his eyes! Those were the eyes of a seer! And he spoke not about the dialogical life, but about the prejudice against God. It was amazing the way he said it. In this lecture of his it became clear to me what Buber meant with his 'I-and-Thou', how he understood the dialogical life. And in this way I got an insight into the Judeo-Christian wisdom, according to which 'loving your neighbor the way you love yourself' is the only way to come to God. (ibid., 58; rough translation mine)

Unlike the 'other' Vilém from Prague—that is, Vilém (Willy) Haas, who lived in exile in Bombay from 1939–1947 and contributed creatively to Indian cinema as well as to the teaching of German literature (see Bhatti 2002)—Vilém Flusser, one of the most influential thinkers of media and cultural theory as well as the philosophy of communication in the second half of the twentieth century, landed in 1940 not on Indian but on Brazilian shores like 'floating wreckage of a ship that is washed ashore':

> One had learnt from Kant that Time and Space are categories of understanding, not realities in themselves. But now, in the bottomlessness of the shadowlike existence, in being uprooted and driven away, as one landed on the shores of Brazil, washed ashore as floating wreckage, what one had learnt theoretically, became part of one's immediate experience.[6] (Flusser 1999, 39; translation mine)

[6] 'Dass es sich bei Raum und Zeit um Wahrnehmungsformen handelt, also nicht um "Wirklichkeiten", das hatte man bei Kant theoretisch gelernt. Aber jetzt, in der Bodenlosigkeit des schattenhaften Daseins, in der entwurzelten Getriebenheit, in der man von den Wellen der Sinnlosigkeit, Strandgut gleich, an die brasilianische Küste geworfen wurde, wurde das theoretisch Erlernte zu unmittelbar Erlebtem.' All subsequent quotes are with page numbers in brackets and have been roughly translated by me.

Bodenlos ('Bottomless/Abyss') is Flusser's 'philosophical autobiography', in which this *Erzähler der Krise*, 'narrator of crisis' (see Neswald 1998), shares with his reader in the chapter 'Das Spiel mit dem Orient und mit dem Selbstmord' ('The Play with the Orient and Suicide') how he turned to these philosophies—not out of any academic interest, but out of an 'existential need'. In Prague itself, while formally studying philosophy, he had felt an instinctive dislike for the specialised form of philosophising as practised in universities. Long before the computer, Flusser thought that this form of philosophy could better be handled by machines than by human beings. He was in search of 'a method which would free him of all thinking, in order that he could get on with the business of living and find a way back into reality' (Flusser 1999, 54).

Flusser was devastated; he had lost his entire family in Auschwitz and Buchenwald. The cultural diversity of Prague, its civilised intellectual and aesthetic richness, and what life as a Prager had taught him about 'being human', had to be bracketed as memory in the sense of Husserl's method of phenomenological reduction. In this utter disorientation he had to learn to find an answer to two statements about life and the world which had kept haunting him, one made by Wittgenstein—'Nicht *wie* die Welt ist, ist das Geheime, sondern *dass* sie ist' ('Not *how* the world is, is the secret, but *that* it is')—and the other by Kafka: 'Ich habe mein Leben damit verbracht, die Lust zu bekämpfen, es zu beenden' ('I have spent my life in fighting the desire to end it') (Flusser 1999, 52). Having arrived at the crossroads where he either had to put an end to life—but 'one was too much of a coward to do that'—or 'give in to a dim feeling that there was probably still a duty he had to fulfill', Flusser decided 'to face the playful horror of daily life' (ibid., 53).[7]

Despite the 'obviousness' with which he turned to the 'Oriental' traditions in this situation, Flusser was aware that he had to consciously let go of the Occidental traditions, not only their various models of thought, but also their foundation. After all, this was what *Bodenlosigkeit* meant. Yet, he emphasised that unlike the American youth a generation later, he was not looking for salvation in India

7 'Dem spielerischen Grauen des täglichen Lebens die Stirn zu bieten.'

or China. But also not in the sense of Otto, Jung, or Eliade, who, Flusser said, were still trying to posit a Being, whereas he had turned to the East because,

> [...] he believed to have found here methods which could lead to a release to which the dialectics of being and not being actually did not apply. This inability to differentiate between the two was in fact the overcoming of thinking, and that precisely was what one was wanting to aim at. In other words, one believed to have understood in the sense of Rilke that we know too well to differentiate and that is where the roots of our confusion and our loss of desire lie.[8] (ibid., 58)

With this understanding, Flusser began his engagement with Indian and Japanese philosophies, taking them to be an 'instruction manual' or a guide that would help him overcome the Self. The Indian 'method' he called the 'Yoga method', which aimed at strengthening the will behind the thinking so that you thought only what needed to be, or had to be, thought. The other he called the 'Buddhist method', which aimed at killing the will to think and therefore at not willing to think at all. He saw soon enough that the two were complementary, for the will which the one sought to strengthen and the other to kill did not mean, as Schopenhauer understood it, suffering or life, but a kind of 'getting out of oneself'—*ein Außersichsein*. 'The Indian method aims at getting out of oneself in order to overcome oneself. The Far Eastern one aims at falling into oneself in order to overcome oneself' (Flusser 1999, 60).[9]

While putting the knowledge of these methods into practice—and it seems he did it for some years—Flusser became increasingly aware of the difference and the tension between what he imagined

---

[8] 'Es schien einem, dass das Vernichten des Denkens durch orientalische Methoden zu einer Auflösung führen kann, von der es keinen Sinn hat, sie als Sein oder Nichtsein bezeichnen zu wollen. Dieses Unvermögen zu unterscheiden war eben das Überwinden von Denken, und dies war es ja, was man erzielen wollte. Mit anderen Worten, man glaubte mit Rilke zu erkennen, dass wir allzu gut unterscheiden und dass darin die Wurzel unserer Verzweiflung und unseres Nichtseinwollens liegt.'

[9] 'Die indische Methode zielt darauf ab, außer sich zu kommen, um sich zu überwinden. Die fernöstliche zielt darauf ab, in sich zu fallen, um sich zu überwinden.'

the methods promised (viz., dissolution of the old self, *Auflösung*; freedom from thinking, *Befreiung vom Denken*; and overcoming the self, *Selbstüberwindung*) and what he actually experienced. While the promises do not come true, he feels on the one hand that the whole thing was just 'intellectual masturbation', the honest admission of which was extremely humiliating, and on the other, he feels at times as if he were experiencing something similar to the 'virtuosity of a gymnast in a circus', or as if he were a 'clown' who kept throwing up at the sight of himself and wished he could take his own life. He can no longer sustain these 'illuminating' practices because he is so disgusted with what he sees and experiences. After 'a few good moments' and 'many bad ones', he by and large perceived himself as a 'Fakir with crooked limbs', not an 'emancipated Sadhu' (Flusser 1999, 60).

The stifling feeling of disgust with these 'spiritual' practices, which to Flusser lacked any sense for the aesthetic, any sense of creatively and actively participating in life and the world, made him abandon them, but the insights into his own inner world—into the nature of his 'I' as a virtual reality, as culturally formed, as a programmed construct—'catapult[ed] him into the outer spaces' with an energy and passion never experienced before. There is now a narratological dimension to his life and work, a distance between his self, the observer, and his self, the actor. The process of becoming a 'Brazilian writer' follows: writer as a 'nomad', as an 'immigrant', as a 'translator', between cultures, between worlds, hovering over cultures, and at the same time aware of this moving 'third space', this floating above cultures as progressive transcendence of the I, as progressive self-alienation: 'You see yourself as hovering, and since you perceive yourself as an I that has been formed by one of the transcended cultures, you experience this hovering as a continuous transcending of your own self, or as a progressive self-alienation' (ibid., 76).[10]

Flusser describes in detail this complex cultural experience as that of a 'classic immigrant' who, living in the border region between cultures, also finds himself witnessing an active dialectic

---

10 'Man sieht sich selbst in der Schwebe, und da man sich selbst als ein "Ich" erkennt, das von einer der überstiegenen Kulturen geformt wurde, erlebt man das Schweben als ein fortschreitendes Übersteigen des eigenen Ich, als progressive Selbstentfremdung.'

of remembering, forgetting, and again remembering, while trying to learn Portuguese as a language in which he could express this experience and finding that he himself was changing substantially in the process:

> The dialectics that characterises each relation between the subject attempting to inform some material, and that material which is to be informed, thus came between you and the material. Epistemologically, this means that you tried to arrive at the essence of the language in order to change it, and were yourself substantially altered in the process.[11] (Flusser 1999, 79)

These lines cannot but make you think of Benjamin's essay, 'Task of the Translator'. Flusser, who described his life's work as a 'translational activity'—writing in four languages, translating-rewriting his thoughts all the time—understood it more as a 'dialogical' activity in a sense similar to Martin Buber than as a 'discourse'. Flusser's subject has experienced the end of a certain form of history, which had insisted on maintaining the difference between the human subject and the object of its knowledge while creating knowledge through the available means of language and communicating this knowledge to other 'subjects'. It had then witnessed paradigmatic shifts in this methodology, which had resulted in the circular movement of hermeneutics turning the contours of the subject and object of knowledge progressively fluid. It had witnessed how poetic realism had tried to 'save' the subject, and how subsequent movements in the field of art and literature of the *fin de siècle* increasingly included the subject in their focus of attention. Flusser's subject had also been receptive to Buber's dialogical philosophy, which had displaced the inherited worldview based on the subject-object difference and overcome a whole tradition of philosophy based on the subject by introducing the two entirely different original word pairs (*Urwörter*) of I-Thou

---

11 'Die Dialektik, die jedes Verhältnis zwischen dem Subjekt, welches ein Material informieren will, und dem Material, welches informiert werden soll, kennzeichnet, stellte sich also zwischen einen selbst und die portugiesische Sprache. Epistemologische bedeutet das, dass man versuchte, bis zum Wesen der Sprache vorzudringen, um es verändern zu können, und dass man dabei selbst wesentliche verändert wurde.'

and I-It—*Ich-Du* and *Ich-Es*—whereby 'the "I" is no longer a given, but a result of interaction' (Bidlo 2009, 59).[12] Buber had defined the two different attitudes, or stances, which would decide the nature of this interaction.

In this sense, in the *Bodenlosigkeit* of Flusser's subject, the old epistemological insistence is categorically rejected as a paradigm that cannot create new information or give meaning to human life. Without turning into a cultural pessimist, this 'new' subject—a subject who has painstakingly struggled to put the experience of the Holocaust behind it, has fought resentments which, had it given in to them, would have produced another clone of the past subject—is therefore 'free' to investigate the postmodern reality and how technology and the New Media work in it (see Flusser 2013 [1983]).[13] Having understood the old self as a 'projection', as a 'virtual self', accepting the process of continual movement between the *I-Thou* and the *I-It* as a 'continual becoming of the self' (see Steinhoff Smith 1989), Flusser's subject builds further on the understanding of Mauthner, Hofmannsthal, and Buber. There is a 'paradigm shift' (see Ströhl 2002, xiii).[14] The entire tone of Flusser's philosophy is optimistic—'from despair to hope' (see Flusser 2013 [1983], 2).

---

12 For Bidlo, *I-Thou* presents in Buber's philosophical journey a 'sociological turn', which informs his *Kulturkritik* on the lines of Nietzsche and makes it possible to identify similarities between the thought of Simmel, Mead, and Bakhtin.

13 Flusser writes:

> [. . .] it is not possible to condemn Auschwitz and continue to be Western, [. . .] and continue to adhere consciously to the West. Auschwitz is not a violation of Western models of behavior, it is, on the contrary, the result of the application of such models. Our culture allowed its mystifying mask to fall at Auschwitz and reveal its real face. The face of a monster that objectifies man. Our culture has shown that it must be rejected in toto if we admit that the purpose of every culture is to allow for the convivial existence of men that recognize each other mutually as subjects. (2013 [1983], 7)

14 'Thomas Kuhn's hypothesis of the paradigm shift describes a process in which a quantity of existing problems within one discursive model turns into a qualitatively new model. This hypothesis served Flusser repeatedly as a metaphor' (Ströhl 2002, Introduction, xiii).

> In the light of Husserl's notion of the life-world as a network of concrete intentionalities, Flusser foresees the coming technological implementation of a telematic culture that will establish a 'relationship of mutual respect' (Anerkennungsverhältnis) among individuals [....] The 'Enlightenment Project', aiming for the emancipation from restrictions of all kinds, begun in the eighteenth century by philosophers such as Locke, Hume, Rousseau, and Kant and an unfinished project to this very day, runs parallel to developments in technology, for all revolutions are technological revolutions, and they help realize the project for humanization.

Ströhl quotes Flusser:

> A telematized society will be exactly the network of pure relationships that Husserl defines as the concrete structure of the social phenomenon [...]. We can see, then, in what sense it may be said that Husserl has done away with humanism. Instead of the individual man being the supreme value, it is now the dialogue between men that becomes the supreme value, or what Martin Buber, whose thought was profoundly influenced by Husserl, called the 'dialogical life' [*das dialogische Leben*]. (Ströhl 2002, xiv)

That one has inherited a programmed linear mediality, which privileged the written word over the image, need not—must not, and cannot—continue to manipulate the post-historical subject. If that subject chooses to not remain a mere recipient but becomes a 'sender' in the sense of Brecht's Radio Theory (Enzensberger 1979), or an 'Operator-Apparatus' in the sense of Flusser, or an 'Actor-Network' in the sense of Bruno Latour and opens up to the idea of himself as a 'node in a playful network of intermedial relationships', he 'recovers' the medial and communicative nature of a medium which is constantly in danger of being reduced to a mere means of distributing information in the *Kulturindustrie*. Buber had pointed out the difference between the Oriental and the Occidental man, at the risk of being oversimplistic, whereby the 'motoric' Oriental man perceives individual things, including himself, not as existing separately from each other but as 'nodes in an endless movement' of which he is a witness (Buber 2013b).[15]

[15] 'Ich möchte den orientalischen Menschentypus [...] als den motorischen im Gegensatz zum sensorischen ansprechen, [...] Das Weltbild des

What ensues for a subject attracted by such nomadic freedom and convinced that it can help it create new meaning? Flusser says:

> The purpose of human communication is to make us forget the meaningless context in which we are completely alone and incommunicado, that is, the world in which we are condemned to solitary confinement and death: the world of 'nature' [. . . .] Human communication is an artistic technique whose intention it is to make us forget the brutal meaninglessness of a life condemned to death [. . . .] Communications theory is concerned with the artificial texture that enables us to forget our solitude, and it is thus a humanity [. . . .] Human communication is a phenomenon of freedom. (2013 [1983], 3–7)

This subject thus has to learn to become a project to itself—the project of 'becoming human', or 'humanization' (*Menschwerdung*), as Flusser called it. It has to learn to fulfil the 'Obligation to Self-Design' in the sense of Boris Groys (2008, 8), and for that it has to become teachable and open itself up to the Schillerian Programme of Aesthetic Education, learn to play as man, and in the process, become man (Schiller 1975).[16] Such a subject apperceives also the 'neg-entropic'

Orientalen ist von seiner Seelenartung bestimmt. Dem sensorischen Menschen, der unter der Führung des objektivsten Sinnes, des Gesichts, steht, objektiviert sich die Welt als eine Vielheit von Dingen, die sich vor seinen Augen ausbreitet und zu denen auch er selber, sein Leib gehört. Dem motorischen Menschen bekundet sich die Welt als die schrankenlose Bewegung, die ihn durchdringt. Er nimmt die Einzeldinge wahr, aber nicht jedes als ein für sich Seiendes, in sich Ruhendes und Beschlossenes, sondern alle nur als Knotenpunkte der unendlichen Bewegung, die durch ihn selber geht' (I want to refer to the oriental type of man [. . .] as the motoric in juxtaposition to the sensory [. . .] To the sensory man, guided as he is by sight, the most objective of the senses, the world objectifies itself as a multitude of things that spread out before his eyes, and to which he himself, his body, belongs. To the motoric man the world presents itself as the limitless movement that pervades him. He perceives the single objects, but not as beings in their own right, self-immersed and self-contained, but only as nodal points of the endless movement that runs through him') (Buber 2013b, 188–189).

[16] 'Der Mensch spielt nur, wo er in voller Bedeutung des Worts Mensch ist, und er ist nur da ganz Mensch, wo er spielt' ('Man only plays where he is man in the full sense of the term, and only where he plays is he fully a man') (Schiller 1975, 15th Letter, 315).

nature of a communicative form of knowledge creation. *Proxemik* in Flusser's telematic society not only connects the post-historical subject to other subjects, thereby radically questioning the very notion of distance in the sense that Walter Benjamin (1974) discusses it, but simultaneously also makes it answerable to them, in the sense of Buber's *ver-antworten*: 'Mit den Nahegebrachten-Entfernten stehe ich in einer zwischenmenschlichen Beziehung und trage Verantwortung für sie. Das ist, glaube ich, Telematik' (Bidlo 2009, 71).[17]

Flusser is aware of the extremely transitory and weak nature of such a communicative form of knowledge creation as an effort to overcome entropy, as it has been the destiny of all information to fall prey to entropy. And yet he pins his hopes on the new subject who would be willing to put Auschwitz behind and participate in communicative interaction with fellow men to escape the inevitable death and meaninglessness of life (ibid., 67).[18]

Martin Buber had a vision of such *proxemics* in times of an 'Asian crisis' when 'the soul of Asia is murdered' in course of the 'colonisation of India', the self-Europeanisation of Japan, and so on.

---

17 'I am placed in a human relationship with the remote that has been brought near, and I have responsibility for it. This, I believe, is telematics.'

18 'Erst der Akt der Erfindung der Sprache, die Verneinung der Entropie und der Mendelschen Gesetze kann nach Flusser als "das für Menschen kennzeichnende Merkmal" angesehen werden. Aber auch diese Überwindung der Entropie ist nur vorläufig, da schließlich, in kosmischen Dimensionen gerechnet, alle erworbenen Informationen zerfallen und unabwendbar der Entropie zuteil werden. Diese Erfolglosigkeit läßt sich ebenfalls als anthropologisches Merkmal des Menschen erkennen und führt für Flusser auf die existentielle Verfassung des Menschen zu, nämlich durch Kommunikation von Informationen von Mensch zu Mensch dem unabwendbaren Tod zu entfliehen und zugleich dem Leben einen Sinn zu reichen' ('Only the act of inventing language, the negation of entropy and Mendel's Laws, can, according to Flusser, be seen as "the defining feature of man". But also such overcoming of entropy is only preliminary, since, reckoning in cosmic dimensions, all acquired information falls apart and inevitably falls prey to entropy. This failure can also be regarded as an anthropological feature of man, and according to Flusser it leads towards the existential condition of man, namely to escape death by communicating information from man to man, and to bestow a sense to life').

This was a vision of subjects who, as a collective, would look for sanity, turn inward, turn around, and usher in a new era of 'preserving the Orient'; they would promote a relationship of mutual understanding and join hands in creating a new humanitarian society, in which 'neither is Asia devastated by Europe nor does Europe feel threatened by Asia', but both can together discover the great truths about life. And in this 'great historic mission' Buber sees Germany as the ideal mediator, for it has 'inherited all the wisdom and knowledge of the West and yet not lost its essentially oriental roots' (Buber 2013b, 202–203).[19]

Buber finds his dialogical philosophy beautifully put together in a poem of Friedrich Hölderlin: 'Friedensfeier'. His short piece is titled *Ever Since We Are a Dialogue*. Buber focuses on Hölderlin's respective verse:

> Much has man
> Ever since we are a dialogue and listen to each other
> Experienced; but soon we shall be a song
> (Viel hat von Morgen an
> Seit ein Gespräch wir sind und hören voneinander
> Erfahren der Mensch; bald sind wir aber Gesang)

---

[19] The passage from which the quotations in the above paragraph have been taken reads as follows:

> Das Zeitalter [...] wird man einst als das der asiatischen Krisis bezeichnen. Die führenden Völker des Orients sind teils unter die äußere Gewalt, teils unter den innerlich vergewaltigenden Einfluß Europas gekommen; [...] Die Seele Asiens wird gemordet. [...] Selbstbesinnung, Einkehr, Umkehr tut not. Das Volk [...], dessen Leben im Geiste und dessen metaphysische Schöpfung einzig im modernen Europa denen der großen orientalischen Völker verwandt ist, [ist] das deutsche Volk. Es muss sich unterfangen, eine neue Ära [...] zu begründen, [...] in der Asien durch Europa nicht vergewaltigt, sondern aus seinen eignen Keimkräften heraus entfaltet, und Europa durch Asien nicht bedroht, sondern zu den großen Lebenswahrheiten hingeführt wird. Für diese weltgeschichtliche Mission bietet sich Deutschland ein Mittlervolk dar, das alle Weisheit und Kunst des Abendlandes erworben und sein orientalisches Urwesen nicht verloren hat, das berufen ist, den Geist des Orients und den Geist des Okzidents in einer neuen Lehre zu verschmelzen.

He points out that Hölderlin had used the word chorus (*Chor*) in an earlier version and explains why he, too, prefers *Gesang* to *Chor*: 'To be a chorus means: to bring out a song together; but Hölderlin is now asking humans to listen to their being as dialogue as it turns into being as song [....] Only when those whose dialogue we are sing for us, are we WE' (Buber, 83–85).[20]

REFERENCES

Beniston, Judith. 1998. *Welttheater: Hofmannsthal, Richard von Kralik, and the Revival of Catholic Drama in Austria 1890–1934*. MHRA Texts and Dissertations, Book 46 Leeds: Maney.

Benjamin, Walter. 1974. 'Das Kunstwerk im Zeitalter seiner technischen Reproduzierbarkeit'. In Rolf Tiedemann and Hermann Schweppenhäuser (eds), *Gesammelte Schriften*, Vol. I.1, 471–508. Frankfurt am Main: Suhrkamp.

Bhatti, Anil. 2002. 'Haas Willy (1891–1973)'. *Österreichische Literatur im Exil.* 1–9.

Bidlo, Oliver D. 2007. 'Dialog und Kommunikation—Martin Buber und die Kommunikationswissenschaft'. In *Perspektiven philosophischer Forschung. Vorträge der 3. und 4. GPW Graduiertenkonferenz Heidelberg 2004–2005*, 124–140. Essen: Oldib-Verlag.

———. 2009. 'Telematik und Dialog: Vilém Flussers Rekurs auf Martin Buber'. In Oliver Fahle, Michael Hanke, and Andreas Ziemann (eds), *Technobilder und Kommunikologie: die Medientheorie Vilém Flussers*, 57–72. Berlin.

Buber, Martin. 1951. *Two Types of Faith*, Norman P. Goldhawk (trans.). New York: Macmillan.

———. 1996 [1909]. *Ecstatic Confessions* (The Heart of Mysticism), Paul Mendes-Flohr (ed.), Esther Cameron (trans.). Syracuse, NY: Syracuse University Press.

———. 2003. 'Seit ein Gespräch wir sind: Bemerkungen zu einem Vers Hölderlins'. In Asher Biemann (ed.), *Martin Buber Werkausgabe, Vol. 6: Sprachphilosophische Schriften*. Gütersloh: Gütersloher Verlagshaus.

20 '"Ein Chor" sein bedeutet: zusammen Gesang hervorbringen; nun aber verheißt Hölderlin den Menschen, dass aus ihrem Sein als Gespräch ein Sein als Gesang werden soll [....] Erst wenn die, deren Gespräch wir sind, uns singen, sind wir Wir.'

——. 2013a. *Werkausgabe, 2.1 Mythos und Mystik: Frühe religions wissenschaftliche Schriften*, David Groiser (ed.). Gütersloh: Gütersloher Verlagshaus.

——. 2013b. 'Der Geist des Orients und das Judentums'. In David Groiser (ed.), *Band 2.1 Mythos und Mystik: Frühe Religionswissenschaftliche Schriften*. Gütersloh: Gütersloher Verlagshaus. Available at https://www.degruyter.com/document/doi/10.14315/9783641248505-024/html (accessed September 2021).

Dengle, Rajendra. 2001–2002. 'Ending of the Teaching as the Beginning of Learning: Fritz Mauthner's *Der letzte Tod des Gautama Buddha*'. In *Goethe Society of India, Yearbook, 2001/2*, 89–111. New Delhi: Goethe Society of India.

——. 2013. 'Fritz Mauthner und Vilém Flusser—Annäherung zweier Prager Intellektueller an die indische Philosophie'. In *Indienerfahrung und Indiendiskurse europäischer Intellektueller im 20. Jahrhundert*, 27–38. Strasbourg: Presses Universitaires de Strasbourg.

Diersch, Manfred. 1977. *Empiriokritizismus und Impressionismus: Über Beziehungen zwischen Philosophie, Ästhetik und Literatur um 1900 in Wien*. Berlin: Rütten und Loening.

——. 1981. 'Vereinsamung und Selbstentfremdung als Lebenserfahrung Wiener Dichter um 1900'. In Viktor Žmegac (ed.), *Deutsche Literatur der Jahrhundertwende*, 81–106. Königstein/Ts.: Verlagsgruppe Athenäum.

Enzensberger, Hans Magnus. 1979. 'Baukasten zu einer Theorie der Medien'. In Karl-Markus Michel and Harald Wieser (eds), *Kursbuch*, 20, 159–186. Berlin.

Flusser, Vilém. 2013 [1983]. 'The Ground We Tread'. In *Post-History*, A Collection of Flusser's Writings, Rodrigo Maltez Novaes (trans.) and Siegfried Zielinski (ed.), 3–10. Minneapolis: Univocal.

——. 1999. *Bodenlos—Eine philosophische Autobiographie*. Frankfurt am Main: Fischer.

Friedman, Maurice. 1976. 'Martin Buber and Asia'. *Philosophy East and West* 26 (4), 411–426.

Groys, Boris. 2008. 'Die Pflicht zum Selbstdesign'. In Peter Weibel (ed.), *Kunst des Denkens*, 7–24. Hamburg: Philo Fine Arts.

Kant, Immanuel. 1998. 'Critique of Pure Reason'. In *The Cambridge Edition of the Works of Immanuel Kant*, Paul Guyer and Allen W. Wood (trans.). Cambridge: Cambridge University Press.

Kocher, Ursula. 2013. 'Eine gott- und sprachlose Religion. Fritz Mauthners Roman Der letzte Tod des Gautama Buddha (1913)'. In Gerald Hartung (ed.), *An den Grenzen der Sprachkritik—Fritz Mauthners Beiträge zur Sprach- und Kulturtheorie*, 251–270. Würzburg: Königshausen & Neumann.

MacQueen, Graeme. 1998. 'Changing Master Narratives in Midstream: Barlaam and Josaphat and the Growth of Religious Intolerance in the Buddha Legend's Westward Journey'. *Journal of Buddhist Ethics* 5, 144–166.

Mistry, Freny. 1972. 'Hofmannsthal's Oriental Library'. *Journal of English and Germanic Philology* 71 (2), 177–197.

Mauthner, Fritz. 1921. *Der letzte Tod des Gautama Buddha*. München: Müller.

Neswald, Elizabeth. 1998. *Medien-Theologie—Das Werk Vilém Flussers*. Cologne: Böhlau-Verlag.

Schiller, Friedrich. 1975. 'Über die ästhetische Erziehung des Menschen in einer Reihe von Briefen'. In *Über Kunst und Wirklichkeit (Schriften und Briefe zur Ästhetik)*. Leipzig: Reclam.

Steinhoff Smith, Roy. 1989. 'Mourning Becomes Existence: Martin Buber's "Melancholy" Ontology'. *The Journal of Religion* 69 (3), 329–331.

Ströhl, Andreas (ed.). 2002. *Vilém Flusser—Writings*, Erik Eisel (trans.). Minneapolis: University of Minnesota Press.

von Hofmannsthal, Hugo. 1981. *Ein Brief, Reitergeschichte. mit Materialien*. Stuttgart: Klett.

Nine

Indo-German/German-Indian Encounters in the Psychological Sciences[1]

CHRISTIANE HARTNACK

This chapter focuses on the work of Indian psychologists who embarked on projects in Austria and Germany and on the interactions that experts in the psychological sciences from German-speaking Europe had with colleagues in the Indian subcontinent. The topic is of importance because the creation of psychological knowledge was pioneered in both India and German-speaking Europe.

In India, insights into the inner world(s) of a person and the relationship between the inner world and the surrounding human and non-human world have already been documented in ancient Sanskrit texts. State-of-the-art experimental psychology was introduced at Calcutta University in the early twentieth century under the auspices of its long-time Vice-Chancellor, Sir Ashutosh Mukherjee. After the first Department of Psychology at the University of Calcutta opened in 1915, additional departments in Dacca, Patna, Lucknow, Mysore, Delhi, and Lahore were institutionalised soon thereafter. The founding of the Indian Psychoanalytical Society in 1922 and the Indian Psychological Association in 1925 were followed by the first volume of the *Indian Journal of Psychology* in 1926. Nowadays psychology is taught at several hundred academic institutions in India.

From the late nineteenth century onwards, the psychological sciences thrived in German-speaking Europe. In 1879, Wilhelm Wundt founded the world's first psychological laboratory in Leipzig. His methodological innovations—derived from physics—were experiments with research objects, that is, the systematic study of others. As a result, psychology eventually moved away from philosophy and became an independent academic discipline. In the

[1] The term 'psychological sciences' comprises the fields of psychology, psychoanalysis, and psychiatry.

1920s and early 1930s Berlin, famous for its groundbreaking school of Gestalt psychology, became one of the world's leading centres of psychological research. Around 1900, Emil Kraepelin transformed psychiatry by classifying psychiatric disorders. In the early twentieth century, Sigmund Freud developed psychoanalysis in Vienna. His publications on the importance of the 'unconscious' had a particularly significant impact on twentieth-century thought, well beyond the field of psychoanalysis.

It is obvious that the transcontinental encounters of German-speaking and Indian experts in the psychological sciences were influenced by their respective political, social, and cultural contexts. The motivation to reach across borders varied widely and the encounters and outcomes were shaped by—amongst other factors—academic discipline (psychology, psychoanalysis, or psychiatry), social skills, personal resilience, and financial resources.

The biographies of these experts and the circumstances of their encounters could hardly have been more diverse. On the Indian side, we have Girindrasekhar Bose, a passionate and creative therapist who combined psychoanalysis with Bengali Hindu traditions, Suhrit Chandra Mitra, an unenthusiastic experimental psychologist who had returned from Leipzig, Kripal Singh Sodhi, a stranded doctoral student who later became the head of Germany's most innovative department of psychology, and Sudhir Kakar, a psychoanalyst who became a successful author. The encounters of German-speaking researchers and practitioners with South Asia were marked by Sigmund Freud's celebration of an intellectual conquest and his resistance to being drawn into the depths of Indian knowledge, and Carl Gustav Jung's appropriation of intellectual findings from Sanskrit texts and his aborted Orientalist infatuation. German-speaking passengers to British India also included Edit Gyömröi, a refugee who found a place to survive, but not a home for herself, in South Asia, and Medard Boss, a philosophically-oriented psychiatrist in search of universal human wisdom.

This contribution outlines the scientific biographies of these eight persons, four from India and four from German-speaking Europe. For almost all of them—the exceptions being Freud and Bose—their interactions included travel to the other continent. The Indian researchers reached out in order to gain insight into the major developments taking place in the psychological sciences in Germany, which included Freudian psychoanalysis, Gestalt psychology at Berlin's psychological institute, and the work being done at the world's first psychological laboratory in Leipzig and at the psychoanalytical institute in Frankfurt. While the researchers from the German-speaking countries had the opportunity to access a wide range of South Asian psychological knowledge, they did so with varying degrees of enthusiasm.

ENCOUNTERS OF INDIAN EXPERTS WITH GERMAN-SPEAKING COLLEAGUES

GIRINDRASEKHAR BOSE (1887–1953)[2]

Bose is a key figure in the history of Indo-German encounters in the psychological sciences for two reasons. He tried to persuade Freud not to naively assume a transcultural validity of his findings and he creatively developed synergies between Bengali-Hindu knowledge and imported European psychoanalysis.

As a medical student in the first decade of the twentieth century in Calcutta, Bose, having been impressed by various articles about Freud's work, obtained all available English translations of Freud's early publications. He claimed that by 1910, he had begun to treat patients in his private medical practice by applying Freud's methods of free association and dream analysis. In the 1910s, his presentations of Freud's work at informal gatherings (*āḍḍā*) in his large family home provided a forum for shaping his ideas. While engaging in congenial discussions about such issues as the unconscious, desires, dreams, and the libido, these socially privileged, Western-educated Bengali Hindu men were at the same time accessing something 'modern' and non-British. The *āḍḍā* also helped Bose to deepen his understanding of his own Bengali Hindu traditions and provided him with opportunities to extend his networks.

2 Depending on the author, Bose's year of birth is stated as 1883, 1886, or 1887. For details, see Hartnack (2001, 115, fn 21).

In addition to being a successful administrator in the fields of psychology, psychoanalysis, and psychiatry, Bose authored numerous books and articles. From 1910 to the late 1940s, he worked as a medical doctor with a private psychoanalytical practice. Although he already had a degree as an MD, when the newly founded Department of Psychology opened at Calcutta University, he registered there as a student in 1915. In 1921, Bose founded the Indian Psychoanalytical Society; from 1922–1953, he was a member of the editorial board of the *International Journal of Psychoanalysis*. A year later, he began lecturing at the Department of Psychology at Calcutta University, and in 1939 he became full professor and head of the department, a post he occupied till 1949. With financial support from his brother Rajsekhar, he opened the Lumbini Park Mental Hospital in 1940. In 1947, he started the Indian psychoanalytical journal *Samiksha*. Bose is also the author of the popular children's book *Lāl'kālo*, which can be read as an allegory of the colonial situation.

In his quest to combine elements of ancient Hindu psychological knowledge with twentieth-century scientific findings and practices, Bose asked a guru to guide him in self-experimentation with introspection and a pandit to help him understand the deeper meaning of Sanskrit texts. The resulting publications include *The Psychological Outlook of Hindu Philosophy* (1930a), 'Sattva, rajaḥ, tamaḥ' (1930b), *Purāṇ prabeś* (1934), *Gītā* (1931), and *Yoga Sutras* (1935).

In 1921, Bose sent Freud his Ph.D. thesis in psychology, titled *The Concept of Repression*. Freud replied with a friendly note, and thus began a correspondence that lasted till 1937 (Bose and Freud 1956). Although Bose was thirty-five years younger than Freud and still an unknown Bengali medical doctor and lecturer, his interactions with Freud showed stunning persistence and self-confidence. Anchored in his *Bhadralok* social structure, anti-British sentiment, and Bengali Hindu intellectual traditions, Bose had enough self-confidence to criticise Freud, question his assumptions, and explicitly contradict him. Bose also tried to convince Freud as to why cultural adaptations in psychoanalytical theory and clinical practice are necessary and kept him informed about his theoretical and therapeutic innovations: his theories of opposite wishes and the see-saw mechanism. In several of his letters, Bose further criticised Freudian concepts as not universally applicable. Controversial topics included the structure and the dissolution of the Oedipus complex and Bose's emphasis on the importance of the feminine (goddesses, wishes to be female), which contradicted Freud's androcentric and monotheistic worldview (Bose 1949).

SUHRIT CHANDRA MITRA (1895–1962)

Mitra was about a decade younger than Bose and his successor in many respects. Like Bose, he was well-connected to Calcutta's Western-educated Bengali Hindu elite; he also had links with anti-British circles. After studies in philosophy, mathematics, and English literature at the Scottish Church College of the University of Calcutta, Mitra joined the newly founded department of psychology there. His motivation behind this decision was supposedly his interest in yoga (Sinha 1962, 172).[3] Between 1920 and 1923 he worked at the Department of Psychology, University of Calcutta as a lecturer. In October 1923, Mitra left for Leipzig, from where he returned in 1926 with a doctorate degree in experimental psychology. The transfer was initiated by the University of Calcutta's Vice-Chancellor, Sir Ashutosh Mukherjee, who was known not only for his anti-colonial stance, but also for his ambition to turn the University of Calcutta into a research university (ibid.). His support for Mitra's decision to carry out postgraduate research at the world's first and, at that time, most famous institute of experimental psychology was thus a very deliberate move.

Despite possessing a doctorate degree from a prestigious institution, Mitra's academic career did not proceed as fast as one would have expected. In 1950, at the age of fifty-five, he finally became full professor. In the same year, he succeeded Bose as head of the Department of Psychology at Calcutta University, a position he held till 1959. Mitra's studies in Germany eventually resulted in the founding of the Institute of Applied Psychology at Calcutta University in 1938, but this did not lead to thriving experimental research (*Indian Journal of Psychology* 1942). In 1961, at the end of

[3] See also Special Centenary Issue on S. C. Mitra, *Psychological Research Journal* 22, 1998. I thank Amitranjan Basu for providing me with information on Suhrit Chandra Mitra.

his career, he confessed, 'Laboratory experiments in psychology never satisfied me wholly'.[4]

In 1925, while he was a student in Leipzig, he received financial support from the Indian Psychoanalytical Society, which enabled him to attend the ninth International Psychoanalytical Congress in Bad Homburg, near Frankfurt. After his return to Calcutta, he underwent analysis with Bose and praised this experience (The Indian Psychoanalytical Society 1926).[5] Although he never practised as a psychoanalyst, he seemed to be especially interested in psychoanalysis; out of forty-one published writings, the majority deal with psychoanalytical topics. After Bose's death in 1954, Mitra became president of the Indian Psychoanalytical Society, a position he occupied till his death in 1962. Like Bose, Mitra also supported research on traditional Indian psychological knowledge at the University of Calcutta and integrated elements of his Sanskrit learning into his publications.

Mitra played a role in the transmission of ideas from the German-speaking world to British India. He was an active member of the Baṅgīya Jārmān Bidyā Saṃsad, the Bengali Society of German Science, where he presented lectures on psychoanalytical topics. Influenced by the legendary fighter for India's independence, Subhas Chandra Bose, who was his childhood friend (both had studied at the Scottish Church College) and relative (his brother was married to Bose's sister), Mitra published several articles on anti-colonial themes.[6]

KRIPAL SINGH SODHI (1911–1961)

What follows is the biographical sketch of a dedicated researcher and lecturer whose stellar career ended abruptly and tragically. The son of a doctor in civil service, he grew up in an upper-middle class Sikh family, studied psychology, philosophy, history, literature, and economics,

4 *Special Centenary Issue on S. C. Mitra*, 8.

5 Ibid., 9.

6 On the relationship between S. C. Bose and Mitra, see Mallick (1998). Mitra's articles with a political content include: 'The Spirit of the Nation in War and Peace' (1927).

and graduated in 1936 with an MA in psychology from Punjab University in Lahore (Holzkamp 1961; Manz 1993; Rösgen 2003). After reading an English translation of Wolfgang Köhler's *Gestalt Psychology*, an introduction to the cutting-edge work being done in holistic experimental psychology in Germany, he decided to continue his studies in Berlin with Köhler. But when Sodhi arrived there in 1937, he found that Köhler had fled Nazi Germany for political reasons and emigrated to the US. Sodhi nevertheless remained in Berlin, where he was supported for some time by a Humboldt Fellowship offered by the Deutsche Akademie.[7] Once war was declared in 1939, the British authorities repeatedly asked him to leave Germany, but he stayed in Berlin and continued his research. In 1941, he successfully obtained his doctoral degree with a dissertation on his experiments with depth perception. Thereafter, he lectured at the Department of Psychology at Humboldt University, and continued his research on the psychological aspects of vision. In February 1945, during a bombing raid on Berlin's imperial castle where the Department of Psychology had its laboratories, Sodhi risked his life in an attempt to save his research files. He survived, but lost all his data to the flames.

After the war, Sodhi taught psychology at an American university for US soldiers stationed in Berlin. Thanks to a visiting research fellowship at Swarthmore College in Pennsylvania, where Köhler had found a teaching position after his emigration, Sodhi was finally able to meet with his—until then imaginary—mentor in 1948. While in the United States, he also became acquainted with Richard S. Crutchfield and with Solomon Asch, who both shared with him the latest research in North American experimental social psychology.

When West Berlin's newly founded Free University opened in 1949, Sodhi was appointed lecturer in its Department of Psychology. Three years later, he submitted his second substantial research work (his dissertation being the first), the 'habilitation', a prerequisite for being appointed to a professorship in Germany. The research focussed on the importance of social context in shaping opinions (Sodhi 1951). In his subsequent work on national stereotypes, Sodhi creatively combined three different influences: (*i*) his personal experiences as a

[7] I thank Kris Manjapra for this information.

non-German who had by then spent over a decade in a racist social-political context and its aftermath;[8] (*ii*) the latest empirical social psychological methods he had come to know while in the United States; and (*iii*) the intellectual traditions of German psychology.

Based on his solid empirical research record, his innovative and also critical use of methods in social psychology, and his international reputation, in 1954 Sodhi was placed at the top of the list to become head of the Department of Psychology at the Free University. Influential Berliners and their networks, however, successfully managed to ensure that the position was offered to Philipp Lersch, who ensured continuity in the use of established methods. Only on 1 January 1959—after Lersch had decided to stay at the University of Munich in the position he had held continuously since 1942 and after Sodhi was offered a professorship in Cairo via the UNESCO—did he finally become full professor and head of a department that he had already run successfully for four years as acting director.

In the winter of 1960–1961, after having been abroad for twenty-four years, he was finally able to visit his relatives in India and establish ties with Indian universities. Four weeks after his return to Berlin, on 3 May 1961, Sodhi died suddenly of a heart attack. He was not even fifty years old.

Sodhi left behind his German wife Sigrid and their 15-year-old son Rana, as well as a research agenda which, under his assistant, colleague, and successor Klaus Holzkamp, became the nucleus of the Berlin School of Critical Psychology (Painter, et al. 2009).

SUDHIR KAKAR (B. 1938)

Kakar's reputation is based on sixteen published books of non-fiction, five novels, and several collected works, most of which are available in German translation. Some of his publications were translated into over twenty languages. His most important work, *The Inner World* (1978), is currently in its sixteenth edition. Kakar has been honoured with numerous prizes; in Germany, he received the highest honour

8 The German émigrés to the United States, Max Horkheimer and Theodor W. Adorno, had similarly worked on prejudices. The émigrés' personal situation obviously contributed to choosing this theme.

of the Federal Republic of Germany, the Order of Merit as well as the Goethe Prize of the city of Frankfurt, and also a fellowship and membership on the board of the Centre for Advanced Study in Berlin (Wissenschaftskolleg).

A Punjabi Hindu born into an upper-middle-class family (his father was a magistrate in the colonial government), Kakar belongs to the generation of Indians who grew up in an epoch in which Europe and the United States were idealised and—whenever possible—considered attractive destinations to move to. Kakar's first encounter with Germany was Hamburg's shipyard, where he interned as an engineer. He then studied business administration in Mainz and then Mannheim before going on to teach at the Indian Institute of Management (IIM) in Ahmedabad. The beginnings of Kakar's interest in psychoanalysis lay in a chance encounter with Erik Erikson, who had stayed at the IIM Ahmedabad for his research on a psychobiography of Gandhi, and whose books he subsequently read (Kakar 2011, 161; Sharma 2000, 254). In his autobiography, Kakar mentioned that Erikson had told him, 'If you get your doctorate in the next two or three years, I'll try my best to get you to Harvard to work for me' (Kakar 2011, 161).

Both Kakar and Erikson did their part to bring this about. Kakar obtained his Ph.D. in economics in Vienna, and indeed went from there to work as Erikson's assistant at Harvard University (1966–1971), followed by training analysis at the renowned Sigmund-Freud-Institut in Frankfurt. In 1975, after his return to India, Kakar began working as a psychoanalyst. In his private practice in New Delhi, he treated mostly foreigners and wealthy Indians. In due course, he received more and more scholarships and invitations to teach from abroad. Besides holding visiting appointments at universities in Vienna and Cologne, he obtained fellowships from other universities, including Harvard, McGill, Princeton, Hawaii, Chicago, Melbourne, and Fontainebleau.

These extended and frequent stays abroad enabled Kakar to view India from both an outsider's and an insider's perspective. He created contrasts between these worlds in an—especially for the Western readers—informative and, above all, lucidly written way. Kakar increasingly began to turn away from applied psychoanalysis and cultural psychology to explore the healing work of mystics and shamans, Indian erotic culture, Hindu–Muslim communal violence, myths, folk tales, and popular culture. He also published psychobiographies of Gandhi, Vivekananda, Ramakrishna, and Tagore. Like Sodhi, Kakar could add a third dimension, the US-American. In his thinking, however, the India–Germany–US triangle is not equilateral. As evident from Kakar's publications, from *The Inner World* (1978) to *Young Tagore: The Making of a Genius* (2013), his early and sustained contact with his 'guru' Erikson shaped his thinking more than his encounters with German intellectual traditions.

ENCOUNTERS OF GERMAN-SPEAKING EXPERTS IN THE PSYCHOLOGICAL SCIENCES WITH THEIR COLLEAGUES IN SOUTH ASIA

SIGMUND FREUD (1856–1939)

Freud's contact zones with India are ambiguous. On the one hand, his writings reflect the Eurocentric attitudes common to that time. For him, the non-European world did not contain regions to learn from; rather, these regions were—at best—locations to conquer with his ideas. Freud also expressed resistance towards Indian visitors. Nevertheless, a closer reading of his letters and the accounts written by his contemporaries reveal a hint of knowledge and even an air of fascination vis-à-vis classical Sanskrit texts. However, he backed off again and again from these inklings of interest. He never reached towards anything Indian in an active way, but instead responded at will to various advances to draw him into Indian culture.

In 1904, Bruno Goetz, then a student of Indology at the University of Vienna, told Freud about a class in which the *Bhagavadgītā* was read (Goetz 1969, 7–8). According to Goetz's narrative, Freud jumped out of his chair, walked back and forth through the room, and warned him: 'Careful, young man, careful! . . . do not get beguiled, do not get entangled. . . . The Bhagavad Gita is great literature, but it is very deep and terribly abysmal.' He reminded Goetz of one of the most famous poems in German literature, *The Diver* by Friedrich Schiller, which tells of the beauty of the deepest waters, a lure that is eventually fatal for the diver. Freud then continued:

> If you dive without the help of a very sharp mind into the world of the Bhagavad Gita where nothing appears to be fixed and everything merges with one another, you will suddenly lose ground.... Indian Nirvana is not nothing, but something that lies beyond all contradictions. (ibid., 9)

Assuming that these reminiscences of Goetz's are accurate and not later creations, Freud appears to have been familiar with the content of the *Bhagavadgītā*. In a letter written on 19 January 1930 to Romain Rolland, the French Nobel Prize winner in literature, Freud confirmed that he indeed had some insights into Indian cultural traditions:

> I shall now try with your guidance to penetrate into the Indian jungle from which until now an uncertain blending of Hellenic love of proportion, Jewish sobriety, and philistine timidity have kept me away. I really ought to have tackled it earlier, for the plants of this soil shouldn't be alien to me; *I have dug to certain depths for their roots.* (Fisher 1976, 38–39; emphasis mine)

In his letters to Girindrasekhar Bose, Freud appeared to be attentive to Bose's work, but then shied away from questioning elements of his own psychoanalytic theory. On 9 March 1929, Freud wrote to Bose: '... I confess I am by no means more convinced of the validity of my own assumptions. We have not yet seen through this intricate Oedipus matter. We need more observations' (Bose and Freud 1956, 9 March 1929). And on 1 January 1933, Freud wrote:

> I [...] reproach myself for not having given attention to your ideas before [....] It needs more time and effort to overcome the feeling of unfamiliarity when confronted with a theory so different from the one professed hitherto [...] I am still bewildered and undecided. I see that we did neglect the fact of the existence of opposite wishes [....] (ibid., Freud to Bose, 1 January 1933)

While Freud—rather loyally—answered all of Bose's letters, personal rapport with Indian celebrities was another matter. In October 1926, Freud met with Rabindranath Tagore in Vienna at the latter's request, and, a little while later, with Surendranath Dasgupta, a professor of philosophy at Calcutta University. After these encounters, Freud remarked to Ferenczi that 'my need of Indians is for the present fully satisfied'.[9] This attitude of Freud's obviously continued. The Bengali linguist Suniti Kumar Chatterji visited Freud in 1935, and after Chatterji had finished reciting a hymn from the Brahma Samhita in both Sanskrit and English, Freud remarked gravely, 'So.' After exactly half-an-hour, Freud asked Chatterji to leave, because he expected his doctor to come at any time (Chatterji 1949).

In 1931, when the Indian Psychoanalytical Society sent Freud a statue of Vishnu along with a Sanskrit poem on the occasion of his seventy-fifth birthday, he did not show any interest in the cultural symbolism of the gift. The only thing Freud did with respect to this statue was give it a special place on his desk, but as a symbol of his conquest, not reciprocity.[10]

There is no doubt about Freud's enthusiasm for Greek culture. He even used Greek names for his concepts (for example, Oedipus complex or libido). Sander Gilman (1991) claims that his preference for Greek over Latin derived from his emotional rejection of Catholicism (where Latin remained the main language). Similarly, his attitude towards India might be in opposition to the fascination that German intellectuals—who tended to be Protestant—had with respect to Sanskrit learning. Carl Gustav Jung was one of these.

CARL GUSTAV JUNG (1875–1961)

While Freud shied away from the lure of the potential depth of Indian knowledge, Jung did just the opposite: he appropriated India's intellectual assets as though they were precious minerals and freely embedded these in his oeuvre.

Primarily because of his non-Jewish family background and personal charisma, Jung, a Swiss medical doctor and psychiatrist, was initially chosen by Freud to be his intellectual 'son and heir'.

9 Freud to Ferenczi, in a letter dated 13 December 1926. *Cf.* Jones (1957, 128).

10 In his letter of thanks to the Indian Psychoanalytical Society, Freud wrote: 'The Statuette is charming. I gave it the place of honor on my desk. As long as I can enjoy life it will recall to my mind the progress of Psychoanalysis [,] the proud conquests it has made in foreign countries' (Bose and Freud 1956, Freud to Bose, 1931).

Jung reciprocated these feelings and considered Freud a god-like father figure. Yet by 1913, their initially very intense relationship, begun in 1907, had turned into fierce competition. Among the reasons for this split—and one of its long-lasting results—was that Jung developed an intellectual profile that was different to Freud's. He explored not only occult visual arts and literature, but also alchemy and astrology, and he incorporated elements of all of these in his voluminous oeuvre.

In 1917, Jung mentioned '[his] intensive unconscious relation to India' in his *Red Book* (Collins and Molchanov 2013, 12).[11] A couple of years later, because of a patient's dream, he studied Sir John Woodroffe's work on the serpent goddess Kundalini. In his lectures on Kundalini yoga at the Psychological Club in Zurich in 1930 and 1931, Jung then presented these 'Indian parallels' to his own psychological discoveries (Jung 1996). In the following year, Jakob Wilhelm Hauer, a professor of Indology and religion from the University of Tübingen, joined him in this lecture series.[12] Another source for Jung to learn about Sanskrit texts was Heinrich Zimmer, a professor of Indology at Heidelberg University.[13] Beginning in 1933, Jung and Zimmer attended several of the annual Eranos gatherings at Monte Verità in Ascona, which dealt with East-West topics.[14] As a result of these

[11] Jung's visual and literary expressions of his dreams and thoughts were posthumously published in Shamdasani (2009).

[12] From 1933–1944, Hauer was also Untersturmführer of the SS (Membership No. 107.179). In 1934, he published a book on the *Bhagavadgītā*, titled *Eine indo-arische Metaphysik des Kampfes und der Tat* (*Indo-Aryan Metaphysics of Combat and Deed*), which also revealed his Nazi ideology. For details on Hauer's life and work, see Dierks (1986).

[13] The relationship between Jung and Zimmer was a highly complex one. As Jung did not hide his success in intellectual, material, and social respects, Zimmer, in a letter to a friend, characterised Jung as, 'for all his great qualities, a power-loving fox, inflated by a legitimate self-confidence because of his mind and abilities and by the adoration of devoted, big-moneyed femininity' (Letter from Zimmer to Herbert Nette, November 1931, in Case 1994, 71). Despite Zimmer's initial envy, the two stayed in contact even after Zimmer had emigrated to the US.

[14] Jung also invited Zimmer to open his Berlin seminar with a lecture on yoga, and in 1935 he invited Zimmer to address the International

encounters with Hauer and Zimmer, Jung freely incorporated imagery and philosophical concepts from translations of the Vedas and the Upanishads into his theories (Sorge 2013).

Jung's dalliance with Indian spiritual and intellectual traditions came to an abrupt end after the British government invited him to visit their 'Jewel in the Crown' on the occasion of the celebration of the Silver Jubilee Congress of the Indian Science Congress Association (Sengupta 2013). Jung travelled in India between December 1938 and February 1939. While there, he was awarded honorary doctorates from the universities in Benares, Calcutta, and Allahabad. It appears that during this trip, Jung was hardly receptive to new impressions. Throughout the journey he continued reading about European alchemy as if to shield himself from gaining new insights or from questioning his uninhibited use of Sanskrit terms which he had interspersed throughout his writings. A bout of amoebic dysentery led to a life-threatening sickness and states of delirium while he stayed at the American hospital in Calcutta, thus finally putting an end to Jung's attraction to Sanskrit knowledge.

Jung's publications relating to contemporary India as it was in the late 1930s reflect his stereotypes and prejudices. He repeated the strictly binary division that he adhered to in his thinking and concluded that while European culture is dynamic, Indian culture is timeless and static. Jung also characterised India's population as passive, childlike, feminine, and lacking individuality (Jung 1939, 1964).[15]

Ironically, Jung's aborted interest in the psychological content of Sanskrit scripts left certain traces behind. Jung's early publications on *maṇḍalas*, *cakras*, *kuṇḍalinī*, etc., initiated a flourishing global business in which the creation of psychological experiences that carry such labels have become sought-after commodities. Moreover, study trips to India are offered to learn about mystic traditions in 'Jung's footsteps' (excluding, of course, Calcutta's hospital).

Psychotherapy Congress with a lecture on 'Indian Views on Psychotherapy' (*cf.* Zimmer 1935).

15 For further details on Jung's views on non-Europeans, see Dalal (1988).

EDITH GYÖMRÖI (1896–1987)[16]

Gyömröi differs from all the other persons presented in this chapter in that she was a woman, and that she did not voluntarily sail across the sea between Europe and India. Unlike Jung, she went to South Asia not to be honoured, but simply to survive. Thanks to the financial help of the British psychoanalyst Ernest Jones, she eventually managed to escape racist and political persecution in Nazi-occupied Central Europe.

Gyömröi was born into a rich and well-connected Jewish Hungarian family (her father had owned a furniture factory; after he had 'Magyarised' his original name 'Gelb' and converted to Catholicism, he was elevated to the nobility). Against her parents' wishes, she quit a school for interior design, married at the age of eighteen, had a child, and was soon divorced. In 1923, Gyömröi moved to Berlin, where she survived on income from odd jobs as a translator, photographer, and costume designer. She had joined the Communist Party, wrote for the 'Rote Hilfe', one of its publications, and was trained in psychoanalysis by the Marxist psychoanalyst Otto Fenichel. Eventually, she began to settle down in Berlin as a psychoanalyst. In 1933, however, after she learned that she would no longer be safe in Nazi Germany, she left for Prague, where she contributed to the formation of a psychoanalytical association. From Prague she moved back to her hometown, Budapest, where she became a member of the Hungarian Psychoanalytical Society. When even Hungary became dangerous for her, she searched for options to flee. On 8 February 1939, she and her husband left Trieste on board a vessel bound for Sri Lanka (then Ceylon).

After her husband's death in 1940, she decided to move to Los Angeles where Fenichel had emigrated.[17] She was already in

[16] Her family names are also Renyi, Glück, Ujvari-Gyömröi, Ludowyk-Gyömröi. Her first name also appears in the original Hungarian spelling as 'Edit'. *Cf.* Schröter (1995) and Ludwig-Körner (1999).

[17] In Sri Lanka, she was not only a member of the Indian Psychoanalytical Society, but—like in Germany—also of the Communist Party. Between 1934 and 1945, she belonged to a closed Marxist psychoanalytical circle around Otto Fenichel whose members secretly exchanged letters, the so-called 'Rundbriefe'. In 1940, she wrote in one of these letters: 'You must combine the Eastern

the United States and well on her way to settling in there when a pile of letters reached her. In these, the literature professor and public intellectual Lyn Ludowyk (1905–1985) pleaded with her to return to Colombo. In August 1941, she married Ludowyk. Henceforth she lived in a grand tropical estate and studied the history of religion at Colombo University. In 1944 she obtained her Ph.D. with a thesis titled 'Miracle and Faith in Early Buddhism'. She also initiated a socialist women's association in Colombo and saw some patients. Based on her analysis of a Sinhalese teenaged girl, she published an article on the puberty rites of Sri Lankan girls (Gyömröi 1955). In keeping with her political commitments as a Marxist and her liberal views on sexuality, in this article she claimed that the prudish Victorian views on sexuality that had been brought to South Asia with British colonialism had had a negative impact on the sexual development of Sri Lankan girls.

As soon as her husband was able to retire, they left for London, where Gyömröi was affiliated with Anna Freud's Hampstead Clinic (now the Anna Freud Centre). Although she published an important article about her analysis of a young concentration camp victim, her main strengths were direct interactions with people through her teaching, training analysis, and networking (Gyömröi 1963). She was also active in re-establishing psychoanalytic training in then-socialist Hungary.

Gyömröi kept the experiences of her sixteen years in South Asia and her transcultural reflections hidden from the outside world. It is only in her novels, and not in her psychoanalytic publications, that she integrated some of her Sri Lankan encounters (Ludwig-Körner 2014).

MEDARD BOSS (1903–1990)

In 1925, Medard Boss—then a medical student from Zurich, Switzerland, spending a year abroad to study at Vienna University—was analysed by Freud (Condrau 1973; Pongratz 1973; Rattner 1995).

---

character, the inhibiting education, the religious bias and the difficulties typical for all colonies—and you will have an idea about the circumstances in which I am working here' (Mühlleitner and Reichmayr 1998, 1281).

His later intellectual pursuits as a professor of psychiatry and practising psychiatrist in Zurich did not, however, turn in the direction of Freud's causal, linear, and progress-oriented scientific reasoning. Boss instead tended towards a different philosophical direction in which intuition and openness to complexity played an important role. Inspired by Edmund Husserl's phenomenology and influenced by his close friend Martin Heidegger, Boss became a proponent of the so-called 'Daseinsanalysis', a school of psychiatry that does not conceptualise the individual as separate from other human beings and the world around her/him, but integrates this 'being' in a holistic way with the life worlds around them (Boss 1963, 2001). As Boss and Jung both lived in the German-speaking part of Switzerland and as their professional experiences and philosophical orientations were highly compatible, between 1938 and 1948 they regularly exchanged their views and influenced each other in monthly meetings.

Boss had a stellar international career. From the early 1950s until late in his life, he was the recipient of several international honours, including the 'Great Therapist Award' by the American Psychological Association. As president of the International Federation for Medical Psychotherapy (1954–1967), he received many invitations to prestigious medical and psychotherapeutic institutions, including the University of Washington, University of Madison, Helsinki University, Harvard University, and universities in Buenos Aires, São Paulo, Djakarta, Tokyo, Kyoto, and Nagoya.

In 1956, Boss accepted an offer to teach a semester in Lucknow, staying in India for five months and returning again for sojourns of four months each in 1958 and 1966. Before going to India, Boss had learned basic Hindi and studied Sanskrit texts in German, English, and French translation. These studies led to his desire to meet with Indian sages and gurus and to learn from them in his search for Indian knowledge and wisdom about the inner world. In addition to his stays in Lucknow, he travelled to Madras, Bombay, and into the Himalayas.

Boss's first two stays in India resulted in his book, *A Psychiatrist Discovers India* (1965).[18] Its first German edition, published in 1959,

[18] In German: *Indienfahrt eines Psychiaters*. Pfullingen: Günther Neske, 1959. [Herder (ed.), Freiburg: i. Br, 1966, 2e; Hans Huber (ed.), Bern, 1976,

immediately turned out to be a great success. Three further editions were issued in German, and it was also translated into English, French, Swedish, and Japanese. The book reads like a mirror held up to and reflecting Europe. In it, Boss criticises Western attitudes of cognitive superiority and Europe's emotional poverty and intellectual reductionism, which leaves out experiential learning. Boss also cites the divisions between body and mind, subject and object, human being and nature in European thought, and shows a deep respect for Indian knowledge and its transmitters; in this, the book can be read as an ode in praise of Indian culture.

Although it was likely not Boss's intention, his book became a component of the psychological and philosophical canon of the early 'flower power generation' as it constructed its own 'Orientalist', idealistic version of Indian spirituality, of which the young Beatles, who went to Rishikesh in 1968, were part.

CONCLUSION: ON THE FLOW OF PERSONS, KNOWLEDGE, AND METHODS IN THE PSYCHOLOGICAL SCIENCES

In trying to weave together the warp and woof threads of these different biographies, it becomes evident that the movements between German-speaking Europe and South Asia do not create a structured tapestry. The motivations for developing Indo-German/German-Indian thought or contact zones and the results of these encounters varied widely. There is thus little in these flows that can be generalised. The political contexts, synergies, and impact of these encounters among these eight persons even show that the divergence was often due less to differences in German and Indian cultures than it was to other factors.

POLITICAL CONTEXTUALISATION

The transmission of ideas between the German-speaking world and (British) India was set in a complex colonial and postcolonial context

3e; Hans Huber (ed., enlarged and illustrated), Bern, 1987, 4e.] Swedish translation, 1967, French, 1971, and Japanese, 1972.

with different alliances. The Indian psychologists who lived during British rule and had contacts with Germany all conveyed anti-colonial sentiments. By contrast, my reading of Kakar's (the only representative of postcolonial India in this chapter) publications showed that he refrained from analysing the impact of Western political, economic, and cognitive hegemony on India's culture and population.

Freud's language reflects that he lived during the time of European colonial conquests in Asia and Africa; again and again he spoke of the 'proud conquests' psychoanalysis has made. Although Freud did not raise any political issues in his correspondence with Girindrasekhar Bose, a hidden colonial element in their communication surfaced nonetheless. When Bose sent Freud an imaginative sketch of him, Freud remarked to Lou Andreas Salomé that the image made him look like a British officer (Pfeiffer 1972, 114). Jung and Boss were Swiss citizens, and thus not directly involved in the German National Socialist activities, but they were nevertheless ideologically linked to supporters of German National Socialist ideology. Jung had worked closely with the Indologist Hauer who, between 1933 and 1945, was a high-ranking SS officer, and he also personally benefitted from the forced exodus of psychoanalysts from Nazi Germany and Austria. In her work on Sinhalese girls, Gyömrői explicitly included the psychological impact of the colonial system, and in her work on the trauma suffered by a concentration camp victim, she obviously connected political and psychological conditions.

SYNERGIES

In scientific terms, the core question of this contribution is how and to what extent the encounters between purveyors of different psychological concepts and practices resulted in confluences or creative developments as a result of their crossing of intellectual borders. In fact, most of these authors explicitly incorporated elements of their intercultural theoretical entanglements or personal experiences into their published scientific work. Among the synergies that developed out of the Indo-German contacts, Bose's theory of opposite wishes and his so-called 'see-saw mechanism' stand out, in that these were creative combinations of selected Bengali Hindu and Freudian concepts and therapeutic procedures. In his socio-psychological research on national prejudices, Sodhi introduced innovations to post-war German experimental social psychology based on his personal experiences as an émigré. Kakar related elements of Western psychoanalysis to Indian family structures and myths and to his study of the biographies of eminent Indians. As long as India remained in the realm of his projections and imaginations, before he visited the subcontinent, Jung imported a number of classical Indian concepts into his analytical psychological theory, as a result of which he became known. Boss's encounters in India, shaped by his search for knowledge and wisdom about the inner world as conveyed to him by Indian sages and gurus, also contributed substantially to his oeuvre.

IMPACT

Although the works of some of the people presented here were groundbreaking at the time, the fruits of these encounters did not prove to be sustainable. In India as well as in Europe, only works by Jung and Kakar continue to be read. While Sodhi laid the groundwork for the Berlin School of Critical Psychology, his writings are now outdated. The publications by Mitra, Gyömröi, and Boss are likewise gathering dust in the basements of antique book sellers and/or archives. It is unlikely that any of their writings—perhaps with the exception of Boss—will be rediscovered. Although Bose's critiques of Freud's assumption of cross-cultural validity and Bose's evidence of the cross-cultural relativity of psychoanalytic concepts could potentially garner interest in postcolonial discourse, his psychotherapeutic concepts and methodological innovations remain largely unnoticed.

OUTLOOK

Contemporary research done in the psychological sciences in German-speaking countries has by now lost the status it enjoyed at the beginning of the twentieth century. As a result, the influence of German psychological sciences in India belongs to the past. There will hardly be any more Boses, Mitras, Sodhis, or Kakars striving to learn from the state-of-the-art work being done by their German counterparts. It will be easier and more rewarding for their scientific (great-)grandchildren to look towards the United States or elsewhere.

Moreover, several decades after India's independence, Indian scientists' fascination for Germany as a politically attractive alternative to the cultural and political hegemony of the British Empire has become anachronistic.

On the other hand, the burgeoning output of psychological research at Indian universities nowadays, as well as the revival of so-called 'indigenous' psychology in India, might spark renewed interest in scholars from the German-speaking world. Similar to ayurveda or yoga, psychological knowledge as contained in Sanskrit texts, once taken out of its historical and social context and thus construed and cherished as a timeless and caste-less intellectual treasure, cannot only be politically co-opted in service of nationalistic self-affirmations against global or local non-Hindu influences. It is likely also to become attractive to both Indian and European psychological experts as something that can be globally commercialised.

REFERENCES

Bose, Girindrasekhar. 1921. *Concept of Repression.* Calcutta: G. Bose.

———. 1930a. 'The Psychological Outlook of Hindu Philosophy'. *Indian Journal of Psychology* 5, 119–46, repr. *The Modern Review*, January 1931, 14–25.

———. 1930b. 'Sattva, rajaḥ, tamaḥ'. *Prabāsī* 30, 2 (1), 1–5.

———. 1931. 'Gītā'. *Prabāsī* 31, 2 (1), 9–16.

———. 1934. *Purāṇ prabeś.* Calcutta: M. C. Sarkar.

———. 1949. 'The Genesis and Adjustment of the Oedipus Wish'. *Samiksha* 3, 222–240.

———. 1957. 'Yoga Sutras'. *Samiksha* 11, 44–63, 157–185, 217–237.

Bose, Girindrasekhar, and Sigmund Freud. 1956. *Correspondence.* Calcutta: Indian Psychoanalytical Society.

Boss, Medard. 1963. *Psychoanalysis and Daseinsanalysis.* New York: Basis Books.

———. 1965. *A Psychiatrist Discovers India*, Henry A. Frey (trans.). London: Wolff.

——— (ed.). 2001. *Martin Heidegger: Zollikon Seminars.* Evanston, Illinois: Northwestern University Press.

Case, Margaret H. 1994. *Heinrich Zimmer: Coming into His Own.* Princeton, NJ: Princeton University Press.

Chatterji, Suniti Kumar. 1949. 'An Interview with Sigmund Freud'. Library of Congress, Sigmund Freud Papers: Interviews and Recollections, 1914–1998; Set A, 1914–1998.

Collins, Al, and Elaine Molchanov. 2013. 'A Chronology of Jung and India'. *Jung and India, Spring: A Journal of Archetype and Culture* 90 (Fall), 11–17.

Condrau, Gion. 1973. *Medard Boss zum 70. Geburtstag*. Bern: Huber Verlag.

Dalal, Farhad. 1988. 'The Racism of Jung'. *Race and Class* 29 (3), 1–22.

Dierks, Margarete. 1986. *Jakob Wilhelm Hauer, 1881–1962*. Heidelberg: Kohlhammer.

Fisher, David James. 1976. 'Sigmund Freud and Romain Rolland: The Terrestrial Animal and His Great Oceanic Friend'. *American Imago* 33, 1–59.

Gilman, Sander L. 1991. 'Reading Freud in English: Problems, Paradoxes and a Solution'. *International Review of Psychoanalysis* 18, 331–344.

Goetz, Bruno. 1969. *Das ist alles, was ich über Freud zu erzählen habe: Erinnerungen an Sigmund Freud*. Berlin: Friedenauer Presse.

Gyömröi, Edit. 1955. 'Pubertätsriten der Mädchen'. In Maria Pfister-Amende (ed.), *Geistige Hygiene, Forschung und Praxis*, 237–51. Basel: Benno Schwabe.

———. 1963. 'The Analysis of a Young Concentration Camp Victim'. In *The Psychoanalytic Study of the Child*, Vol. 18, 484–510. New York: International University Press.

Hartnack, Christiane. 2001. *Psychoanalysis in Colonial India*. New Delhi: Oxford University Press.

Holzkamp, Klaus. 1961. 'In Memoriam Kripal Singh Sodhi (1911–1961)'. *Kölner Zeitschrift für Soziologie* 13, 383–385.

Indian Journal of Psychology. 1942. 'Report on the Working of the Applied Section of the Department of Psychology, Calcutta University'. *Indian Journal of Psychology*, Special Issue, 1–45.

The Indian Psychoanalytical Society. 1926. Reports. *International Journal of Psychoanalysis* 7, 291.

Jones, Ernest. 1957. *The Life and Work of Sigmund Freud, Vol. 3: The Last Phase 1919–1939*. New York: Basic Books.

Jung, Carl Gustav. 1939. 'What India Can Teach Us'. *Asia* 39, 97–98.

———. 1964. 'The Dreamlike World of India'. In *Collected Works*, Vol. 10, 515–524. Princeton, NJ: Princeton University Press.

———. 1996. *The Psychology of Kundalini Yoga: Notes on the Seminar Given in 1932 by C.G. Jung*, Sonu Shamdasani (ed.), Bollingen Series 99. Princeton, NJ: Princeton University Press.

Kakar, Sudhir. 1978. *The Inner World: A Psychoanalytic Study of Childhood and Society in India*. Delhi: Oxford University Press.

———. 2011. *A Book of Memory: Confessions and Reflections*. New Delhi: Penguin Viking.

———. 2013. *Young Tagore: The Makings of a Genius*. New Delhi: Penguin Random House.

Ludwig-Körner, Christiane. 1999. 'Edit Ludowyk-Gyömröi'. In Christiane Ludwig-Körner (ed.), *Wiederentdeckt: Psychoanalytikerinnen in Berlin*, 119–148. Berlin: Psychosozial Verlag.

———. (ed.). 2014. *Edit Gyömröi: Gegen den Strom*. Berlin: Selbstverlag. [The Hungarian translation of *Die Aussöhnung* (*The Reconciliation*) published as *Megbekeles*. Budapest: Magvetö Kiado, 1979.]

Mallick, Amal Kumar. 1998. 'Psychology and Tales of two Friends Suhrit and Subhas: A Psycho-historiographical Study'. *Psychological Research Journal*, Special Issue, 22 (1&2), 21–32.

Manz, Wolfgang. 1993. 'Kripal Singh Sodhi'. In H. E. Lück and R. Miller, *Illustrierte Geschichte der Psychologie*, 199–202. München: Quintessenz.

Mitra, Suhrit Chandra. 1927. 'The Spirit of the Nation in War and Peace'. *Indian Journal of Psychology* 2, 84–89.

Mühlleitner, Elke, and Johannes Reichmayr (eds). 1998. *Otto Fenichel: 119 Rundbriefe (1934–1945)*. Frankfurt/M.: Stroemfeld.

Painter, Desmond, Athanasios Marvakis, and Leendert Mos. 2009. 'German Critical Psychology: Interventions in Honor of Klaus Holzkamp'. *Theory & Psychology* 19, 139–147.

Pfeiffer, Ernst (ed.). 1972. 'Freud to Lou Andreas-Salomé, 21 March 1921'. In *Sigmund Freud and Lou Andreas-Salomé: Letters*, W. & E. Robson-Scott (trans.). New York: Harcourt Brace Jovanovich.

Pongratz, Ludwig J. (ed.). 1973. 'Medard Boss'. In *Psychotherapie in Selbstdarstellungen*, 75–106. Bern: Huber.

Rattner, Josef. 1995. 'Medard Boss'. In Josef Rattner, *Klassiker der Psychoanalyse*, Vol. 2, 700–725. Weinheim: Beltz.

Rösgen, Petra. 2003. 'Kripal Singh Sodhi und die Anfänge der Sozialpsychologie in Berlin nach dem Zweiten Weltkrieg'. In Lothar Sprung and Wolfgang Schönpflug (eds), *Zur Geschichte der Psychologie in Berlin*, 2. Auflage, 451–469. Wiesbaden: Peter Lang.

Schröter, Michael. 1995. 'Edith Gyömröi. Eine biographische Skizze'. *Luzifer Amor. Zeitschrift zur Geschichte der Psychoanalyse* 8, 102–115.

Sengupta, Sulagna. 2013. *Jung in India*. New Orleans: Spring Books.

Shamdasani, Sonu (ed.). 2009. *The Red Book: A Reader's Edition*, Sonu Shamdasani, John Peck and Mark Kyburz (trans.). New York: W. W. Norton and Company, and Düsseldorf: Patmos.

Sharma, Dinesh. 2000. 'A Conversation with Sudhir Kakar'. *International Journal of Group Tensions* 29 (3 and 4), 253–283.

Sinha, S. 1962. 'Professor Suhrit Chandra Mitra (1895–1962)'. *Psychologia* 5 (3).

Sodhi, Kripal Singh. 1951. *Urteilsbildung im sozialen Kraftfeld.* Göttingen: Hogrefe.

Sorge, Giovanni. 2013. 'Jung's Hermeneutic of the Yantra and the Mandala: The Influence of Heinrich Zimmer's Kunstform und Yoga im indischen Kultbild'. *Spring: A Journal of Archetype and Culture* 90 (Fall), 77–104.

Zimmer, H. 1935. 'Indische Anschauungen über Psychotherapie', *Zentralblatt für Psychotherapie* 8, 147–161.

Ten | Colonial Bilinguality in Dialogue

Girindrasekhar Bose Manoeuvring His Readers, Indian Traditions, and Freud[1]

Hans Harder

Various assessments of Girindrasekhar Bose (1887–1953) have highlighted his pioneering role in the dissemination of psychoanalysis in India and his stature as an original thinker and practitioner who, far from only spreading Freudian doctrines, also developed his own take on the discipline and elaborated independent theories. Bose's oeuvre, falling into almost equal halves of Bengali and English writings, shows that he communicated on different planes and with different audiences.

One question repeatedly raised in assessments of Bose concerns the nature of this 'colonial bilinguality'. Did addressing different readerships through these languages also predetermine the content of his writings and the spin he gave them? Was Bose more creative in Bengali, as Ashis Nandy (1995) contends, and did he pursue entirely different projects through Bengali and English, reserving Bengali for an underlying mission of nationalist identity formation (Manjapra 2014)? Another question running through this debate is whether psychoanalysis as a discipline helped Bose overcome colonial hierarchies. Did his relation with Sigmund Freud, with whom he corresponded directly for a number of years, get trapped in the colonial set-up of the time, as Christiane Hartnack (2001) and Ashis Nandy (1995) have argued? Or, following Manjapra's (2014) assessment, were Freud's Austrian nationality and the German legacy

[1] I thank Agniva Ghosh for discussing the topic with me and for guiding me through the source material. I am also indebted to the participants in the workshop for their constructive comments on an earlier version of this chapter, as well as to Dhruv Raina and the anonymous peer reviewer for their feedback on the final draft.

of psychoanalysis an escape from colonial bifurcations, enabling Bose to take a less ambivalent position? Did Bose's interaction with Freud result in a stance of defiance towards the latter, as Alf Hiltebeitel (2018) suggests?

This chapter looks at Bose's engagements in terms of dialogues on separate, but interlinked planes—the mediated dialogues that Bose engaged in with his readers in the Bengali and English mediums, his metaphorical dialogue with intellectual traditions of the Indian past, and the literal epistolary, rather barren dialogue with Freud by sea mail. Through a detailed discussion of three texts, Bose's *Svapna* ('Dreams'), *The Yoga Sutras*, and *The Bose-Freud Correspondence*, I first demonstrate that while Bose did adhere to a nationalist project of enriching the Bengali language and public domain, there is no neat division of labour between English as an outer 'trade language' and Bengali as a medium of inner identity formation (Manjapra 2014). Second, I argue that Freud and psychoanalysis did initially provide Bose with an impetus to reach across colonial constraints towards a universalist level, but due in part to the lack of fruitful interaction with Freud, this took a regressive turn at a later stage, resulting in a deplorable historic case of failed dialogue.

Introduction

Girindrasekhar Bose[2] (1887–1953) is considered the main founding figure for the introduction of psychoanalysis in India, and is often referred to as the 'Father of Indian Psycho-Analysis' (*cf.* Bose 2009 [1945], front cover). Born to a wealthy Kayastha family of northern Calcutta, he studied science and medicine at Presidency College and passed his second MB exam in 1910. He became one of the first students of psychology in the country: when the subject started to

[2] The English spelling of his name varies in his different publications. In this chapter, I spell it as Girindrasekhar Bose in the main body of the text for sake of consistency, but stick to the actual, often divergent spellings in bibliographical references. For Bengali sources, accordingly, the Bengali forms (Girīndraśekhar or Girīndra Śekhar Basu) are used.

be taught at Calcutta University in 1916,[3] he enrolled, excelled in his exams, and even won a prize of Rs 500. Bose received his doctorate in 1921 with a dissertation on the concept of repression (see Basu 2009 [1920]). In that same year, he founded the Indian Psychoanalytical Society and his own practice at his dwelling house at 14, Parsi Bagan Lane (Image 10.1) (*cf.* also Nandy 1995, 96). The society proved to be a successful undertaking, financially as well, until his death, after which its fate deteriorated. Apparently the society mirrored the larger picture: Bose's life marked the high tide of the early years of psychoanalysis in India, a tide that was never again reached afterwards. Today, the Indian Psychoanalytical Society still resides in Parsi Bagan Lane and upholds his memory in various ways, not least by preserving the library and reprinting most of his books and publications.[4]

Girindrasekhar Bose was a prolific writer: he authored altogether ten books, three in English and seven in Bengali, as well as some forty articles in both these languages, from the early 1920s until his death in 1953.[5] A few of these writings are literary works: *Lāl'kālo* ('Red and Black', 1930–1931) is a Bengali children's classic, a short book about a battle between red and black ants that has been interpreted as an allegory about the struggle between coloniser and colonised, even though an attentive reading of the text rather discourages such

3 *Cf.* Hartnack (2001, Chapter 3), and especially the sub-chapter on 'The Institutionalization of Psychology and Psychoanalysis in Calcutta' for a detailed account.

4 A good and concise overview of his life and works can be found in Dāś (1996 [1971]).

5 Dāś (1996 [1971]) lists the following (for complete bibliographical references, as far as is available, see the bibliography): *Concept of Repression*, 1920; *Svapna* ('Dreams'), 1928–1929; *Lāl'kālo* ('Red and Black'), 1930–1931; *Purān prabeś* ('Entry to the Puranas'), 1934–1935; *Jīban yātrāẏ manobidyār praẏog* ('Use of Psychology in the Course of Life'), 1934; *Reconstruction of Andhra Chronology*, 1939; *Everyday Psycho-Analysis*, 1945; *Bhagabadgītā*, 1948; *Manobidyār paribhāṣā* ('Terminology of Psychology'), 1953; *Paurāṇikī* (on Puranas), 1956. Other posthumous publications were *The Yoga Sutras* (1957, in *Samiksha* and later as a book) and the *Bose-Freud Correspondence* (1964).

Image 10.1: Entrance Gate of 14, Parsi Bagan Lane, Central Kolkata, Bose's Domicile and Headquarters of the Indian Psychoanalytical Society
Source: Hans Harder, 2014.

an interpretation.[6] Apart from this tale and some poems, the bulk of Bose's works consists of discursive prose that falls mainly into two thematic and almost equal parts: first, expositions and specialised research articles on psychoanalytical issues, comprising four books both in Bengali and English, almost all of his English articles, and some Bengali articles; and second, writings on and translations of classical Indian mythological and philosophical texts in altogether five books and the majority of his Bengali articles.

[6] Dhirendranath Nandi (signing as ex-chairman of the All India Psychoanalytical Society) in his introduction to the 2008 edition calls *Lāl'kālo* an allegory: 'When reading it one naturally feels that Dr. Girindrasekhar Basu has provided a hidden hint at the fight of the subdued Indians against the English rulers' (Basu 2008, n.p.). Ashis Nandy does not seem to advocate a reading of *Lāl'kālo* in terms of colonial simile, but just mentions the book and one drawing in it in appreciation of Girindrasekhar Bose's creativity. In fact, the book is famous for its original illustrations, drawn partly by Bose himself and partly by the well-known illustrator Yatindra Mohan Sen.

These two fields of psychology and mythology may, at a superficial glance, seem somewhat unrelated, but on closer perusal it becomes clear that they are very overlapping and, in fact, interrelated concerns.[7] To these publications we have to add one more outstanding series of texts: the Bose-Freud correspondence, published posthumously in 1964 and consisting of a selection of the letters Freud and Bose exchanged in English between 1921 and 1937.[8]

Girindrasekhar Bose's role in the history of psychoanalysis and his positionality as an intellectual in a colonial situation have been dealt with in a number of studies on the history of psychoanalysis in India, among them Ashis Nandy's *The Savage Freud* (1995), Christiane Hartnack's *Psychoanalysis in Colonial India* (2001), Shruti Kapila's article 'The "Godless" Freud and his Indian Friends' (2007), and Alf Hiltebeitel's *Freud's India* (2018). Bose is also discussed in some detail in a chapter of Kris Manjapra's *Age of Entanglement* (2014) on Indo-German interactions during the age of Empire, and his work features prominently in a so far unpublished Bengali doctoral thesis on the reception of psychoanalysis in Bengal by Agniva Ghosh (2017).

Hartnack (2001) and Nandy (1995) view Girindrasekhar Bose primarily as a colonial intellectual. Hartnack connects her argument with Partha Chatterjee's hypothesis regarding the common bifurcation of domains in colonised society, with the public domain being open to 'the West' and the private, inner domain of the family and women becoming the abode of tradition and spiritual retreat.[9] She narrates Bose's uneasy trajectory between his propagation of Western thought

[7] Mythology was a concern he shared with his brothers, particularly his elder brother Rajshekhar (1880–1960), the famous Bengali short story writer and humorist, who authored abridged Bengali translations of the *Mahābhārata* and *Rāmāyaṇa* besides his narrative fiction.

[8] Regarding the selective nature of the published correspondence and missing letters, *cf.* Dāś (1996 [1971], 69) and Hiltebeitel (2018, 11).

[9] *Cf.* Chatterjee (1994, Ch. 1, esp. 9; also Ch. 6, where Chatterjee speaks of 'nationalism's success in situating the "women's question" in an inner domain of sovereignty, far removed from the arena of political contest with the colonial state. This inner domain of national culture was constituted in the light of the discovery of "tradition"' (p. 117).

and his 'national pride' and 'anti-colonial stance' (Hartnack 2001, 96). The relationship between Bose and Freud, according to Hartnack, was characterised by a 'great cultural and personal distance'. Freud's decision to concentrate on the unconscious and not on the other 'dark continents' of his days, on women, or on the non-Western world, resulted in psychoanalysis remaining Eurocentric, and he 'missed the chance to learn from colleagues abroad' (ibid., 137, 149).

Ashis Nandy, partly with reference to an earlier version of Hartnack's work, paints a nuanced portrait of Bose's personality against the background of nineteenth-century colonial India/Calcutta. Psychoanalysis, he argues, played an ambivalent role. While it seemed to provide an internal critique and subversion of European hegemony, it compensated for this deviation by its smashing Eurocentric critique of the non-West (Nandy 1995, 81f.). For non-Western practitioners, this bias created opportunities in that Freud could be used 'as a radical critic of the savage world and, at the same time, a subverter of the imperial structures of thought that had turned the South into a dumping ground for dead and moribund categories of the Victorian era' (ibid., 136). Regarding Bose's bilinguality, Nandy suggests that he was at greater ease in Bengali than in English when it came to demonstrating the 'theoretical daring born of cultural self-consciousness' (ibid., 372). Nandy also deals with Freud's role in Bose's trajectory, and repeatedly stresses Freud's paternalistic attitude, at times aligning it right away with a typical coloniser's mindset.[10]

Kris Manjapra (2014), in his survey of Bose's writings, including the correspondence, is less intent on emphasising the bias in that exchange, but stresses two other points. He argues that for Bose, Freud held a third position outside the colonial set-up and his being Austrian enabled an engagement that was not predetermined by the coloniser-colonised divide.[11] Second, Manjapra takes up the issue

[10] *Cf.* Ashis Nandy's remark on Freud's reaction to the 'imaginative portrait' made by a member of the Indian Psychoanalytical Society and then sent to him, to which Freud had remarked that he looked like an Englishman (Nandy 1995, 101f), and the related discussion below.

[11] 'Girindrasekhar Basu did not see himself as adopting a European science, but as practicing a non-British one. Psychoanalysis did not have its roots in the Anglophone cultural world'; 'Girindrasekhar always referred to Freud

of bilinguality from Nandy and accentuates it further, claiming that there was a division between English as a 'trade language' enabling international communication in the field and Bengali for 'centering the identity of Bengali practitioners' out of nationalist motivation (ibid., 227).

The most recent, and most intense, reconstruction of the interaction between Bose and Freud is Alf Hiltebeitel's monograph, *Freud's India* (2018). Hiltebeitel does not leave it at an in-depth investigation into the actual dialogue between the two personalities, but engages in carrying it further towards what it could have become. A scholar of Indian mythology, Hiltebeitel thoroughly dialogises the ideas of these thinkers with Indian philosophical and mythological traditions. He also painstakingly researches Freud's reservations about engaging with Indian thought and how that adversely affected his openness towards Bose's ideas.

This chapter has nothing to add to the historical and psychological insights that these studies have yielded. What it aims to achieve comes down to two points: re-examine Bose's colonial bilinguality and reconsider his positionality as it played out in his dialogues. An exercise in textual scholarship, it focuses on some of Bose's writings and through them, on the communicational mechanics at work in his interactions with a Bengali and an English-reading public. What, in terms of colonial bilingualism,[12] is the relationship between Bose's English and Bengali writings? In order to check and modify the assessments summarised above, we will examine Bose's practice of bilinguality. Through a detailed examination of two examples from his early and late work, we will look for some clues as to how his choice of either English or Bengali impacted on his mediation and scaling of information and the way he addresses his readers. In addition, we will revisit the correspondence and interpret the position that

as a Viennese doctor, not as a Western or European one, and located Freud specifically in the atmospheric Viennese world of modernism' (Manjapra 2014, 220, 225).

12 *Cf.* Veena Naregal (1999) who, however, uses the concept more poignantly to demonstrate how nineteenth-century Marathi journalists strategically used their skills in both Marathi and English to cement their elite position in colonial society.

Freud occupied in Bose's perception. Does the juxtaposition English vs Indian or coloniser vs colonised supply a valid matrix in the case of Freud? Where is Freud positioned between outer and inner knowledge—a dichotomy so fundamental to Indian nationalist and indigenist discourse in colonial times, claiming inner or spiritual knowledge for India while outer knowledge, comprising science, technology, warcraft, etc., was identified with the West?

It appears convenient to use the notion of the dialogue, the key idea of this volume, as the overarching framework to ponder about the nature of Bose's writings. While this element of dialogue is obvious in his correspondence with Freud, traces of dialogue can also be found in his outwardly monological treatises: either with his varying audiences or, quite prominently, with classical Indian tradition. In the following, I will present three of his texts and sketch the particular kinds of dialogue underway in them. Two of these, his Bengali treatise *Svapna* (1928–1929) and his English introduction to and translation of the *Yogasūtra* (titled *The Yoga Sutras*, first published posthumously in *Samiksha*, 1957), were his first Bengali and last English book, respectively. Thereafter, I will also briefly deal with his correspondence with Freud (1921–1937). The order in which this last body of texts will be discussed defies chronology, but for a good reason, since the analysis of the correspondence with Freud will furnish a possible explanation for a shift in tone noticeable from Bose's early to his later phase.

DREAMS IN BENGALI

In 1928, Girindrasekhar Bose published a book of about 140 pages titled *Svapna*, 'Dreams'.[13] It can broadly be qualified as an exposition for an informed lay Bengali-reading public, and is to this day regarded as an authoritative Bengali classic on the topic. The treatise carries a rather lengthy *Bhūmikā* (Introduction, 4–38) that provides a survey of Freudian psychoanalysis along such central concepts as the unconscious, wishes and their suppression, symbol formation, sexual

13 The page numbers in the following refer to the reprint of 2008 as given in the References.

desire and its sublimation, etc. Bose also cursorily contextualises Freud's approach in the contemporary state of psychology and sketches further developments connected with Jung and Adler. In the main text, Bose starts by describing dreaming as an all-pervasive human phenomenon. He introduces Freud's premise that dreams serve the purpose of fulfilling unfulfilled wishes (§48, 45ff.), and that their meaning can be decoded by what he calls the *abādh bhābānusaṅga paddhati*, that is, the free association method (§50, 48ff.). After a section on the particular distortions of dreams (visualisation, displacement, condensation, dramatisation—§81, 77ff.), he treats the role of the mind (Bengali: *man*) in repressing wishes and the way in which these wishes reappear in dreams. Thereafter, Bose discusses a number of dream types, such as childhood memories in dreams, dreams of fear, supernatural happenings in dreams, dream conversations with deceased persons, etc.[14] The book ends with a general index and a chart of English psychoanalytical terms with their Bengali equivalents.[15]

This short summary suggests that *Svapna* is a work closely related to Freud's oeuvre, and indeed the book is sometimes referred to as a 'translation' or 'Bengali version' of Freud's *Traumdeutung* of the year 1900. But a more thorough look at the text disperses such an impression. The book, for one, construes a central perspective that is entirely fixed in India, Bengal, or even more specifically, Calcutta. For instance, when establishing the cultural significance of dreaming, Bose right away gives examples from Chittaur's Rana Lakshman Singh and the Mughal king Jahangir, as well as unnamed rich Marwaris dreaming of markets heating up; he points to the 'Sanskrit books' for specific explanations of dreams and repeatedly exemplifies dreams of fear with tigers (pp. 39–40) or dreams of uncontrollable desires with rasagollas, a famous variety of Bengali sweets (p. 47). His section 42 starts as follows:

[14] The respective sections start with §102, 92, and basically go on until the end of the text in §145, 128.

[15] This *Pāribhāṣik śabder nirghaṇṭa* contains altogether 133 entries in English and Bengali in accordance with the convention used by Calcutta University. For a summary of *Svapna*, *cf.* also Ghosh (2017, 74–75).

> In our Sanskrit *śāstras*, there are various reasonings about the production of dreams. On this topic there are two opinions in the *Bṛhadāraṇyaka-Upaniṣad* regarding dreams: (a) the soul creates a new world in the dream by imitation from things seen in the outer world; (b) the soul leaves the body and wanders around ad libitum in the world. (p. 41)

Bose adds dream-related statements from the Vedānta and dismisses their authority: 'None of all these reasonings can however be classified as scientific definitions.' But, as he clarifies in the following section, since scientists were concerned with 'determined things' (*nirdiṣṭa jinis*), dreams had been outside the realm of science not only in India, but also anywhere else, including Europe, until Freud had come up with his *svapnar tattva* or theory of dreams (pp. 40–41).

It is important to note that the first-person plural 'we' that Girindrashekhar Bose uses to create his reader address actually refers to a Bengali reading public in more than a merely circumstantial sense. On one level, he consistently relates his observations to classical Indian concepts; for instance, he identifies *suṣupti* as dreamless deep sleep, calls upon the *Brahmavaivartapurāṇa* when establishing the relationship between awake experience and dreams, mentions discussions on dreams in the Vedas, *Brahmavaivartapurāṇa, Sāmaveda, Vāyu-* and *Matsyapurāṇas*, as well as the Āyurveda, and adds a list of old Indian standard dream explanations (pp. 43–48). In conclusion, he states:

> Such interpretations of dreams are common in western countries as well. There, too, many books have been written about the theory of dreams, and in all those books meanings of dreams are given. It goes without saying that all these explanations have no particular value by scientific standards. (p. 48)

While these explanations are thus quite irrelevant for Bose's scientific argument, they have an obvious symbolic value because of the culture-specific resonances they convey. His repeated dismissals of their accuracy do not stop him from continuously referring to *Pauranic* sources in his exposition of dreams.[16]

16 There are references to the *Manusmṛti* (p. 84), Vatsyayana, author of the *Kāmasūtra* (p. 77), and again to the *Brahmavaivartapurāṇa* (p. 96);

Along with these invocations of classical Sanskrit texts, we also find another level with more specifically Bengali layers of reference. Bose quotes the common expression *niśite pāoẏā* for somnambulance or the expression *yame ṭāniẏāche* for death wishes, and points out that just like Coleridge's *Kubla Khan*, some works of Rabindranath Tagore were received in dreams. He also invents a lowly office clerk or *kerāni* called Rambabu and his dream of success in the office to illustrate dream compensations for frustrations (pp. 44–46). Other examples are drawn from well-known Bengali literature of the time and of earlier times. There are references to novelist Sharatchandra Chattopadhyay, Bengali folk tales (see p. 71 for both), famous children's author Sukumar Ray (p. 77), premodern poet Chandidas, and short story writer Prabhat Kumar Mukhopadhyay (p. 83), alongside Oscar Wilde and William Shakespeare. Examples such as Bengali writer Trailokyanath Mukhopadhyay (p. 91) and the popular *Baṅgabāsī* periodical (p. 97) are also cited. In two instances, even popular *dehatattva* imagery, that is, the tantric symbolic language of the Bauls, is referred to for the elucidation of a dream (pp. 75, 105).[17]

Moreover, Bose's textual localisation strategy does not only hinge on a thorough integration of references to Bengali literature, but also extends to the realm of his practice. Thus, for instance, when the readers are introduced to one *Ka Bābu* ('Mr A', p. 47), they realise that the Bengali case studies of dreamers throughout the book are hardly ever citations of Freud's examples. They are drawn from Girindrasekhar Bose's own patients, whose dreams can be interpreted only by entering the semantic texture of colonial Bengal: for example, Haribabu's Ganga bath as a cover for his suicidal wish (p. 58). The patients were generally persons of privileged social standing: people with property, servants, etc., just like Bose himself.

Bose usually addresses the readers as *pāṭhak* and, as noted above, often uses the first-person plural to guide the reading process, construe a Bengali readership, and at times, refer to humans in

---

Bose also cites the Purāṇas and other Indian mythological accounts in favour of interpreting dreams in which something taken out of the water is seen as symbolising the wish for children (p. 97), and introduces the Sanskrit term *svapnāntika* to denote a dream within a dream (p. 92).

[17] Especially the house symbolising the body; *cf.* below.

general. However, the first-person singular is also employed, not only as a narratorial device, but also to signal his agency as a doctor and scholar. And while Freud gets all the credit for the new approach to dream interpretation in *Svapna*, Bose's first-person 'I' self-consciously announces also those places where he differs with Freud, for example, his theory of the opposite wish.[18] He states quite nonchalantly: 'In this book I shall discuss a little Freud's research on dreams and the opinions of other psychologists. Along with that I will also give my own views' (p. 40).

Bose also takes great pains to deal with the supposed predispositions of his readers and prepare them to accept his approaches, whether it be the fundamental role of the libido in human activity (p. 73ff.) or the rational explanations of supernatural dreams (p. 95ff.). The length at which he deals with these is apparently in direct proportion to the alleged dominance of such beliefs amongst his readers.

Such differences of opinion also include instances in which he argues for culture-specific deviations from Freud's theory, for example, in the dreams of exposing one's nude body in public, which according to Freud are extremely common. Bose explains that these indicate a wish to regain the freedom to show one's body that one had in childhood, but contends that such dreams are not frequent in India: 'In comparison to the West, there are more occasions to show one's body in our country, and therefore this wish has less chances to be repressed' (p. 84). Similarly, Bose alludes to *dehatattva* songs, characterised by the use of esoteric Bengali code language to describe the human body and a set of secret bodily practices,[19] to demonstrate that certain images, such as the equivalence of the body and a house, can be culturally acquired, and to disprove what he labels as Freud's biologism.[20] If all this is read as instances of cultural embedding, it is very clear that Bose goes quite some way towards taking the message of his *Svapna* home to his addressees, a lay Bengali-language readership.

---

18 *Cf.* Hiltebeitel (2018, 95–124) for an extensive discussion of this theory.

19 For further information on *dehatattva*, see Das (1992) as well as Harder (2011, sub-chapters 5.7.13 and esp. 5.7.14, 264–270).

20 *Manojagate jīb bidyā mūlak byākhyā samīcīn nahe*: 'In the realm of the mind, interpretations based on biology are not accurate' (p. 105).

Wherever possible, he thoroughly connects the psychoanalytical theories to traditional and contemporary Bengali ideas on the topic, guides his readers attentively through the text, and sometimes persuades them to accept new perspectives. And significantly, Bose moderates Freud as the most important, but not unfailing voice on the topic; he does not simply present Freud, but rather his own original take on Freud's theory, thought through independently on the canvas of classical and contemporary South Asian/Bengali culture. So *Svapna* goes far beyond a simple adaptation of psychoanalysis and does achieve a certain re-centring of Freudian dream theory. Freud's ideas are verily transposed both in terms of practice and cultural resonances, and are in the process also submitted to a critical examination.[21]

However, the decisive point for our present argument is the following: notwithstanding Bose's careful cultural embedding of dreams in the South Asian and Bengali context, there is no conscious attempt in *Svapna* to appropriate dream psychology as something inherently Indian, or particularly close to the Indian tradition. Premodern, pre-psychoanalytical interpretations of dreams are treated as evidence of the longstanding concern with dreaming in the cultures concerned, and by extension, in human societies in general. Dream analysis thus addresses a complex that the tradition in both realms had tried to tackle multifariously, but equally unscientifically. In *Svapna*, Bose distinguishes between traditional and modern models of dream explanation, or scientific and unscientific ones—and not between West and East. In this scheme, premodern Indian traditions are not portrayed as privileged, but by and large projected on par with Western ones. This assessment changed considerably towards the later phase of his life, as we shall now see.

---

[21] An English version of *Svapna* is contained in a much later publication by Girindrashekhar Basu, in his *Everyday Psycho-Analysis* of 1945 (pp. 150–215). As stated in the Preface (p. v), this book comprises the lectures that Bose 'delivered at different times to lay audience on various aspects of psycho-analysis'. The 'Dreams' section appears to be an abridged version of *Svapna*. While the instances of disagreement with Freud are there in the English text, some of the cultural specifications (for example, the *dehatattva* example quoted above) are lacking. However, I know too little of the editorial policy underlying this publication to draw any strong conclusions for a theory of bilingual topic assortment.

YOGA IN ENGLISH

The Yoga Sutras is Bose's last book and thus a suitable counterpart to *Svapna* when it comes to gauging the *longue durée* evolution of his positions. The *Yogasūtra* had fascinated Bose ever since his youth (Nandy 1995, 92), but he left it to his final years to write this treatise-cum-text-cum-translation. *The Yoga Sutras* can be profitably contrasted with *Svapna* on at least two counts: the text is written not in Bengali but in English, and (outwardly, at least) is not about psychoanalysis, but Bose's second great concern, ancient Indian mythology and philosophy. How, we shall ask, is psychology placed in this work? Does the implied audience differ from the one Bose addresses in *Svapna*? And how is the relationship between the 'East' and the 'West' conceived here?

The Yoga Sutras appeared posthumously in four instalments in the journal *Samiksha* in 1957, and a reprint was published by the Indian Psychoanalytical Society, but without a date.[22] I have been unable to trace the exact time of composition, but it seems almost certain that he wrote this text in the early 1950s, that is, in the last years of his life. Comprising altogether 134 pages, it has a long introduction (pp. 1–74), summaries of the text of Patanjali's *Yogasūtra* (pp. 75–85), the Sanskrit text in a Romanised diacritical version (pp. 86–92), and the translation with Bose's commentary (pp. 93–134). In the following, given our preoccupation with his voice in these exchanges, the emphasis will be placed on the introduction which, rather than narrowly focusing on his engagement with the *Yogasūtra*, spins off a fairly independent treatise on the role of the psychological in classical Indian culture.

Bose starts off by citing the contemporary interest in Yoga in India as well as in European countries and in America. He then places the *Yogasūtras* in the context of the six classical philosophical systems and proposes to study them through an 'intrinsic' approach, as opposed to the 'extrinsic' method preferred, as he says, by Western scholars:

---

[22] It is this edition that I will refer to in the following as Bose (n. d.), as given in the References.

> The first method deals with such questions as the date of composition of the work, how far the author has borrowed from previous workers on the subject, what is his influence on later thought, how many times a particular technical term has occurred in the work, in what different ways and with what different connotations certain terms [have been used], etc.

For the intrinsic approach, on the other hand, he states:

> The subject matter of the work under consideration is the only important thing to be discussed in this method of approach; the question of interpolation as such, that of the authorship, the date of composition and all such items are entirely irrelevant from this point of view [....] The 'intrinsic' approach is certainly the method of choice but it can always be supplemented with advantage by considerations of 'extrinsic' nature. (Bose n. d., 4)

Such extrinsic considerations, however, are declared to be of an entirely academic and potentially dull nature. The same applies to traditional Indian scholarship: while Bose names quite a few of the important commentaries and secondary Sanskrit works on Yoga, he claims to have avoided any detailed discussion of them in the interest of the 'general reader'.[23] Thereupon, under the heading 'Psychological Outlook in Hindu Philosophy' (Bose n. d., 6), he bluntly states that there is an extraordinarily strong connection between classical Indian philosophy and the modern discipline of psychology:

> Hindu philosophy when compared with Western systems stands on a peculiar footing. In no European system of philosophy has the psychological material been so dominant. The outlook of the Vedanta, the Samkhya, the Yoga and the Vaisesika systems is almost purely psychological. (ibid., 7)

Bose establishes this fundamentally psychological orientation for the Upanishads and takes the argument towards the question of whether pure consciousness is possible (pp. 16–19) in order to then juxtapose two theories of creation: one from matter (of the modern scientists)

---

[23] 'I have studiously refrained from giving the book a learned appearance so as not to scare away the general reader from this extremely interesting subject' (Bose n.d., 6).

and another from consciousness/mind (of the 'Indians', meaning the ancient philosophers, and mainly the Sāṃkhya system), and develops a creationist standpoint of sorts for himself. In another sub-chapter, Bose takes up the three *guṇas* (*sattva, rajas, tamas*). He refers to Friedrich Max Müller's inability to understand them as evidence that the meaning of the *guṇa* classification is difficult to realise, and then offers a psychological explanation, interpreting *sattva* as inward-oriented and thus psychological knowledge; *rajas* as outward-looking and 'divert(ing) the mind'; and *tamas* as the knowledge-hindering opposite of both (pp. 40–42).[24]

Next, Bose discusses karma and rebirth, stating that free will is mostly negated by psychoanalysis also, and examining the theories of inheritance of the karma approach in terms of Sāṃkhya philosophy (p. 49f.). These are compared to Freud's ideas, backed up by biologists, about inheritance being stored in the *id*:[25]

> The conception of a microscopic immortal germ plasm carrying unit characters or hereditary traits of almost infinite variety from generation to generation [...] is not easier of comprehension than the idea of numbers of more or less similar immortal subtle bodies constituting functional personality units and controlling the propagation of a species by producing hereditarily similar organisms. As a theory therefore the doctrine of karma may be said to be almost as good or as bad as the accepted doctrine of heredity [....] (Bose n. d., 58)

In the last part of his introduction, Bose deals with the terminologies of the mind (*manas, citta, buddhi*) employed by the so-called 'Hindu psychologists', meaning the ancient authors on the topic. He describes the *saṃskāras* as that which stores unfulfilled wishes by leaving an indelible impression on the *citta*, and is transmitted to the subtle body and ultimately to the next birth. Mental concentration in Yoga is interpreted as identification with an object. He ends his introduction by questioning 'our' disbelief in the miraculous powers of yogis, at

---

24 *Cf.* his Bengali article 'Sattva rajaḥ tamaḥ' in *Prabāsī* (1930) and Ashis Nandy's remarks on it (Nandy 1995, 126).

25 In works such as *The Ego and the Id*, *General Introduction to Psychoanalysis*, *Totem and Taboo*, and *Moses and Monotheism* (Bose n. d., 51–52).

least in the past (p. 70f.), claiming that an open scientific mind should not negate the possibility.

We do not know exactly when this work was written, but we can safely assume a gap of more than twenty years between *Svapna* and *The Yoga Sutras*. Despite the initial assurance of not wanting to scare away the general reader, Bose's audience is definitely learned and expert, and other than in *Svapna*, there are no textual markers that would identify the readers as a Bengali audience. Whether the actual readers were overwhelmingly Bengali or not is hard to ascertain. The journal *Samiksha* apparently circulated internationally and thus reverberated in circles beyond Bose's immediate surroundings, but the ensuing undated monograph version of the text that the Indian Psychoanalytical Society brought out does not suggest any such outreach. For the latter, we may assume that a major part of the audience was Bengali and significantly overlapped with that of *Svapna*. But the point is that in *The Yoga Sutras*, the readers are not addressed as a Bengali community but as partakers in modern enlightened discourse, or as modern citizens. In general, the reader address is less pronounced, making the text more academic and sober in tone. Stylistically it is not inferior to the Bengali of *Svapna*, but betrays the experienced author in both languages that Bose had become since the still 'clumsy' diction of his doctoral thesis[26]—the many printing mistakes notwithstanding, for his level of English mastery at this stage suggests that they probably were not his.

In terms of content, there is no clear rupture between *Svapna* and *The Yoga Sutras*, but rather frequent synapses that make the texts appear like parts of a continuum. Bose's basic ideas about the inherent psychological dimension of Indian philosophy and mythology had announced themselves already in *Svapna*, and the same is true for

26 Ashis Nandy seems particularly critical of Bose's competence in English, calling his dissertation a 'clumsy work, still clumsier by Bose's awkward and cluttered English' (1995, 95), and stating that his writings, 'especially his English works, [were not] free of inelegance, crudity and simplification' (ibid., 131). Hartnack limits the criticism to his thesis and concedes that his English improved afterwards (2001, 107). Her assessment, rather than Nandy's, is in sync, I argue, with the English writing skills Bose displays in *The Yoga Sutras*.

the distinction between outer/extrinsic and inner/intrinsic knowledge. However, this recessive state is now turned into a dominant one, as both are considerably amplified in the introduction to *The Yoga Sutras* and serve to realign his reasoning with popular cultural discourses of his time. For there cannot be much doubt that Bose's distinction comes close to one particular conceptual opposition that had evolved in the nineteenth century and can be found in Brahmo Samaj circles and with Bankimchandra Chattopadhyay, Vivekananda, and others, namely that between *bahirbiṣaẏak/bahirmukh* and *antarbiṣaẏak/antarmukh jñān* (knowledge directed towards outer and inner objects).[27] This scheme had been taken to task for explaining nothing less than colonial domination: while the Indians had always excelled in 'inner knowledge', it was the West's mastery of 'outer knowledge' (science, technology) that had caused India's colonial subjugation, and an assimilation of this outer knowledge was the historic task, accomplishing which India would arise again and attain freedom.

The direct comparison between *Svapna* and *The Yoga Sutras* would then suggest that over time, Bose gave in to this keynote of a dominant trend in Indian nationalism—not because the earlier of these works shows any strong resistance to such a position, but because there is much more concern with it in the later one. While in *Svapna* the new theory of dreams sits above two regionalised traditions, one Indian, the other Western, and is projected as a universalist approach in a dynamics of extension, in *The Yoga Sutras* the psychological discipline is conjugated into an Indian philosophical and religious tradition in a reverse dynamics of contraction. Following Manjapra's (2014) contentions regarding the differential content assortment in Bengali and English, one would have expected this to be the other way round, namely that the move of identity-bestowing contraction would have taken recourse to Bengali, and the universalist extension to English. It thus appears that the Bengali in-group reference—which no doubt plays its role and also has a nationalist agenda behind it—can nevertheless not be equated in as straightforward a manner

27 *Cf.* Nandy (1995, 126), who translates *antarmukh jñān* in Bose's texts as inner-directed knowledge. On this opposition in Bankimchandra Chattopadhyay's novel *Ānandamaṭh* (1882), *cf.* Harder (2019, 68f).

with manoeuvres of identity formation as Manjapra claims. Soumen Mukherjee therefore seems to be right in saying that '[Manjapra's] argument of a Bengali/English cleavage is overstated' (Mukherjee 2018, 6). Of course, two texts are in no way a sufficient number of samples to thoroughly probe the ratio behind Bose's linguistic choices, but they certainly go some way towards complicating the story. What they show is that there is no straightforward equation between contextualisation for a cultural in-group and the articulation of nationalist and indigenist claims. While a strong degree of cultural embedding in the Bengali medium seems rather predictable, it is striking that the claim regarding a substantial involvement with psychology in the Indian tradition is, in our examples, reserved to the English medium.

BOSE AND FREUD

What does our discussion so far tell us about Bose's attitude towards Freud? It appears that in *Svapna*, despite the occasional disagreements, Bose perceived Freud essentially as a pathbreaking ally who helped him transcend fortified borders in his genuine and independent psychological quests. In *The Yoga Sutras*, by contrast, we find him subsuming Freud's explanation of inheritance in a re-reading of karma theory. Can we draw an easy equation here and see this as a move to align Freud with the West and the coloniser, and dismantle his hegemonic take by a recourse to Indian tradition? I am not sure about this and suggest, among other things, that Freud's nationality as a non-British Austrian ought not to be underrated.

Earlier discussions have questioned the relevance of this factor. Ashis Nandy (1995, 101) and Christiane Hartnack (2001, 139) alike point out that the portrait a contemporary of Bose's had made of Freud from imagination, never having seen Freud or a picture of him, had looked like an Englishman to Freud, as he remarked in a letter to Lou Andreas-Salomé in 1922. Hartnack takes this as proof that '[...] such a portrayal reflected that Bose saw Freud as not essentially different from the colonizer' (Hartnack 2001, 139). And Nandy adds that, '[n]one pointed out to the ageing patriarch the analytic implications of his casual remark and the political tragedy that lay unarticulated in it' (Nandy 1995, 101). The analytic implications Nandy hints at appear to be precisely the identification of Freud with the English colonisers on the part of his Indian admirer and his own resistance to this identification—even though, as Hiltebeitel remarks, this hardly agrees with Freud's pleasant surprise upon seeing the picture because he was 'glad to look like an Englishman, and not Jewish'.[28] Shruti Kapila seems to follow Hartnack and Nandy in stating that while the felt need to represent Freud physically spoke for the immense stimulus of Freud's ideas, 'his representation as an Englishman is suggestive of the pervasivity (and the colonial) in any imaginative exercise [...]' (Kapila 2007, 128).

However, one can ask to what extent the template for European physiognomy available to Calcutta-based Indians at the time allowed for variations to accommodate 'Austrian' looks, and thus enabled some visual proto-provincialising of Europe. If this element of identifying Freud with the coloniser can be shown to be contrived, then Freud's remark is appropriately casual and does not throw the long shadow that Nandy conjures up. In any case, a proper judgement is impossible without a discussion of the picture, which is not available to me; and the reason for stressing this point is only that this chapter aims at de-emphasising the 'colonial Freud' in favour of another reading in which Freud, at least initially, functions as a third party employed to address the colonial situation. I argue that despite such a stereotypical depiction of a European by a Bengali who, moreover, was not Girindrasekhar Bose himself, Freud's non-Englishness mattered a lot to Bose and in a way helped him transcend the colonial divide. The differentiated reception of non-English Europe in colonial Bengal is amply borne out by a random look at the press of those days, and certainly shows that some provincialising of Europe, to borrow Dipesh Chakrabarty's famous phrase, was taking place in those days already. Whether Freud's non-English nationality remained his long-term advantage in his interactions with Bose is an entirely different question, and one that will probably have to be answered in the negative. Some hints to that may be found in the following proper dialogue, the Bose–Freud correspondence.

---

28 *Cf.* Hiltebeitel (2018, 18), quoting from a recollection by Anna Freud, given in Hartnack (2001, 197).

In 1964, the Indian Psychoanalytical Society brought out a slim booklet titled *The Beginnings of Psychoanalysis in India: Bose-Freud Correspondence*, and has had it reprinted twice since then: a compilation of twenty-six short letters, some no more than postcard length. The correspondence started in 1921 when Bose sent his doctoral thesis on repression to Freud and stopped after altogether twelve letters in 1923. It was again revived in 1929 (when Freud responded to a letter by Bose which is not included in the compilation) and continued uninterrupted until 1933. A small coda in 1937 consists basically of a congratulations by Freud. According to the preface of the booklet, the extant letters were requested by Anna Freud in 1938 and sent by Bose's wife to be published, after which they were republished in India.

Christiane Hartnack (2001, 139–143) has dealt with this correspondence in detail and aptly points out that it is rather meagre in outcome. It has to some extent even the nature of a mere paratext, in that it accompanies and wraps up various postal packages containing portraits, articles, books, and even a bust—items that travelled one-way from Calcutta to Vienna with only one exception: an asymmetrical exchange indeed. Of late, Alf Hiltebeitel (2018) has furnished a meticulous analysis of the correspondence, reading it in parallel to Freud's letter exchange with Romain Rolland in order to keep track of Freud's attitude towards India, and particularly the oceanic feeling structure that Rolland had discovered in India, which acted as a repellent to Freud. Hiltebeitel also reads the silences in the correspondence, particularly a year's break between two New Year's greeting cards (ibid., 19f.).

If there is little substantial debate on issues of psychoanalysis to be found in those letters, these investigations amply demonstrate how interesting they are in terms of rhetoric and tone. As stated above, I hesitate to read overtly colonialist underpinnings into this inherent asymmetry as Hartnack and Nandy have done; I lack the knowledge of other correspondences of Freud, but would imagine that this state of affairs might be a recurring pattern elsewhere, too.[29] In Bose's

[29] Hiltebeitel's examination of Freud's correspondence with Romain Rolland shows that it displayed far greater warmth and affection indeed, but arguably the constellation between the correspondents along the parameters

case, there are a number of factors that may account for an unequal distribution of interest and engagement between the two parts of this dialogue. First, the correspondents were divided by thirty-one years of age—a proper generation gap. Second, the meeting ground for the correspondents being psychoanalysis, and Freud having become eponymous with it, it was also clear who held the central position in this arena and who was the newcomer.[30] Further, the correspondence took place at a time when Freud was already looking back on most of his life's work and declared himself to be 'too old to come over to India and very busy here' (*The Beginnings of Psychoanalysis*, 8) in 1922, and held his own mind to be 'still active although not productive' (ibid., 13) in 1929.

As Hartnack and Hiltebeitel show, the few instances in the correspondence where topical debates arise do suffer from Freud's lack of interest—he does not seriously engage with Bose's theory of the opposite wish which leads to repression, nor does he take up the argument regarding the less pronounced occurrence of castration fear in India as opposed to Europe. Freud duly reads the works Bose sends him and briefly comments upon them, at times also expressing his disagreement in very frank terms. But it is true that he never really catches on, and his remarks rather seal the debate than take it further. For example, reading through a number of Bose's articles, Freud answers as follows: 'You directed my attention on the Oedipus wish especially and you were right in doing so. It made a great impression on me. In fact I am not convinced by your arguments' (*The Beginnings of Psychoanalysis*, 16).[31]

There is quite a rupture between declaring to be greatly impressed and not being convinced, it appears. Is this sudden change in tone, one

of age, cultural familiarity, etc., was so different that a comparison is hardly feasible (Hiltebeitel 2018, 59–81).

30 Kris Manjapra (2014, 221f.) seems right in his rather sober assessment of the correspondence, pointing out that both were divided by a generation: 'Freud commanded the dominant position in their exchange given that he was the founder of this counter scientific field, and yet Girindrasekhar showed a remarkable scope to critique and challenge some of Freud's central theses within the psychoanalytic arena of discourse.'

31 Also quoted and discussed in Hartnack (2001, 140).

feels prompted to inquire, an instance of the opposite wishes within Freud to be polite to his Indian correspondent and to be faithful to his own ideas? It is certainly not Freud's lack of competence in English, for his letters display a reasonable fluency in that language. But after some seven sentences of explanation, he concludes as follows: 'But I confess I am by no means more convinced of the validity of my own assumptions. We have not yet seen through this intricate Oedipus matter. We need more observations' (*The Beginnings of Psychoanalysis*, 16).

This does not signal readiness to delve deeper into the debate, but should rather be read as appeasing gestures to close it, or, as Hartnack calls it, an attempt 'to balance his criticism' (2001, 140). But on the positive side, it will also not be far-fetched to appreciate this gesture as a sign of the general openness that Freud displayed towards Bose, despite the limiting factors of age difference, shortage of time, and lack of specific interest in India.

To sum up, the correspondence clearly does not develop into a proper dialogue at all, and never goes beyond the pattern of rather isolated propositions and equally isolated reactions to them. But it appears overdrawn to read the conspicuous asymmetries that are at work in it directly in terms of the colonial divide. Nevertheless, and even if it seems a mistake to blame Freud for it, it is only natural to suppose that this lack of direct dialogue should have played its part in estranging Bose from Freud, and may also have strengthened the revivalist trend in Bose's research that we can note from *Svapna* towards *The Yoga Sutras*. It is on this level that the colonial framework had its decisive impact, as will be argued in the conclusion.

CONCLUSION

No doubt a comprehensive study of the whole corpus of Bose's writings and other relevant material is needed to settle the issues raised in this brief investigation. But even the selected texts under discussion offer some indications that Bose's relation with Freud and his positioning of psychoanalysis do follow a discernible pattern. So what is the overall picture that emerges from this analysis, and what are its implications for this Indo-Austrian dialogue? Reverting to the guiding questions posed in the beginning, we can sum up the answers as follows.

First, the relationship between Bose's English and Bengali writings, on the basis of the samples that have been investigated, does not obey any simple ratio. Towards the later phase of his life, Bose arguably had become almost equally proficient in English as in Bengali, and while his choice of language carried implications regarding the intended readership, we do not find the revivalist arguments reflected in Bengali and the sober psychoanalytical ones in English; in fact, in the chosen texts it is rather the opposite.

Second, it does not seem that the binary of English/European vs Indian, or coloniser vs colonised works in the case of psychoanalysis and Freud, or at least not in any straightforward manner. In *Svapna*, Freud is clearly an ally who helps Bose cross the opposites of outer and inner knowledge or science and 'Indian tradition' and find a middle way of combining them. Freud is ambiguous in this scheme as a 'scientist' who nevertheless discloses *inner* knowledge.

However, while it was Freud's theory that enabled this interaction, it seems that the lack of substantial direct dialogue in the correspondence ultimately had a repelling effect on Girindrasekhar Bose. It was indeed a missed chance (Hartnack 2001, 149; Hiltebeitel 2018, 17). Freud's lack of engagement left Bose to himself, with the only original option of contributing to the Indian rather than the psychoanalytical side of his endeavour. This last point is what, in retrospect, seems so deplorable about this 'dialogue', and it is here that the colonial factor plays out, despite all well-meaning intentions. The Bose–Freud correspondence was one of the rather few instances in the history of colonial India when direct contact between an exponent of metropolitan European disciplinary developments and one of his colonial colleagues was established.[32] Given Bose's level of expertise, it carried the potential of opening up a broader vision of the psyche that would be malleable to cultural specificities in a way that went beyond Freud's own capacities and those of his European followers. One can only speculate about the boost for psychology that a more intense

[32] Other famous interactions being the correspondences between Rammohan Roy and Jeremy Bentham, Satyendranath Bose, and Albert Einstein, and also Rabindranath Tagore's celebrated meeting with the latter.

interaction between these two interlocutors might have provided. But as things stand, the dialogue remained rudimentary and, for lack of direct interaction, fell back on an internal conversation between Indian tradition and a largely imagined 'West'. This was the typical set-up that colonialism imposed in so many cases on intellectuals in the colonies, and which was predestined to lead to ideas of revivalism and the celebration of the indigenous rather than to an understanding on enlarged universal terms.

REFERENCES

A. Books by Girindrasekhar Bose

Basu, Girindraśekhar. 2009 [1920]. *Concept of Repression*. Kolkata: Bangiya Kala Kendra (1st edn, Calcutta/London: Kegan Paul, Trench, Trubner & Co.).

———. 1980 [1928–1929]. *Svapna*. Kalikātā: Baṅgīẏa-Sāhitya-Pariṣat. Reprint, Kalikātā: Bibekānanda Buk Seṇṭār, 2008.

———. 2008 [1930–1931]. *Lālˈkālo*. Kalikātā: Bibekānanda Buk Seṇṭār.

———. 1934. *Jībanˈyātrāẏ manobidyār praẏog*. No place indicated: Author's publication.

———. 2012 [1934–1935]. *Purāṇ prabeś*. Kalikātā: Bibekānanda Buk Seṇṭār.

———. 1939. *Reconstruction of Andhra Chronology*. Calcutta.

———. 2009 [1945]. *Everyday Psycho-Analysis*. Kolkata: Vivekananda Book Centre.

———. 1948. *Bhagabadgītā*. Kalikātā: Author's publication.

———. 1953. *Manobidyār paribhāṣā*. No place indicated: Author's publication.

———. 1956. *Paurāṇikī*. No place indicated: Author's publication.

———. n. d. [1957]. *The Yoga Sutras*. Calcutta: Indian Psychoanalytical Society.

The Beginnings of Psychoanalysis in India: Bose-Freud Correspondence. 1999 [1964]. Calcutta: Indian Psychoanalytical Society.

B. Secondary Literature

Chatterjee, Partha. 1994. *The Nation and its Fragments: Colonial and Postcolonial Histories*. New Delhi: Oxford University Press.

Das, Rahul Peter. 1992. 'Problematic Aspects of the Sexual Rituals of the Bauls of Bengal'. *Journal of the American Oriental Society* 112 (3), 388–432.

Dāś, Debajyoti. 1996 [1971]. *Girindraśekhar Basu (1887–1953). Sāhitya-Sādhak-Caritˈmālā 108*. Kalikātā: Baṅgīẏa-Sāhitya-Pariṣat.

Ghosh, Agniva. 2017. `Manaḥsamīkṣā o biś śataker bāṅāli mānas tattva' ('Psychoanalysis and Twentieth-century Bengali Psychology'). Unpublished Ph.D. thesis, Jadavpur University.

Harder, Hans. 2011. *Sufism and Saint Veneration in Contemporary Bangladesh: The Maijbhandaris of Chittagong*. London: Routledge.

——. 2019. 'Bankimchandra Chattopadhyay and Modern Hinduism'. In Torkel Brekke (ed.), *The Oxford History of Hinduism: Modern Hinduism*, 54–71. Oxford: Oxford University Press.

Hartnack, Christiane. 2001. *Psychoanalysis in Colonial India*. New Delhi: Oxford University Press.

Hiltebeitel, Alf. 2018. *Freud's India: Sigmund Freud and India's First Psychoanalyst Girindrasekhar Bose*. New York: Oxford University Press.

Kapila, Shruti. 2007. 'The "Godless" Freud and his Indian Friends: An Indian Agenda for Psychoanalysis'. In Sloan Mahone and Megan Vaughan (eds), *Psychiatry and Empire*, 124–152. Houndmills/New York: Palgrave Macmillan.

Manjapra, Kris. 2014. *Age of Entanglement: German and Indian Intellectuals Across Empire*. Cambridge, Mass./London: Harvard University Press.

Mukherjee, Soumen. 2018. 'Recovering Wisdom of the "Ancient *Rishis*": Girindrasekhar Bose, Indra Sen, and the Psy-disciplines in Modern India'. *South Asian History and Culture* June, 1–27.

Nandy, Ashis. 1995. *The Savage Freud and other Essays on Possible and Retrievable Selves*. Princeton, NJ: Princeton University Press.

Naregal, Veena. 1999. 'Colonial Bilingualism and Hierarchies of Language and Power: Making of a Vernacular Sphere in Western India'. *Economic and Political Weekly* 34 (49), 3446–3456.

Notes on the Contributors

Rajendra Dengle taught at the Centre of German Studies, JNU, for forty-two years, retiring in July 2021. His research interests have been Philosophy of Language, Theories of Literature, Communication and the New Media. He has been Secretary of the Goethe Society of India and Editor of its Yearbook. Apart from his academic work, he has been Dean of Students and Dean of the School of Language, Literature, and Culture Studies of JNU.

Martin Fuchs, trained in Sociology and Anthropology, Professor for Indian Religious History, Max Weber Centre for Advanced Cultural and Social Studies, University of Erfurt, Germany. He is member and temporarily Director of the M.S. Merian—R. Tagore International Centre of Advanced Studies in the Humanities and Social Sciences 'Metamorphoses of the Political' (ICAS: MP) in New Delhi, India. His research interests lie in Cultural and Social Theory and South Asia studies. Among his recent publications are *Religious Interactions in Modern India* (2019) and two co-edited volumes on *Religious Individualisation: Historical Dimensions and Comparative Perspectives* (2019).

Hans Harder has been Professor of Modern South Asian Languages and Literatures at the South Asia Institute, Heidelberg University, Germany, since 2007. His research interests are modern literatures in South Asia, particularly Bengali, religious movements, and colonial and postcolonial intellectual history. Books authored by him include *Sufism and Saint Veneration in Contemporary Bangladesh: The Maijbhandaris of Chittagong* (2011) and *Bankimchandra Chattopadhyay's* Śrīmadbhagabadgītā*: Translation and Analysis* (2001). He has edited *Asian Punches: A Transcultural Affair* (2013) and *Literature and Nationalist Ideology: Writing Histories of Modern Indian Languages* (2010).

Christiane Hartnack has been teaching since 2000 at the Institute for South Asia, Tibet and Buddhist Studies, at the University of Vienna,

Austria. In 2006/2007, she was Visiting Professor at the School of Social Sciences at Jawaharlal Nehru University in New Delhi. She also taught briefly at the University of Iowa and at Wellesley College in Massachusetts. From 2001–2015 she was Head of the Centre for Intercultural Studies at Danube University, Krems in Austria. Her publications focus on inter- and transcultural theoretical issues and on the travel of persons and ideas between India and Europe.

Angelika Malinar has held positions at the University of Tübingen, Free University Berlin, and University of London (SOAS), and since 2009, is Professor of Indology at the University of Zurich. Key areas of her research are Sanskrit epic and puranic literature, classical and modern formations of Hinduism, Indian philosophy, and the entangled history between India and Europe in the colonial period. Her publications include *The Bhagavadgītā: doctrines and contexts*, *Time in India: Concepts and Practices* (editor), *Asia and Europe interconnected: Agents, Concepts, and Things*, and the multi-volume *Brill's Encyclopedia of Hinduism* (co-editor).

Axel Michaels is Senior Professor of Classical Indology at the South Asia Institute, Heidelberg University. From 2007–2017, he was one of the Directors of the Cluster of Excellence 'Asia and Europe in a Global Context' and Founding Director of the Centre for Asian and Transcultural Studies (CATS). His fields of interest are social history and the history of Hinduism, theory of rituals, as well as the cultural and legal history of Nepal. He has authored *Cultural History of Nepal* (forthcoming), *Homo ritualis. Hindu Rituals and its Significance for Ritual Theory* (2016), *Present and Hinduism. Past* (2004), *Śiva in Trouble. Rituals and Festivals at the Paśupatinātha temple of Deopatan, Nepal* (2008).

Roddam Narasimha joined IISc in 1962 and built up an active fluid mechanics group. After serving as Chairman of AE Department and Dean (Engineering), and founding a Centre for Atmospheric Sciences at IISc, he took over as Director, National Aerospace Laboratories in 1984 till 1993. He headed the National Institute of Advanced Studies from 1997–2004, where he started the series of lectures on History of Ideas. Some of his publications include *Nature and Culture* (2011), *Encyclopedia of Classical Indian Sciences* (2007), and

Verses for the Brave (2005). He has been honoured with the Bhatnagar Award, the AIAA Fluid Dynamics Award (2000), Trieste Science Prize (2008), and elected to all the academies of science and engineering in India, the Royal Society London, the US National Academies of Engineering as well as Science. He was awarded the Padma Vibhushan in 2013.

Dhruv Raina is Professor at the Jawaharlal Nehru University, New Delhi, where he teaches the history and philosophy of science. His research has focused on the politics and cultures of scientific knowledge in South Asia, both in historical and contemporary contexts, as well as the history and historiography of mathematics. His published works include *Situating the History of Science: Dialogues with Joseph Needham* (1999), *Social History of Sciences in Colonial India* (2007), and *Images and Contexts: The Historiography of Science and Modernity* (2003), among others. He has been a visiting professor of the Maison des Sciences de l'Homme, Paris; a Fellow of the Wissenschaftskolleg, Berlin; and the first incumbent of the Heinrich Zimmer Chair at Heidelberg University. He is also an elected Fellow of the Indian National Science Academy.

Benjamin Zachariah is currently Senior Research Fellow at the Georg Eckert Institute in Braunschweig. His research interests include historical thinking in public arguments, historiography and historical theory, the movements of ideas in the twentieth century, international revolutionary networks, and global fascism. He is the author of *Nehru* (2004), *Developing India: An Intellectual and Social History, c. 1930–1950* (2005), *Playing the Nation Game: The Ambiguities of Nationalism in India* (2011), and *After the Last Post: The Lives of Indian Historiography in India* (2019).

Index